GAYLO

PLYMOUTH ROCK
and the PILGRIMS

and Other Salutary Platform Opinions

Books by Charles Neider

Fiction

OVERFLIGHT

NAKED EYE

THE AUTHENTIC DEATH OF HENDRY JONES

THE WHITE CITADEL

Nonfiction

BEYOND CAPE HORN: TRAVELS IN THE ANTARCTIC

EDGE OF THE WORLD: ROSS ISLAND, ANTARCTICA

SUSY: A CHILDHOOD

MARK TWAIN

THE FROZEN SEA: A STUDY OF FRANZ KAFKA

Edited by Charles Neider

PLYMOUTH ROCK AND THE PILGRIMS

THE SELECTED LETTERS OF MARK TWAIN

THE AUTOBIOGRAPHY OF MARK TWAIN

THE COMIC MARK TWAIN READER

MARK TWAIN

PLYMOUTH ROCK
and the PILGRIMS

and Other Salutary Platform Opinions

Edited with an introduction and commentary by
CHARLES NEIDER

1817

HARPER & ROW, PUBLISHERS, New York

Cambridge, Philadelphia, San Francisco,
London, Mexico City, São Paulo, Singapore, Sydney

PLYMOUTH ROCK AND THE PILGRIMS AND OTHER SALUTARY PLATFORM OPINIONS. Copyright © 1984 by Charles Neider. All rights reserved. Printed in the United States of America. No part of this book may be used or reproduced in any manner whatsoever without written permission except in the case of brief quotations embodied in critical articles and reviews. For information address Harper & Row, Publishers, Inc., 10 East 53rd Street, New York, N.Y. 10022. Published simultaneously in Canada by Fitzhenry & Whiteside Limited, Toronto.

FIRST EDITION

Designed by Ruth Bornschlegel

Library of Congress Cataloging in Publication Data

Twain, Mark, 1835-1910.
    Plymouth Rock and the Pilgrims and other salutary platform opinions.

    Collection of his speeches.
    Bibliography: p.
    Includes index.
    1. After-dinner speeches.   I. Neider, Charles,
1915-   . II. Title.
PS1302.N43   1984   815'.4   84-47603
ISBN 0-06-015353-9

84 85 86 87 88 10 ⁹ 8 7 6 5 4 3 2 1

To the warm and supportive faculty of Stevenson College
of the University of California at Santa Cruz

Contents

Introduction

The present volume is not a collection of all of Mark Twain's speeches. From the many speeches available, I have chosen eighty-two which I believe represent him at his best in terms of variety of subject, literary style, autobiographical illumination and inspired humor, the kind of casual or sometimes wild humor which only he was capable of. I have admired all of these speeches and all have given me great pleasure. I have excluded speeches which bored me or which seemed to me to be too dated or too trivial. Genius though he was, Mark Twain was not always an inspired speaker. Nor, for that matter, was he always an inspired writer. While pleasing myself, I have tried to make available again for the general reader after a lapse of more than sixty years some of Mark Twain's finest and at the same time least known work.

The first collection of his speeches, consisting of ninety-four items, was issued by Albert Bigelow Paine in 1910, the year of Clemens's death. The speeches were not in chronological order. As a matter of fact, they possess no order discernible to me. The volume contained a brief preface by William Dean Howells, Clemens's friend, but lacked an introduction by Paine, the friend of Clemens's last several years, his official biographer and his literary executor. Most of the titles are by Paine or were accepted by him from sources at his disposal. Some examples are "Dedication Speech," "Dinner to Mr. Jerome," "Dinner to Whitelaw Reid," "Galveston Orphan Bazaar," and "Russian Sufferers."

In using such titles Paine gives the impression of being more concerned with the occasion for a speech rather than with the content of it. In Clemens's case, sometimes the guts of a speech had little relevance to the occasion, as when he was autobiographically humorous at a benefit for victims of a social or a natural disaster—humorous but never insensitive, for he was profoundly imaginative and compassionate. Too often Paine's titles are insufficiently revealing of the contents of the speeches to be useful today, and possibly they were not of much more use in 1910. Occasionally, as in the case of "Russian Sufferers," a title is opaque to the point of being misleading. "Russian Sufferers" refers to a speech Clemens made at a benefit for Russian *Jewish* victims of the abortive revolution of 1905.

The second collection of Mark Twain's speeches, brought out by Paine in 1923, contained eighty-four items, most of which were drawn from the earlier edition, while the rest made their first appearance in book form. The speeches were now in chronological order. On the whole, Paine retained the earlier titles. Occasionally he quietly retitled a speech. He reprinted Howells's preface and added an introduction by himself. The 1923 edition also appeared as Volume XXVIII of the Definitive Edition of Clemens's works, published that same year.

Paine's editions were designed for the general reader and were published by Harper & Brothers, Clemens's publisher. In 1976 the University of Iowa Press brought out the third collection of Clemens's speeches (the last one prior to my own), this one intended primarily for scholars: *Mark Twain Speaking*, edited by Paul Fatout, a volume evidencing a full battery of scholarly apparatus and containing, in its 195 items and 688 pages (excluding the introduction), lectures and readings as well as speeches. Like Paine's editions and my own, the Fatout edition is not a complete collection. The text of the majority of the speeches is a "composite" one, that is, the best that the editor, in his opinion, depending on variant texts, could construct. The titles are often elusive regarding both content and occasion. For example, I counted seven speeches with the same title, "Curtain Speech."

A few words about the textual sources of Clemens's speeches. Some of the speeches survive only in Paine's editions, and one is at a loss to explain what happened to his sources. Others survive only in contemporary newspaper accounts and transcripts. Sometimes there is no record of how a speech was originally written—or exactly delivered. There is a distinction to be made here between prepared text and actual delivery, for it was Clemens's practice to depart from his text whenever he thought it advantageous to do so to create an impromptu effect or one of easy, graceful flexibility.

Which is to say that there is a paucity of, first, the perfect manuscript indications of what Clemens had in mind when he conceived a speech, and, second, a paucity of clear indications as to the final, spoken product. Sometimes there are variant texts of the same speech, one text representing the prepared text which he may have handed in advance to newspaper reporters, and another indicating what he actually said, or what some reporter believed he heard him say. And if Clemens gave the same speech, or more or less the same, on more than one occasion, he was sure to invent variations of emphasis, phrasing and even, now and then, of anecdote.

Despite the foregoing, there is ample evidence that Clemens rarely made speeches which were pure exercises in improvisation. He almost always wrote them out with as much care as he devoted to work meant for publication. In his time, key speeches and lectures were news. They were reported in the newspapers, and with a degree of stenographic accuracy. Because of his early fame as a speaker, not to mention his renown as an author, he soon realized that his lectures and speeches *were* news and often would be published whether he liked it or not (he liked it). To assure greater authenticity of text, he early formed the habit of making available to reporters in advance written or typed copies of his speeches. Later, on occasion he even made proof sheets available.

Having written the speeches, he memorized them with avid attention to detail concerning emphasis and delivery. In Howells's words, "He studied every word and syllable, and memorized them by a system of mnemonics peculiar to himself, consisting of an arbitrary arrangement of things on a table—knives, forks, salt-cellars; inkstands, pens, boxes, or whatever was at hand—which stood for points and clauses and climaxes, and were at once indelible diction and constant suggestion." When Clemens delivered his speeches and lectures, including the after-dinner ones, he suggested by his casual demeanor, and occasionally by stammers, pauses or by slips of grammar, that they were impromptu, and he did so with great naturalness.

"He was a most consummate actor," Howells reported, "with this difference from other actors, that he was the first to know the thoughts and invent the fancies to which his voice and action gave the color of life." Howells went further. "He studied every tone and gesture, and he forecast the result with the real audience from its result with that imagined audience. Therefore, it was beautiful to see him and to hear him; he rejoiced in the pleasure he gave and the blows of surprise which he dealt; and because he had his end in mind, he knew when to stop."

So much for method and manner. As for matter, one cannot but agree with Howells that "it is good matter, glad, honest, kind, just." And so because the speeches were crafted carefully, because they were not mere momentary extemporized efforts, they rank in importance with his other short writings. Which gives the present collection an interest far beyond one's usual expectations of such a volume.

The year 1985 will mark the hundred and fiftieth anniversary of Clemens's birth and the seventy-fifth of his death. With so much distance between us and his time, it is fascinating to have a look at how he appeared to his contemporaries—appeared as a living presence—and also to catch glimpses of his effect on them. The *San Francisco Examiner* of October 3, 1866, under the headlines "Local Intelligence/Mark Twain's Lecture," had the following to say about his maiden platform appearance.

"Until last evening there were but few people in this city who knew what manner of man the correspondent of the Sacramento Union, whose letters, signed 'Mark Twain,' had so often amused them, might be. Nor had 'Mark' himself as yet drawn aside the curtain which concealed his individuality, or made his bow to the public that was so well acquainted with his mind, in *propria persona*. There was naturally a good deal of curiosity felt by all who knew his writings (and their name is legion) to ascertain if the man himself was like the ideal conjured up by his letters, if he spoke as he wrote, if he could enchain the interest of an audience by the utterances of his lips as he has so successfully done by the emanations of his pen. Many fears were expressed, to speak the truth, as to the issue of the experiment—for it *was* an experiment. He had never before, so far as we know, spoken in public, which was one disadvantage. And again it was not unnaturally feared that like many other clever humorists on paper, he would prove but a Dryas-dust in speech.

"Still his reputation was so great, and the desire to know how he would come out of the ordeal so strong and general, that the Academy of Music last night was crowded to its utmost capacity, with an audience who may be considered as having represented the most critical elements of a particularly fastidious community. Whatever that audience should endorse, would be a success. That appeared to us almost a certainty, as we looked around the house previous to the appearance of the lecturer. No doubt the audience was disposed to be good-humored; but also, no doubt, they were determined not to be bored with impunity, nor to endorse a humbugging lecturer because he was a good writer."

Clemens was almost thirty-one then, and stage-frightened, and he and his friends had taken the precaution to "paper" the house.

"He came before them; he began to speak, and, in five minutes, all doubt as to his ability as a lecturer was dispelled. The most delightful discovery made was, we think, this: that he spoke as he writes. The same unexpected jokes—the same inimitable drollery—the same strong sense embodied in quaint phraseology. He is sometimes a little too rough; of that there can be no doubt. He verges, indeed, occasionally, upon coarseness; but his roughness is the roughness of the crude diamond through the opaque incrustation of which flashes ever and anew a ray of that fountain of light which is the essence of the gem.

"We have no intention of analyzing his lecture of last night. It is to be hoped that he will repeat it, and it is much better that people should judge by themselves as to the matter, than we should attempt to direct their tastes. With the style alone we are dealing now—and the style is excellent.

"We confess that we have always preferred Mark Twain to Artemus Ward, as a humorist. We do not much respect that species of wit which has sprung up into a school in the United States so recently, and the fun of which rests chiefly upon labored cacography. In nine cases out of ten, the jokes which have a show of humor when clothed in blundering orthography, would, divested of their ragged covering, and written in plain English, appear but dreary jests. But apart from writing, we like Mark Twain's style of delivery better than that of Artemus Ward. There is more life, more quaintness and drollery in it; more evidence of genius indeed, we think.

"And there is a power which Mark developed last night which adds very much to our estimate of his abilities. He can talk seriously as well as humorously, and his serious descriptions are, if possible, even better than his drolleries. His picture of the volcano of Kilauea was an admirable piece of word painting. It was eloquent, and it showed, at least for us, that Mark Twain is something more than a mere humorist; he is a poet. There is no true poet to whom humor is a stranger, and there can be no true humorist without something of the *divine afflatus* in his breast."

Curiously, aside from the mention of Kilauea, the *Examiner* writer has said nothing about the subject of Clemens's lecture: the Sandwich Islands, which Clemens had visited earlier that year for four months. Nor does he mention that the islands were the subject of Clemens's letters to the *Sacramento Union*.

"Mark Twain has undergone the test," he concludes, "and has come out triumphant from the ordeal. He has received the hall mark of approbation from a public whose endorsement is not to be despised or lightly thought of, and he will hereafter be recognized as the greatest humorist, not only of the Pacific slope, but of the United States of America."

Reporting on the same lecture, the San Francisco *Daily Alta California* made many of the same points, and closed by saying, "Mark Twain has thoroughly established himself as the most piquant and humorous writer and lecturer on this coast, since the days of the lamented 'John Phoenix.'"

The East Coast was as charmed by the newly celebrated Clemens as the West Coast was. A little more than three years later he was still working the Sandwich Islands materials. The *Philadelphia Evening Bulletin* (December 8, 1869) regarded him as "the very best of the humorists of his class." It said he was more extravagant and preposterous than John Phoenix, and superior to Artemus Ward because he had a decent regard for the English language, and that Josh Billings was not to be compared with him.

"Mark Twain indulges in humor because it is his nature to do so," the *Evening Bulletin* said. "It is impossible to read his productions or to hear him speak without being impressed with the conviction that his cleverest utterances are spontaneous, natural, unpremeditated. Like all men of his temperament he has a hearty hatred of sham, hypocrisy and cant, whether in religion, social life or politics. Some of his sturdiest blows have been aimed at the follies of the times; and we believe that he may, if he chooses, exercise a very considerable influence as a reformer. Ridicule, cleverly used, is one of the most powerful weapons against pretension and humbug; for it not only robs them of their false dignity, but it appeals strongly to the popular reader, and finds ready acceptance where serious discussion would not be permitted. . . . There may be some who will regard his calling as of smaller dignity than that of other men. Perhaps this is the class with which he is at war. The mass of intelligent people will agree with us that genuine humor is as rare and excellent a quality as any other, and that it is as respectable to amuse mankind as to stupefy them."

A review in the Washington, D.C., *Daily Morning Chronicle* (December 9, 1869) is interesting because the writer was not entirely sold on Clemens. Again Clemens had delivered his Sandwich Islands lecture. The reviewer gave him high marks but ranked him below Artemus Ward.

Clemens worked his Sandwich Islands material heavily but almost always with fresh turns, and with increasing fame. The newspapers seemed to be competing with each other to describe his manner as droll. An unidentified clipping of no date in the Mark Twain Papers at the University of California at Berkeley affords a particularly vivid picture of him on the lecture platform.

"The apparently unconscious drollery of the lecturer began almost with his opening sentences, in which he deprecated any criticisms upon his inability to explain, or even to understand, why the Sandwich Islanders were placed so far away from everywhere else. From that time forth he held the audience in his hand. His hearers never laugh in the wrong place. Perhaps this is because he never indicates either by voice or manner what he thinks the right place for a laugh; and hence his audience has to listen sharply. . . . After you have listened to his wild extravagances for an hour, you are astonished to perceive that he has given you new and valuable views of the subject discussed. Every sentence may be burlesque, but the result is fact. And what insures his success as a teacher is that his manner is so irresistibly droll that it conquers at the first moment the natural revolt of the human mind against instruction."

It is extremely interesting to glimpse Clemens not only as Americans saw him but Europeans as well. The *Northern Whig* of Belfast, Ireland, in a clipping of no date (again in the Mark Twain Papers in Berkeley) provides a particularly detailed portrait. On the clipping Clemens wrote, "I can't get halls in Ireland on dates that are satisfactory—lose too much time—so I don't lecture in Ireland at all.—Mark." A probable date for the clipping is early January 1874.

"We regret to learn that in consequence of other engagements Mr. S. L. Clemens ('Mark Twain') has been compelled to relinquish the intention of giving his now celebrated 'lecture' in Belfast, prior to his return to America on the 13th inst. The people of Belfast have missed a great enjoyment, for Mr. Clemens's 'lecture' is perfectly unique, and is one of the most singular, most humorous, and most exhilarating discourses that can be imagined. It is, in point of fact, impossible to form, without having heard him, an adequate conception of the steady deliberate gravity with which Mark Twain for an hour and a half pours out an even stream of jokes, and stories, and ludicrous phrases, his countenance remaining stonily impassive, whilst his auditors are shaking and screaming with laughter. Hardly changing his position, never moving the muscles of his face, speaking in a tone which is almost melancholy, with what the French call 'tears in his voice,' when he is saying the funniest things, the lecturer is the only person in the room who preserves a semblance of gravity or maintains any personal dignity. The closest attention is demanded from the audience, for often the finest bits of humour and the best hits are quietly dropped out parenthetically, as if the speaker either wasn't aware there was any fun in them or didn't notice it himself. Hearing Mark Twain's lecture is a perfect cure for low spirits, and as a hearty laugh is a very good thing alike for body and mind, we are sorry that, for the present at any rate, our readers are not to have a call from Mr. Clemens on his way home."

From the above quotations the reader may be led to think that Clemens was invariably successful with his platform lectures and after-dinner speeches. Such was not the case, however. There were some striking exceptions. His lecture tour of several months in the lyceum season of 1871–1872 was on the whole disappointing until he switched from "Reminiscences of Some Uncommonplace Characters Whom I Have Chanced to Meet," and later a lecture on Artemus Ward, to western materials garnered from his forthcoming *Roughing It*. And the after-dinner speech he gave in Boston in December 1877, titled "The Whittier Birthday Speech," was by all odds his most painful failure, judging by his reaction to it. For a while he believed the reports that he had been "irreverent beyond belief, beyond imagination" (his own words) toward New England's literary idols, Emerson, Holmes, Longfellow and Whittier, all of whom had been present at that ill-fated dinner. But the reader may judge for herself (or himself) the degree of his irreverence by examining both the speech and Clemens's emotional and copious comments on it which follow it.

Once again it is fascinating to examine the contemporary records for the light they shed on Clemens and his time. For example, the *Boston Advertiser* of December 18, 1877, devoted much of its front page to the celebrated dinner, with appropriate headlines. "Whittier's Birthday./ Testimonial in Honor of the/Quaker Poet./Dinner at the Brunswick Hotel Last/Evening—Gathering of the Con-/tributors of the Atlantic Monthly." Poets were stars in Boston then, the equivalent (at least in terms of news) of our sports stars, film stars, or astronauts fresh from outer space.

Poor Clemens, with his western jokes he set himself up to seem the upstart crow in such a company. And if New England's literary establishment felt threatened by him, it had good cause, for his was the rising literary power. A splendid dinner it certainly was, and the *Advertiser* writer made the most of it. At times his prose seems to drip with idolatry.

Two of the speeches in the present collection are being reprinted for the first time, or rather one and the major portion of a second. They are "Author and Publisher" (1887) and "Caprices of Memory" (1908). Paine used only the tail end of "Author and Publisher" in his 1910 edition and he omitted it from his 1923 edition. The reader may be curious to know something about the mechanics of coming upon forgotten speeches by Mark Twain ninety-six and seventy-five years respectively after their delivery and almost three-quarters of a century after the author's death. "Author and Publisher" was found not by accident but rather by systematic searching through the annual so-called Documents Files and the various newspaper scrapbooks in the Mark Twain Papers in Berkeley. The trick was to know what speeches had already appeared in book form. "Caprices of Memory" was brought to my attention through the kindness of Thomas Tenney, a Mark Twain scholar who like myself was working in the reading room of the Bancroft Library in Berkeley.

Tenney, aware that I was preparing the present volume, told me he was under the impression that "Caprices of Memory" had not previously been reprinted, and he generously offered his photocopy of it so I could copy it for my book. He was correct, and the speech proved too good to leave out of the collection. When I asked him how he had come upon it, he replied that it had come to him in his general search for Mark Twain material in libraries in the United States and abroad. He had sent out a total of nearly five thousand inquiries, one of which had gone to the public library in Hamilton, Bermuda. The Hamilton library had notified him that they had something, and he had ordered photocopies of everything they had on Clemens.

"So, it wasn't a brilliant burst of intuition that told me there'd likely be something in the library at Hamilton," he wrote to me later, "and in particular I didn't know there was going to be a speech. I just asked if they had anything, and ordered copies when they said they did. This isn't carving out research material with a scalpel; I used a blunt instrument."

Speaking of finding things, I remember a time when I was in Christchurch, New Zealand, on my way to Antarctica. One morning I walked from my hotel to the Canterbury Museum, where John Wilson, the librarian (now the director), showed me an album that had been kept by J. J. Kinsey, the man who had been so helpful to Scott and Shackleton, the famous Antarctic explorers. It contained a photograph of Shackleton looking young and happy, a poem by him about Mt. Erebus in his own hand— and an excellent photograph of Mark Twain, taken by Kinsey in November 1895 during Clemens's visit to Christchurch on his round-the-world lecture tour. My journal of that day notes, "Will see this material at greater leisure on my return to New Zealand from Antarctica." But when I returned to Christchurch I was too busy dealing with the consequences, both public and private, of a helicopter crash near the summit of Mt. Erebus. The photograph which I found in the album may be seen on the front of the dust jacket of the present book, and another, also taken by Kinsey at that time, adorns the frontispiece. The photographs were taken on the verandah of Kinsey's home at Clifton, Christchurch.

Among the eighty-two items here, there is a great variety of topics, as even a casual glance at the Contents will show. There are also many and varied moods: political, philosophical and deeply moving ones. And there are speeches pursuing fun for its own sake. Above all there is great humor. After more than the quarter of a century during which I have worked with Clemens, I am still astonished that he can continue to elicit belly laughs in me. There is no humor in the world like it, and I believe none matches it. As for his humanity, its breadth too is a constant source of surprise and inspiration to me.

I have arranged the speeches in chronological order and have provided most of the titles. I have edited the text for consistency and, following Bernard DeVoto's practice in *Mark Twain in Eruption* (1940) as well as my own as long ago as *The Autobiography of Mark Twain* (1959), have modernized the punctuation by deleting countless commas, semicolons, dashes and ampersands. It is probably a pity to take liberties with Clemens's punctuation, but the practice in this instance is not without some justification, as I believe the reader will agree from the foregoing discussion of texts. In most cases it is impossible to discover what part of the punctuation is Clemens's and what part a newspaper reporter's, or a newspaper editor's, or a compositor's, or Paine's. An interesting sidelight on this problem occurs in the margin of a typescript page of the Autobiographical Dictations in the Mark Twain Papers. "*Private*: Discard the stupid Harper rule for once: don't put a comma after 'old'—I can't *have* it ! SLC." The notation is in Clemens's hand. He was referring to a phrase—"beyond that old safe frontier."

The reader will notice that Clemens sometimes repeats himself. The stolen watermelon, the deliberately dropped watermelon, the moonlit naked corpse and the bucking plug were all anecdotes that he used on many public occasions, but whenever he recycled such material he always offered it with remarkable freshness.

Alameda, California
February 29, 1984

PLYMOUTH ROCK
and the PILGRIMS

and Other Salutary Platform Opinions

1

On March 5, 1866, Clemens, now thirty, decided to accept an offer by the *Sacramento Union* to write twenty or thirty letters about a trip to the Sandwich (Hawaiian) Islands, "for which they pay me as much money as I would get if I staid at home," he wrote to his mother and sister. "My friends seem determined that I shall not lack acquaintances . . . and they have already sent me letters of introduction to everybody down there worth knowing. I am to remain there a month and ransack the islands, the great cataracts and the volcanoes completely." Actually he remained in the islands for four months and wrote twenty-five letters for the *Union*. The following are extracts from his first lecture, originally given at Maguire's Academy of Music in San Francisco on October 2, 1866, and repeated many times in the United States and Great Britain.

THE SANDWICH ISLANDS

To cut the matter short, the Sandwich Isles are 2,100 miles southwest from San Francisco. But why they were put away out there in the middle of the Pacific so far away from any place and in such an inconvenient locality is no business of ours. It was the work of Providence and is not open to criticism.

The subject is a good deal like many others we should like to inquire into. Such as What mosquitoes were made for. But under the circumstances we naturally feel a delicacy about doing it.

They are a dozen in number, of volcanic origin, eight of them inhabited and four of them the most marvelously productive sugar land in the known world. Eighty years ago there was a population of 400,000 on the islands, but there are only 50,000 now. The Kanaka race is rapidly passing away. . . .

It is said by some, and believed, that Kanakas won't lie. But I know they *will* lie. Lie like auctioneers. Lie like lawyers. Lie like patent-medicine advertisements. They will almost lie like newspaper men. They will lie for a dollar when they could get a dollar and a half for telling the truth. They *never* tell a traveler the right road or right distance to a place.

Christian Kanakas will go into court and swear on the Bible and then stand up and lie till the lights burn blue around them. And then go home and go through a lot of purifying idolatrous ceremonies and the thing is all straight. There is only one way of getting them to tell the truth on the stand or anywhere else, and that is to swear them on the Great Shark God, which seems to have been the most potent personage in their idolatrous mythology. In old times when the priests fancied that the shark god was angry or out of sorts about anything and stood in need of a sacrifice to compose his spirits, they used to go forth and lasso a poor wretch of a plebeian native and cast him into the sea where the sharks could devour him.

And to this day in the island of Hawaii they fear and respect this deity, and when they swear by him they keep the oath and tell the truth. And yet the unsagacious judges go on swearing such witnesses on the Scriptures and refuse to profit by our keener judgment. When we have a Chinese witness on an important case we swear him on a butchered chicken.

And cheat? They will cheat anybody. They used to be arrant thieves in old times, and now they are arrant rascals, arrant knaves. They measure a stranger by the eye and begin to average him as soon as he gets into their cabin. If he knows the language and is only pretending to be a stranger he will hear them comment on him and his probable errand very freely. They will wonder if he is a missionary, and shake their heads and say no, looks too worldly for a missionary. And wonder if he is a Californian—no, not quick-motioned enough for a Californian. And so on.

If they determine that you are a missionary they will offer to have family prayers. If they decide that you are a Californian they will proceed to swindle you. To them, anybody who doesn't live in the islands is usually a Californian, no matter where he comes from.

If you merely want to stay all night, stay and welcome. Eat their poi and raw fish and welcome. Make yourself at home, for theirs is the freest hospitality in the world. It is customary to pay them but the offer must come from *you*. They would never ask it. But if you want to trade, if you want to buy anything, they will manage to get ahead of you somehow or other nearly every time.

They have always got a sore-back horse lying around somewhere to sell to the stranger. They will sell him a young chicken and then cook him one that remembered Noah's ark and the Deluge. A Kanaka will hire a stranger a horse for a dollar and then demand $2.50 when he gets back, and say he doesn't know anything about the original bargain—his *brother* made it and then went to the country.

These natives are strange people. They can die whenever they want to. Don't mind dying any more than a jilted Frenchman. When they take a notion to die they *die* no matter whether anything matters or not. They will lie right down sometimes and say they are going to die, and can't be persuaded otherwise. Have got ready to die, made up their minds to die, and *will* die in spite of all. A gentleman in Hawaii asked his servant if he wouldn't like to die and have a big funeral.

He said yes and looked happy.

And the next morning the overseer came and said, "That boy of yours laid down and died last night and said you were going to give him a fine funeral."

They are more civilized and Christianized than they used to be but still they believe an enemy can offer incantations to the idols and pray them to death. Three Kanakas on one whaleship that left the islands last year died one after the other from no apparent cause, and each said it was no use to try to save them, for they knew some enemy at home was praying them to death. I know there is something in it albeit it is rank idolatry, and I sincerely feel for these poor creatures. Even in this Christian city I went to church last Sunday and came mighty near getting prayed to death myself.

The Kanakas are passionately fond of dogs. Not great magnificent Newfoundlands or stately mastiffs or graceful greyhounds. But a species of little, puny, cowardly, sneaking, noisy cur that a white man would condemn to death on general principles. They love these puppies better then they love one another—better than their children or their religion. They feed them, stuff them with poi and fish from their own calabashes when the supply is scanty and even the family must go hungry. They sleep with them. They don't mind the fleas. Men and women carry these dogs in their arms always. If they have got to walk a mile the dog must be carried—or five miles, for that matter—while the little children walk. The dog travels in the schooners with them.

I have seen a puppy hugged and caressed by a mother, and her little, tired, sore-footed child cuffed and slapped for stumbling to the ground and crying. When the woman rides on horseback she often carries the puppy in front of her on the horse. And when the man rides (they nearly always go in a keen gallop) the puppy stands up behind the saddle, "thortships," as a sailor would say, and sways gently to and fro to the motion of the horse. No danger of its falling. It is educated to ride thus from earliest puppyhood. They passionately love and tenderly care for the puppy and feed it from their own hands until it is a full-grown dog. And then they cook it and eat it.

I did not eat any dog. I ate raw salt pork and poi and that was bad enough. But I was lost in the woods and hungry.

I do not see where old Kamehameha got his fierce warriors. He was a great warrior, you know, a Kanaka Napoleon, and in the old times, when the feudal system prevailed and the islands were so divided up that there was an average of three kings to an acre, he held four aces once and took them all in and combined the whole concern under one sovereignty. He fought many great battles but I cannot think where he got his fighting material, for certainly the Kanakas of the present day are the most peaceable, inoffensive, unwarlike creatures imaginable. One would as soon expect a rabbit to fight as one of these.

You often see them quarreling, doubling their fists and striking them together and making frightful grimaces and hurling curses and the deadliest insults at one another, even striking out savagely within an inch of one another's faces. And just as you think blood is going to flow, just as you think there is going to be a Kanaka for breakfast, it all ends in smoke. They go off growling and viciously shaking their heads.

The army of the Hawaiian Islands consists of two hundred men. They have got a Secretary of War there. And a Secretary of the Navy too, for that matter, but not any ships. And a Minister of Finance also—Harris—and if he stays there they won't have any money shortly. The army consists of two hundred men but it is not on a war footing now, happily. Some of the muskets haven't got any locks to them. And the others haven't got any ramrods.

Kanakas are fond of horses and they have got plenty of them. They seldom walk anywhere. They nearly always ride. Whenever you see a lot of men and women at work in a sugar plantation you will see as many horses hitched at hand for them to ride a quarter of a mile home on. These horses are worth on an average about seven dollars and a half apiece (you can often buy them for less, though), and they have to pay a government tax of a dollar a head on them.

But that doesn't matter. A Kanaka with an income of fifty dollars a year will keep half a dozen horses if it breaks him. And he is as unkind and as unmerciful to his horse as he is disgustingly fond of his puppy. His horse is seldom well fed and is always hard ridden. And they can make a horse go when a white man can't. If there is any of that capacity in a horse the Kanaka will get it out.

I once rode over a mountain in Mani with a white man whose horse was so lean and spiritless and worthless that he could not be persuaded or spurred out of a walk. And he kept going to sleep, besides—at least he seemed to. But the man said that when he got to Maaleo Bay he would find one of his own horses there, a blooded animal that could outstrip the wind.

He got his blooded animal and gave the slow horse to a Kanaka boy and told him to follow. Then he put his blooded steed to his utmost speed to show him off. But the Kanaka, without spur or whip or scarcely any appearance of urging, sailed by us on the old plug and stayed ahead, and in eight miles he beat us out of sight.

I never could understand how those savages managed to make those wretched horses travel so. They are wild, free riders and perfectly at home in the saddle. They call it a saddle, a little vile English spoon of a thing with a girth that never is tight enough to touch the horse and sometimes without any girth at all. With their loose ideas, they never cinch a Californian's horse tight enough to suit him.

When a Kanaka rides through the country he stops fifteen or twenty minutes at every single cabin he comes to and has a chat. Consequently their horses early acquire an inveterate habit of stopping, and they cannot be cured of it. If you attempt to keep them in the road and go on about your business they grow frantic and kick up and charge around fiercely and finally take the bits in their mouths and carry you to the cabin by main force.

I rode Kanaka horses nearly altogether. When I made the tour of that pleasant country I hadn't any business at any of the roadside cabins but I stopped at them all. The horses wanted to stop and I had to put up with it. That is how I happen to have such an intimate knowledge of the country and the people.

The Kanaka women all ride, and ride well and gracefully. They ride as women *should* ride—astride. To ride sidewise tires the horse, makes his back sore and his footing insecure, and endangers the life of the rider. A sidesaddle is always turning and spilling its precious freight into the mud or on the rocks and bruising the limbs or breaking the neck of the same. For a woman to ride sidewise is to do an awkward, ungainly, absurd and to the last degree foolish and perilous thing.

Kanakas are cruel by nature. They will put a live chicken in the hot embers merely to see it caper about. They used to be cruel to themselves before the missionaries came. They used to tear and burn their flesh or shave their heads or pluck out their eyes or knock out a couple of their front teeth when a great chief died. And if their bereavement were particularly sore and hard to bear they would go out and murder a neighbor. There was no law against it. The largest liberty in the matter of mourning was permitted. But the missionaries have done away with all that.

Down there in the islands they have exploded one of our most ancient and trusted maxims. It was a maxim that we have all of us implicitly believed in and revered and now it turns out to be a swindling humbug. *Be virtuous and you will be happy.* The Kanakas are not virtuous—neither men, women nor children—and yet they are the happiest creatures the sun shines on. They are as happy as the day is long. They wail and carry on grievously when a friend or relative dies but it is all a pretense. They do precisely the same thing when a friend returns from a month's absence. In both instances the tears are manufactured to order and the joy and sorrow counterfeited.

A woman returns from a distance and a lot of her female friends will huddle around her on the ground and twine their arms about her and weep and whine and blubber and howl for an hour. And they would cheerfully repeat the same thing the next day if she died, and dance the hula-hula into the bargain. It is rarely that they show any genuine tribulation. Theirs is a state of placid happiness. All they want is unfettered liberty to eat, drink, sleep, sing, dance, swindle, lie and pray, and then whether school keeps or not is a matter of no interest to them.

The natives do everything wrong end foremost. When you meet one on horseback he turns out on the wrong side. They cinch a horse on the wrong side and mount him from the wrong side. Their lineage and rank come down from the female ancestor instead of the male. The women smoke more than the men. The natives' English "no" generally means "yes." They eat their fish raw and bathe in the middle of the day. Instead of keeping it from a patient that he is likely to die they tell him early. When they beckon to a person to come they motion the hand in the opposite direction.

The only native bird that has handsome feathers has only two, and they are under its wings instead of on top of its head. Frequently a native cat has a tail only two inches long and has got a knot tied in the end of it. The native duck lives on the dry tops of mountains 5,000 feet high. The natives always stew chickens instead of baking them. They dance at funerals and sing a dismal heart-broken dirge when they are happy. And with atrocious perverseness they wash your shirts with a club and iron them with a brickbat.

In old times the Kanaka king was the owner of all the lands and supreme head of church and state. He was absolute. His word was superior to all law. His person was sacred. If a common man passed his house without prostrating himself, if he came near the king with his head wet, if he ventured to stand on a hillock that brought him higher than the level the king stood on, if his intangible and harmless shadow fell upon the king's royal person, that man had to die. There was no salvation for him. Thus sacred was the presence and the belongings of those naked, greasy, mud-colored, regal savages. The king had the power of life and death and liberty over all. He could place a taboo (prohibition) upon any spot or thing or person, and it was death for any man to molest it.

The high priest came next in authority—decreed the human sacrifices and captured the doomed men and butchered them. They regulated and bossed all such matters under the king. The chiefs came next. They held the lands by feudal tenure from the king and owed him service, as in England in the old baronial days. The common Kanakas came next. They were the slaves of the chiefs, sweated and labored for them and were cruelly maltreated in return.

After these came the women, and they were the abject slaves of the men. They were degraded to the rank of brutes and beasts and considered to be no better. They were kept at hard labor and were beaten and contemptuously treated by their lords. By the taboo it was death for them to sit at the tables with their husbands or to eat of the choice fruits of the lands, such as bananas, pineapples, etc., at any time. They seemed to have had a sort of dim knowledge of what came of women eating fruit in the Garden of Eden and they didn't feel justified in taking any more chances. And it is wisdom, unquestionably it is wisdom. Adam wasn't strict enough. Eve broke the taboo and hence comes all this trouble. Can't be too particular about fruit—with women.

They were a rusty set all round, those Kanakas in those days. But the missionaries came and knocked off the shackles from the whole race, broke the power of the king and the chiefs and set the common man free and elevated his wife to an equality with him and got a patch of land set apart and secured to each to hold forever. And the missionaries set up schools and churches and printing presses and taught the people the Christian religion after a fashion, and taught the whole nation to read and write with facility in the native tongue. And now I suppose there is not an uneducated Kanaka in the kingdom.

The natives of the Sandwich Islands are dark brown. Their tropical sun and the easy-going ways inherited from their ancestors have made them rather lazy, perhaps, but they are not vicious. Nor yet virtuous altogether. The missionaries have educated them and have about half civilized and half christianized them. You may well say, "Well done, good and faithful servants!" for mortal man could not have accomplished more with such material to work upon.

The native women in the rural districts wear a single long, loose garment but the men don't. They don't wear anything to speak of. They would cheerfully wear a plug hat and a vest if they had them, but they haven't. . . .

If you would see magnificent scenery, scenery on a mighty scale, and yet scenery which charms with its softness and delights you with its unspeakable beauty at the same moment that it deeply impresses you with its grandeur and its sublimity, you should go to the islands. Each island is a mountain, or two or three mountains. They begin at the seashore in a torrid climate where the cocoa palm grows, and the coffee tree, the mango, orange, banana and the delicious chirinoya. They begin down there in a sweltering atmosphere, rise with a grand and gradual sweep till they hide their beautiful regalia of living green in the folds of the drooping clouds, and higher and higher yet they rise among the mists till their emerald forests change to dull and stunted shrubbery, then to scattering constellations of the brilliant silver sword, then higher yet to dreary, barren desolation.

No trees, no shrubs, nothing but torn and scorched and blackened piles of lava. Higher yet and then, towering toward heaven, above the dim and distant land, above the waveless sea and high above the rolling plains of clouds themselves, stands the awful summit, wrapped in a mantle of everlasting ice and snow and burnished with a tropical sunshine that fires it with a dazzling splendor. Here one may stand and shiver in the midst of eternal winter and look down upon a land reposing in the loveliest hues of a summer that hath no end.

Such is Mauna Loa—16,000 feet high by recent and accurate measurement, and such is Mauna Kea, 14,000 feet high. . . .

The natives are indifferent to volcanic terrors. During the progress of an eruption they ate, drank, bought, sold, planted, builded, apparently indifferent to the roar of consuming forests, the sight of devouring fire, the startling detonations, the hissing of escaping steam, the rending of the earth, the shivering and melting of gigantic rocks, the raging and dashing of the fiery waves, the bellowings and unearthly mutterings coming up from a burning deep. They went carelessly on amid the rain of ashes, sand and fiery scintillations, gazing vacantly on the ever-varying appearance of the atmosphere, murky, black, livid, blazing, the sudden rising of lofty pillars of flame, the upward curling of ten thousand columns of smoke, and

their majestic roll in dense and lurid clouds. All these moving phe-
nomena were regarded by them as the fall of a shower or the running of a brook. While to others they were as the tokens of a
burning world, the departing heavens, and a coming judge.

October 1866

2

When Clemens returned to New York on the *Quaker City* November 19, 1867, he discovered that his travel letters on the journey to the Holy Land, written for the *San Francisco Daily Alta California,* the *New York Tribune* and the *New York Herald,* had made him well known across the country. Two days later Elisha Bliss, Jr., of the American Publishing Company of Hartford, Connecticut, a subscription publisher, wrote to him, expressing strong interest in issuing a book by him, perhaps one based on the travel letters. Clemens was in Washington, trying to scout out a government job for his brother, Orion.

The following talk was given at a banquet of the Newspaper Correspondents Club in Washington in response to the toast, "Woman—the pride of any profession and the jewel of ours." P. T. Barnum exhibited Joyce Heth with the claim that she had been George Washington's nurse and was now a hundred and sixty years old. Lucy Stone and Elizabeth Cady Stanton were American feminists, as was George Francis Train.

WOMAN

I do not know why I should be singled out to receive the greatest distinction of the evening, for so the office of replying to the toast of woman has been regarded in every age. I do not know why I have received this distinction unless it be that I am a trifle less homely than the other members of the club. But be this as it may, Mr. President, I am proud of the position, and you could not have chosen anyone who would have accepted it more gladly or labored with a heartier goodwill to do the subject justice than I—because, sir, I love the sex. I love all the women, irrespective of age or color.

Human intellect cannot estimate what we owe to woman, sir. She sews on our buttons, she mends our clothes, she ropes us in at the church fairs, she confides in us, she tells us whatever she can find out about the little private affairs of the neighbors, she gives us good advice, and plenty of it, she soothes our aching brows, she bears our children—ours as a general thing. In all relations of life, sir, it is but a just and graceful tribute to woman to say of her that she is a brick.

Wheresoever you place woman, sir, in whatever position or estate, she is an ornament to the place she occupies and a treasure to the world. Look at Cleopatra! Look at Desdemona! Look at Florence Nightingale! Look at Joan of Arc! Look at Lucretia Borgia! Well, suppose we let Lucretia slide. Look at Joyce Heth! Look at Mother Eve! You need not look at her unless you want to but Eve was ornamental, sir, particularly before the fashions changed.

I repeat, sir, look at the illustrious names of history. Look at the Widow Machree! Look at Lucy Stone! Look at Elizabeth Cady Stanton! Look at George Francis Train! And, sir, I say it with bowed head and deepest veneration, look at the mother of Washington! She raised a boy that could not tell a lie—could not tell a lie! But he never had any chance. It might have been different if he had belonged to the Washington Newspaper Correspondents Club.

I repeat, sir, that in whatever position you place a woman she is an ornament to society and a treasure to the world. As a sweetheart she has few equals and no superiors. As a cousin she is convenient. As a wealthy grandmother with an incurable distemper she is precious. As a wet nurse she has no equal among men.

What, sir, would the people of the earth be without woman? They would be scarce, sir, almighty scarce. Then let us cherish her, let us protect her, let us give her our support, our encouragement, our sympathy, ourselves—if we get a chance.

But, jesting aside, Mr. President, woman is lovable, gracious, kind of heart, beautiful—worthy of all respect, of all esteem, of all deference. Not any here will refuse to drink her health right cordially in this bumper of wine, for each and every one has personally known and loved and honored the very best one of them all—his own mother.

January 1868

3

This lecture was based on Clemens's experiences on the *Quaker City* excursion of 1867. The material was also used in *The Innocents Abroad*, the triumphant result of the excursion. Clemens repeated the lecture many times between November 1868 and March 1869. *The Innocents Abroad* was published in July 1869. By the end of January 1870 more than 30,000 copies had been sold.

AMERICAN VANDAL ABROAD

I am to speak of the American Vandal this evening but I wish to say in advance that I do not use this term in derision or apply it as a reproach, but I use it because it is convenient. And duly and properly modified, it best describes the roving, independent, free-and-easy character of that class of traveling Americans who are *not* elaborately educated, cultivated and refined and gilded and filigreed with the ineffable graces of the first society.

The best class of our countrymen who go abroad keep us well posted about their doings in foreign lands. But their brethren vandals cannot sing their own praises or publish their adventures.

The American Vandal gallops over England, Scotland, Spain and Switzerland and finally brings up in Italy. He thinks it is the proper thing to visit Genoa, the stately old City of Palaces, whose vast marble edifices almost meet together over streets so narrow that three men can hardly walk abreast in them and so crooked that a man generally comes out of them about the same place he went in. He only stays in Genoa long enough to see a few celebrated things and get some fragments of stone from the house Columbus was born in. For your genuine Vandal is an intolerable and incorrigible relic gatherer. It is estimated that if all the fragments of stone brought from Columbus's house by travelers were collected together they would suffice to build a house fourteen thousand feet long and sixteen thousand feet high. And I suppose they would.

Next he hurries to Milan and takes notes of the Grand Cathedral (for he is always taking notes). Oh, I remember Milan and the noble cathedral well enough, that marble miracle of enchanting architecture. I remember how we entered and walked about its vast spaces and among its huge columns, gazing aloft at the monster windows all aglow with brilliantly colored scenes in the life of the Savior and his followers. And I remember the side shows and curiosities there, too.

The guide showed us a coffee-colored piece of sculpture which he said was considered to have come from the hand of Phidias, since it was not possible that any other man, of any epoch, could have copied nature with such faultless accuracy. The figure was that of a man without a skin. With every vein, artery, muscle, every fiber and tendon and tissue of the human frame represented in minute detail. It looked natural because it looked somehow as if it were in pain. A skinned man would be likely to look that way—unless his attention were occupied by some other matter.

The Vandal goes to see the ancient and most celebrated painting in the world, "The Last Supper." We all know it in engravings: the disciples all sitting at a long, plain table and Christ with bowed head in the center. All the last suppers in the world are copied from this painting. It is so damaged now by the wear and tear of three hundred years that the figures can hardly be distinguished. The Vandal goes to see this picture, which all the world praises, looks at it with a critical eye and says it's a perfect old nightmare of a picture and he wouldn't give forty dollars for a million like it (and I endorse his opinion), and then he is done with Milan.

He paddles around the Lake of Como for a few days and then takes the cars. He is bound for Venice, the oldest and the proudest and the princeliest republic that ever graced the earth. We put on a good many airs with our little infant of a Republic of a century's growth, but we grow modest when we stand before this gray old imperial city that used to laugh the armies and navies of half the world to scorn, and was a haughty, invincible, magnificent Republic for fourteen hundred years. The Vandal is bound for Venice! He has a long, long, weary ride of it. But just as the day is closing he hears someone shout, "Venice!" and puts his head out of the window, and sure enough, afloat on the placid sea, a league away, lies the great city with its towers and domes and steeples drowsing in a golden mist of sunset.

Have you been to Venice and seen the winding canals and the stately edifices that border them all along, ornamented with the quaint devices and sculptures of a former age? And have you seen the great Cathedral of St. Mark's, and the Giant's Staircase, and the famous Bridge of Sighs, and the great Square of St. Mark's, and the ancient pillar with the winged lion of St. Mark that stands in it, whose story and whose origin are a mystery—and the Rialto, where Shylock used to loan money on human flesh and other collateral?

I had begun to feel that the old Venice of song and story had departed forever. But I was too hasty. When we swept gracefully out into the Grand Canal and under the mellow moonlight the Venice of poetry and romance stood revealed. Right from the water's edge rose palaces of marble. Gondolas were gliding swiftly hither and thither and disappearing suddenly through unsuspected gates and alleys. Ponderous stone bridges threw their shadows athwart the glittering waves. There were life and motion everywhere, and yet everywhere there was a hush, a stealthy sort of stillness that was suggestive of secret enterprises, of bravos and of lovers. And, clad half in moonbeams and half in mysterious shadows, the grim old mansions of the republic seemed to have an expression about them of having an eye out for just such enterprises as these. At that same moment music came stealing over the waters. Venice was complete.

Our Vandals hurried away from Venice and scattered abroad everywhere. You could find them breaking specimens from the dilapidated tomb of Romeo and Juliet at Padua. And infesting the picture galleries of Florence. And risking their necks on the Leaning Tower of Pisa. And snuffing sulphur fumes on the summit of Vesuvius. And burrowing among the exhumed wonders of Herculaneum and Pompeii. And you might see them with spectacles on and blue cotton umbrellas under their arms, benignantly contemplating Rome from the venerable arches of the Coliseum.

And finally we sailed from Naples and in due time anchored before the Piraeus, the seaport of Athens in Greece. But the quarantine was in force and so they set a guard of soldiers to watch us and would not let us go ashore. However, I and three other Vandals took a boat and muffled the oars and slipped ashore at 11:30 at night and dodged the guard successfully. Then we made a wide circuit around the slumbering town, avoiding all roads and houses, for they'd about as soon hang a body as not for violating the quarantine laws in those countries.

We got around the town without any accident and then struck out across the Attic Plain, steering straight for Athens over rocks and hills and brambles and everything, with Mt. Helicon for a landmark. And so we tramped for five or six miles. The Attic Plain is a mighty uncomfortable plain to travel in, even if it *is* so historical. The armed guards got after us three times and flourished their gleaming gun barrels in the moonlight because they thought we were stealing grapes occasionally—and the fact is we *were*, for we found by and by that the brambles that tripped us up so often were grape vines. But these people in the country didn't know that we were quarantine-blockade runners and so they only scared us and jawed Greek at us, and let us go instead of arresting us.

We didn't care about Athens particularly but we wanted to see the famous Acropolis and its ruined temples, and we did. We climbed the steep hill of the Acropolis about one in the morning and tried to storm that grand old fortress that had scorned the battles and sieges of three thousand years. We had the garrison out mighty quick (four Greeks) and we bribed them to betray the citadel and unlock the gates.

In a moment we stood in the presence of the noblest ruins we had ever seen, the most elegant, the most graceful, the most imposing. The renowned Parthenon towered above us, and about us were the wreck of what were once the snowy marble Temples of Hercules and Minerva, and another whose name I have forgotten. Most of the Parthenon's grand columns are still standing. But the roof is gone.

As we wandered down the marble-paved length of this mighty temple the scene was strangely impressive. Here and there in lavish profusion were gleaming white statues of men and women propped against blocks of marble, some of them armless, some without legs, others headless, but all looking mournful and sentient and startlingly human. They rose up and confronted the midnight intruder on every side. They stared at him with stony eyes from unlooked-for nooks and recesses. They peered at him over fragmentary heaps far down the desolate corridors. They barred his way in the midst of the broad forum and solemnly pointed with handless arms the way from the sacred fane. And through the roofless temple the moon looked down and banded the floor and darkened the scattered fragments and broken statues with the slanting shadows of the columns.

What a world of ruined sculpture was about us. Stood up in rows, stacked up in piles, scattered broadcast over the wide area of the Acropolis, were hundreds of crippled statues of all sizes and of the most exquisite workmanship, and vast fragments of marble that once belonged to the entablatures, covered with bas-reliefs representing battles and sieges, ships of war with three and four tiers of oars, pageants and processions, everything one could think of.

We walked out into the grass-grown, fragment-strewn court beyond the Parthenon. It startled us every now and then to see a stony white face stare suddenly up at us out of the grass with its dead eyes. The place seemed alive with ghosts. We half expected to see the Athenian heroes of twenty centuries ago glide out of the shadows and steal into the old temple they knew so well and re-garded with such boundless pride.

The full moon was riding high in the cloudless heavens now. We sauntered carelessly and unthinkingly to the edge of the lofty battle-ments of the citadel and looked down. And lo, a vision! And such a vision! Athens by moonlight! All the beauty in all the world com-bined could not rival it. The prophet that thought the splendors of the New Jerusalem were revealed to him surely saw this instead. It lay in the level plain right under our feet, all spread abroad like a picture, and we looked down upon it as we might have looked from a balloon.

We saw no semblance of a street. But every house, every win-dow, every clinging vine, every projection was as distinct and sharply marked as if the time were noonday. And yet there was no glare, no glitter, nothing harsh or repulsive. The silent city was flooded with the mellowest light that ever streamed from the moon, and seemed like some living creature wrapped in peaceful slumber. On its farther side was a little temple whose delicate pillars and ornate front glowed with a rich luster that chained the eye like a spell. And nearer by the palace of the king reared its creamy walls out of the midst of a great garden of shrubbery that was flecked all over with a random shower of amber lights, a spray of golden sparks that lost their brightness in the glory of the moon and glinted softly upon the sea of dark foliage like the palled stars of the Milky Way. Overhead the stately columns, majestic still in their ruin. Underfoot the dreaming city. In the distance the silver sea. Not on the broad earth is there another picture half so beautiful.

We got back to the ship safely just as the day was dawning. We had walked upon pavements that had been pressed by Plato, Aristotle, Demosthenes, Socrates, Phocion, Euclid, Xenophon, Herodotus, Diogenes and a hundred others of deathless fame, and were satisfied. We got to stealing grapes again on the way back, and half a dozen rascally guards with muskets and pistols captured us and marched us in the center of a hollow square nearly to the sea till we were beyond all the graperies. Military escort. Ah, I never traveled in so much state in all my life.

I leave the Vandal here. I have not time to follow him farther, nor our Vandals to Constantinople and Smyrna and the Holy Land, Egypt, the islands of the sea, and to Russia and his visit to the emperor. But I wish I could tell of that visit of our gang of Quaker City Vandals to the grandest monarch of the age, America's stanch old steadfast friend, Alexander II, Autocrat of Russia.

In closing these remarks I will observe that I could have said more about the American Vandal abroad and less about other things, but I found that he had too many disagreeable points about him, and so I thought I would touch him lightly and let him go.

If there is a moral to this lecture it is an injunction to all Vandals to travel. I am glad the American Vandal goes abroad. It does him good. It makes a better man of him. It rubs out a multitude of his old unworthy biases and prejudices. It aids his religion, for it enlarges his charity and his benevolence, it broadens his views of men and things, it deepens his generosity and his compassion for the failings and shortcomings of his fellow creatures.

Contact with men of various nations and many creeds teaches him that there are other people in the world besides his own little clique, and other opinions as worthy of attention and respect as his own. He finds that he and his are not the most momentous matters in the universe. Cast into trouble and misfortune in strange lands and being mercifully cared for by those he never saw before, he begins to learn that best lesson of all, that one which culminates in the conviction that God puts something good and something lovable in every man his hands create, that the world is not a cold, harsh, cruel prisonhouse stocked with all manner of selfishness and hate and wickedness.

It liberalizes the Vandal to travel. You never saw a bigoted, opinionated, stubborn, narrow-minded, self-conceited, almighty mean man in your life but he had stuck in one place ever since he was born and thought God made the world and dyspepsia and bile for his especial comfort and satisfaction.

So I say, by all means let the American Vandal go on traveling. And let no man discourage him.

about November 1868

ᦞ 4 ᦞ

According to Albert Bigelow Paine, this speech was given "at a social meeting of literary men in New York." The occasion was a dinner sponsored by the publisher of *The Aldine*, a New York monthly magazine. A variation of the anecdote about Jim Wolfe, together with other colorful material about him, appear in *The Autobiography of Mark Twain.*

JIM WOLFE

When I was fourteen I was living with my parents, who were very poor, and correspondently honest. We had a youth living with us by the name of Jim Wolfe. He was an excellent fellow, seventeen years old and very diffident. He and I slept together—virtuously. And one bitter winter's night a cousin Mary (she's married now and gone) gave what they call a candy pulling in those days in the West, and they took the saucers of hot candy outside of the house into the snow, under a sort of old bower that came from the eaves (it was a sort of an ell then, all covered with vines) to cool this hot candy in the snow, and they were all sitting there. In the meantime we were gone to bed. We were not invited to attend this party. We were too young.

The young ladies and gentlemen were assembled there, and Jim and I were in bed. There was about four inches of snow on the roof of this ell, and our windows looked out on it, and it was frozen hard. A couple of tom cats—it is possible one might have been of the opposite sex—were assembled on the chimney in the middle of this ell, and they were growling at a fearful rate and switching their tails about and going on, and we couldn't sleep at all.

Finally Jim said, "For two cents I'd go out and shake them cats off that chimney."

[20]

So I said, "Of course you would."

He said, "Well, I would. I have a mighty good notion to do it."

Says I, "Of course you have. Certainly you have. You have a great notion to do it."

I hoped he might try it but I was afraid he wouldn't.

Finally I did get his ambition up and he raised the window and climbed out on the icy roof with nothing on but his socks and a very short shirt. He went climbing along on all fours on the roof toward the chimney where the cats were.

In the meantime these young ladies and gentlemen were enjoying themselves down under the eaves. And when Jim got almost to that chimney he made a pass at the cats, and his heels flew up and he shot down and crashed through those vines and lit in the midst of the ladies and gentlemen and sat down in those hot saucers of candy.

There was a stampede, of course, and he came upstairs dropping pieces of chinaware and candy all the way up. And when he got up there (now anybody in the world would have gone into profanity or something calculated to relieve the mind, but he didn't) he scraped the candy off his legs, nursed his blisters a little, and said, "I could have ketched them cats if I had had on a good ready."

February 1872

๛ 5 ๛

Clemens went to England in 1872 to collect materials for a new travel book but he soon lost himself in socializing. The following was given at the Whitefriars Club in London. David Livingstone was a Scottish missionary and African explorer. Henry Morton Stanley was the British journalist and explorer who found Livingstone in Ujiji, Africa, having been commissioned by the *New York Herald* to do so. This was three years after Livingstone had last been heard from.

STANLEY AND LIVINGSTONE

I thank you very heartily indeed for this expression of kindness toward me. What I have done for England and civilization in the arduous affairs which I have engaged in (that is good: that is so smooth that I will say it again and again)—what I have done for England and civilization in the arduous part I have performed I have done with a single-hearted devotion and with no hope of reward.

I am proud, I am very proud, that it was reserved for me to find Doctor Livingstone and for Mr. Stanley to get all the credit. I hunted for that man in Africa all over seventy-five or one hundred parishes, thousands and thousands of miles in the wilds and deserts all over the place, sometimes riding Negroes and sometimes traveling by rail. I didn't mind the rail or anything else, so that I didn't come in for the tar and feathers.

I found that man at Ujiji—a place you may remember if you have been there—and it was a very great satisfaction that I found him just in the nick of time. I found that poor old man deserted by his niggers and by his geographers, deserted by all of his kind except the gorillas—dejected, miserable, famishing, absolutely famishing—but he was eloquent. Just as I found him he had eaten his last elephant,

[22]

and he said to me, "God knows where I shall get another." He had nothing to wear except his venerable and honorable naval suit and nothing to eat but his diary.

But I said to him, "It is all right, I have discovered you, and Stanley will be here by the four o'clock train and will discover you officially and then we will turn to and have a reg'lar good time."

I said, "Cheer up, for Stanley has got corn, ammunition, glass beads, hymn books, whiskey and everything which the human heart can desire. He has got all kinds of valuables, including telegraph poles and a few cart-loads of money. By this time communication has been made with the land of Bibles and civilization, and property will advance."

And then we surveyed all that country from Ujiji through Unanogo and other places, to Unyanyembe. I mention these names simply for your edification, nothing more—do not expect it, particularly as intelligence to the Royal Geographical Society.

And then, having filled up the old man, we were all too full for utterance and departed. We have since then feasted on honors.

Stanley has received a snuff box and I have received considerable snuff. He has got to write a book and gather in the rest of the credit, and I am going to levy on the copyright and to collect the money. Nothing comes amiss to me—cash or credit.

But seriously, I do feel that Stanley is the chief man and an illustrious one, and I do applaud him with all my heart. Whether he is an American or a Welshman by birth, or one, or both, matters not to me. So far as I am personally concerned I am simply here to stay a few months and to see English people and to learn English manners and customs and to enjoy myself. So the simplest thing I can do is to thank you for the toast you have honored me with and for the remarks you have made and to wish health and prosperity to the Whitefriars Club, and to sink down to my accustomed level.

about October 1872

6

In September of 1872 Clemens was guest of honor at a dinner of the Savage Club, London. Artemus Ward had been a club favorite. Clemens was joking about Leicester Square. The square was in a state of chaos. In the center of it were the remains of an equestrian statue, the king being headless and limbless. He was also kidding about Hyde Park, where public cabs were forbidden. Only private carriages were permitted there. He was, of course, being sarcastic when he placed Prince Albert in the company of Wellington and Nelson.

LONDON

It affords me sincere pleasure to meet this distinguished club, a club which had extended its hospitalities and its cordial welcome to so many of my countrymen. I hope you will excuse these clothes. I am going to the theater. That will explain these clothes. I have other clothes than these.

Judging human nature by what I have seen of it, I suppose that the customary thing for a stranger to do when he stands here is to make a pun on the name of this club under the impression of course that he is the first man that that idea has occurred to. It is a credit to our human nature, not a blemish upon it, for it shows that underlying all our depravity (and God knows and you know we are depraved enough) and all our sophistication, and untarnished by them, there is a sweet germ of innocence and simplicity still.

When a stranger says to me with a glow of inspiration in his eye some gentle, innocuous little thing about "Twain and one flesh," and all that sort of thing, I don't try to crush that man into the earth—no.

I feel like saying, "Let me take you by the hand, sir. Let me embrace you. I have not heard that pun for weeks."

[24]

We will deal in palpable puns. We will call parties named King "Your Majesty," and we will say to the Smiths that we think we have heard that name before somewhere. Such is human nature. We cannot alter this. It is God that made us so for some good and wise purpose. Let us not repine. But though I may seem strange, may seem eccentric, I mean to refrain from punning upon the name of this club though I could make a very good one if I had time to think about it—a week.

I cannot express to you what entire enjoyment I find in this first visit to this prodigious metropolis of yours. Its wonders seem to me to be limitless. I go about as in a dream, as in a realm of enchantment, where many things are rare and beautiful and all things are strange and marvelous. Hour after hour I stand, I stand spellbound, as it were, and gaze upon the statuary in Leicester Square. I visit the mortuary effigies of noble old Henry VIII and Judge Jeffreys and the preserved gorilla and try to make up my mind which of my ancestors I admire the most.

I go to that matchless Hyde Park and drive all around it and then I start to enter it at the Marble Arch and am induced to change my mind. It is a great benefaction, is Hyde Park. There in his hansom cab the invalid can go, the poor sad child of misfortune, and insert his nose between the railings and breathe the pure health-giving air of the country and of heaven. And if he is a swell invalid, who isn't obliged to depend upon parks for his country air, he can drive inside—if he owns his vehicle. I drive round and round Hyde Park, and the more I see of the edges of it the more grateful I am that the margin is extensive.

And I have been to Zoological Gardens. What a wonderful place that is. I never have seen such a curious and interesting variety of wild animals in any garden before—except "Mabille." I never believed before there were so many different kinds of animals in the world as you can find there, and I don't believe it yet. I have been to the British Museum. I would advise you to drop in there some time when you have nothing to do for five minutes if you have never been there. It seems to me the noblest monument that this nation has yet erected to her greatness. I say to her, our greatness—as a nation. True, she has built other monuments, and stately ones, as well. But these she has uplifted in honor of two or three colossal demigods who have stalked across the world's stage, destroying tyrants and delivering nations, and whose prodigies will still live in the memories of men ages after their monuments shall have crumbled to dust. I refer to the Wellington and Nelson monuments and the Albert memorial.

The library at the British Museum I find particularly astounding. I have read there hours together and hardly made an impression on it. I revere that library. It is the author's friend. I don't care how mean a book is, it always takes one copy. And then every day that author goes there to gaze at that book and is encouraged to go on in the good work. And what a touching sight it is of a Saturday afternoon to see the poor, careworn clergymen gathered together in that vast reading room cabbaging sermons for Sunday.

You will pardon my referring to these things. Everything in this monster city interests me and I cannot keep from talking, even at the risk of being instructive. People here seem always to express distances by parables. To a stranger it is just a little confusing to be so parabolic, so to speak. I collar a citizen and I think I am going to get some valuable information out of him. I ask him how far it is to Birmingham and he says it is twenty-one shillings and sixpence. Now we know that doesn't help a man who is trying to learn. I find myself downtown somewhere and I want to get some sort of idea where I am, being usually lost when alone. And I stop a citizen and say, "How far is it to Charing Cross?"

"Shilling fare in a cab," and off he goes.

I suppose if I were to ask a Londoner how far it is from the sublime to the ridiculous he would try to express it in coin.

But I am trespassing upon your time with these geological statistics and historical reflections. I will not longer keep you from your orgies.

'Tis a real pleasure for me to be here, and I thank you for it.

The name of the Savage Club is associated in my mind with the kindly interest and the friendly offices which you lavished upon an old friend of mine who came among you a stranger, and you opened your English hearts to him and gave him welcome and a home—Artemus Ward. Asking that you will join me, I give you his memory.

about September 1872

Clemens sailed for New York on November 12, 1872. That winter he began building his Hartford house on Farmington Avenue. The following talk was given at the Monday Evening Club in Hartford.

SINS OF THE PRESS

The press has scoffed at religion till it has made scoffing popular. It has defended official criminals on party pretexts until it has created a United States whose members are incapable of determining what crime against law and the dignity of their own body is, they are so morally blind, and it has made light of dishonesty till we have as a result a Congress which contracts to work for a certain sum and then deliberately steals additional wages out of the public pocket and is pained and surprised that anybody should worry about a little thing like that.

I am putting all this odious state of things upon the newspaper and I believe it belongs there—chiefly, at any rate. It is a free press, a press that is more than free, a press which is licensed to say any infamous thing it chooses about a private or a public man, or advocate any outrageous doctrine it pleases. It is tied in no way. The public opinion which should hold it in bounds it has itself degraded to its own level. There are laws to protect the freedom of the press's speech but none that are worth anything to protect the people from the press.

A libel suit simply brings the plaintiff before a vast newspaper court to be tried before the law tries him, and reviled and ridiculed without mercy. The touchy Charles Reade can sue English newspapers and get verdicts. He would soon change his tactics here. The papers (backed by a public well taught by themselves) would soon teach him that it is better to suffer any amount of misrepresentation than go into our courts with a libel suit and make himself the laughing stock of the community.

It seems to me that just in the ratio that our newspapers increase our morals decay. The more newspapers the worse morals. Where we have one newspaper that does good, I think we have fifty that do harm. We ought to look upon the establishment of a newspaper of the average pattern in a virtuous village as a calamity.

The difference between the tone and conduct of newspapers today and those of thirty or forty years ago is very noteworthy and very sad. I mean the average newspaper, for they had bad ones then too. In those days the average newspaper was the champion of right and morals and it dealt conscientiously in the truth. It is not the case now. The other day a reputable New York daily had an editorial defending the salary steal and justifying it on the ground that Congressmen were not paid enough, as if that were an all-sufficient excuse for stealing. That editorial put the matter in a new and perfectly satisfactory light with many a leather-headed reader, without a doubt.

It has become a sarcastic proverb that a thing must be true if you saw it in a newspaper. That is the opinion intelligent people have of that lying vehicle in a nutshell. But the trouble is that the stupid people, who constitute the grand overwhelming majority of this and all other nations, do believe and are moulded and convinced by what they get out of a newspaper. And there is where the harm lies.

Among us the newspaper is a tremendous power. It can make or mar any man's reputation. It has perfect freedom to call the best man in the land a fraud and a thief, and he is destroyed beyond help. Whether Mr. Colfax is a liar or not can never be ascertained now. But he will rank as one till the day of his death, for the newspapers have so doomed him. Our newspapers—all of them, without exception—glorify the "Black Crook" and make it an opulent success. They could have killed it dead with one broadside of contemptuous silence if they had wanted to. *Days Doings* and *Police Gazettes* flourish in the land unmolested by the law because the virtuous newspapers long ago nurtured up a public laxity that loves indecency and never cares whether laws are administered or not.

In the newspapers of the West you can use the editorial voice in the editorial columns to defend any wretched and injurious dogma you please by paying a dollar a line for it.

Nearly all newspapers foster Rozensweigs and kindred criminals and send victims to them by opening their columns to their advertisements. You all know that.

In the Foster murder case the New York papers made a weak pretense of upholding the hands of the Governor and urging the people to sustain him in standing firmly by the law. But they printed a whole page of sickly maudlin appeals to his clemency as a paid advertisement. And I suppose they would have published enough pages of abuse of the Governor to destroy his efficiency as a public official to the end of his term if anybody had come forward and paid them for it—as an advertisement. The newspaper that obstructs the law on a trivial pretext for money's sake is a dangerous enemy to the public weal.

That awful power, the public opinion of a nation, is created in America by a horde of ignorant, self-complacent simpletons who failed at ditching and shoemaking and fetched up in journalism on their way to the poorhouse. I am personally acquainted with hundreds of journalists, and the opinion of the majority of them would not be worth tuppence in private. But when they speak in print it is the newpaper that is talking (the pygmy scribe is not visible) and then their utterances shake the community like the thunders of prophecy.

I know from personal experience the proneness of journalists to lie. I once started a peculiar and picturesque fashion of lying myself on the Pacific coast and it is not dead there to this day. Whenever I hear of a shower of blood and frogs combined in California, or a sea serpent found in some desert there, or a cave frescoed with diamonds and emeralds (always found by an Injun who died before he could finish telling where it was), I say to myself I am the father of this child, I have got to answer for this lie. And habit is everything. To this day I am liable to lie if I don't watch all the time.

The license of the press has scorched every individual of us in our time, I make no doubt. Poor Stanley was a very god in England, his praises in every man's mouth. But nobody said anything about his lectures, they were charitably quiet on that head and were content to praise his higher virtues. But our papers tore the poor creature limb from limb and scattered the fragments from Maine to California merely because he couldn't lecture well. His prodigious achievement in Africa goes for naught. The man is pulled down and utterly destroyed. But still the persecution follows him as relentlessly from city to city and from village to village as if he had committed some bloody and detestable crime.

Bret Harte was suddenly snatched out of obscurity by our papers and throned in the clouds. All the editors in the land stood out in the inclement weather and adored him through their telescopes and swung their hats till they wore them out and then borrowed more. And the first time his family fell sick, and in his trouble and harassment he ground out a rather flat article in place of another heathen Chinee, that hurrahing host said, "Why, this man's a fraud" and then they began to reach up there for him. And they got him, too, and fetched him down and walked over him and rolled him in the mud and tarred and feathered him and then set him up for a target and have been heaving dirt at him ever since.

The result is that the man has had only just nineteen engagements to lecture this year, and the audiences have been so scattering, too, that he has never discharged a sentence yet that hit two people at the same time. The man is ruined. Never can get up again. And yet he is a person who has great capabilities and might have accomplished great things for our literature and for himself if he had had a happier chance. And he made the mistake too of doing a pecuniary kindness for a starving beggar of our guild, one of the journalistic shoemaker class, and that beggar made it his business as soon as he got back to San Francisco to publish four columns of exposures of crimes committed by his benefactor, the least of which ought to make any decent man blush. The press that admitted that stuff to its columns had too much license.

In a town in Michigan I declined to dine with an editor who was drunk. And he said in his paper that my lecture was profane, indecent and calculated to encourage intemperance. And yet that man never heard it. It might have reformed him if he had.

A Detroit paper once said that I was in the constant habit of beating my wife and that I still kept this recreation up although I had crippled her for life and she was no longer able to keep out of my way when I came home in my usual frantic frame of mind. Now scarcely the half of that was true. Perhaps I ought to have sued that man for libel. But I knew better. All the papers in America, with a few creditable exceptions, would have found out then, to their satisfaction, that I was a wife beater. And they would have given it a pretty general airing, too.

Why *I* have published vicious libels upon people *myself.* And ought to have been hanged before my time for it, too. If I *do* say it myself that shouldn't.

But I will not continue these remarks. I have a sort of vague general idea that there is too much liberty of the press in this country, and that through the absence of all wholesome restraint the newspaper has become in a large degree a national curse, and will probably damn the Republic yet.

There *are* some excellent virtues in newspapers, some powers that wield vast influences for good. And I could have told all about these things and glorified them exhaustively. But that would have left you gentlemen nothing to say.

March 1873

✂ **8** ✂

This address was given at a gathering of Americans in London, July 4, 1873. Tweed was, of course, the notorious American political boss who headed the Tweed Ring. John Lothrop Motley was an American historian. Jay Gould was the American financier who with Daniel Drew and James Fisk tried to corner the gold market shortly after the end of the Civil War. Samuel C. Pomeroy was a senator from Kansas. General Robert Cumming Schenck was an American soldier and ambassador to Great Britain.

THERE IS HOPE FOR US YET

I thank you for the compliment which has just been tendered me, and to show my appreciation of it I will not afflict you with many words.

It is pleasant to celebrate in this peaceful way, upon this old mother soil, the anniversary of an experiment which was born of war with this same land so long ago and wrought out to a successful issue by the devotion of our ancestors. It has taken nearly a hundred years to bring the English and Americans into kindly and mutually appreciative relations but I believe it has been accomplished at last. It was a great step when the two last misunderstandings were settled by arbitration instead of cannon.

It is another great step when England adopts our sewing machines without claiming the invention—as usual. It was another when they imported one of our sleeping cars the other day. And it warmed my heart more than I can tell, yesterday, when I witnessed the spectacle of an Englishman ordering an American sherry cobbler of his own free will and accord, and not only that but with a great brain and a level head reminding the barkeeper not to forget the strawberries. With a common origin, a common language, a common literature, a common religion, and common drinks, what is longer needful to the cementing of the two nations together in a permanent bond of brotherhood?

This is an age of progress, and ours is a progressive land. A great and glorious land, too, a land which has developed a Washington, a Franklin, a William M. Tweed, a Longfellow, a Motley, a Jay Gould, a Samuel C. Pomeroy, a recent Congress which has never had its equal (in some respects), and a United States Army which conquered sixty Indians in eight months by tiring them out—which is much better than uncivilized slaughter, God knows. We have a criminal jury system which is superior to any in the world, and its efficiency is only marred by the difficulty of finding twelve men every day who don't know anything and can't read. And I may observe that we have an insanity plea that would have saved Cain. I think I can say, and say with pride, that we have some legislatures that bring higher prices than any in the world.

I refer with effusion to our railway system, which consents to let us live, though it might do the opposite, being our owners. It only destroyed three thousand and seventy lives last year by collisions, and twenty-seven thousand two hundred and sixty by running over heedless and unnecessary people at crossings. The companies seriously regretted the killing of these thirty thousand people and went so far as to pay for some of them—voluntarily, of course, for the meanest of us would not claim that we possess a court treacherous enough to enforce a law against a railway company.

But, thank Heaven, the railway companies are generally disposed to do the right and kindly thing without compulsion. I know of an instance which greatly touched me at the time. After an accident the company sent home the remains of a dear distant old relative of mine in a basket, with the remark, "Please state what figure you hold him at, and return the basket."

Now there couldn't be anything friendlier than that.

But I must not stand here and brag all night. However, you won't mind a body bragging a little about his country on the Fourth of July. It is a fair and legitimate time to fly the eagle. I will say only one more word of brag, and a hopeful one. It is this.

We have a form of government which gives each man a fair chance and no favor. With us no individual is born with a right to look down upon his neighbor and hold him in contempt. Let such of us as are not dukes find our consolation in that. And we may find hope for the future in the fact that as unhappy as is the condition of our political morality today, England has risen up out of a far fouler since the days when Charles I ennobled courtesans and all political place was a matter of bargain and sale.

There is hope for us yet.

July 1873

Years later Clemens remarked:

"At least the above is the speech which I was *going* to make. But our minister, General Schenck, presided, and after the blessing got up and made a great, long, inconceivably dull harangue and wound up by saying that inasmuch as speech making did not seem to exhilarate the guests much, all further oratory would be dispensed with during the evening and we could just sit and talk privately to our elbow neighbors and have a good, sociable time.

"It is known that in consequence of that remark forty-four perfected speeches died in the womb. The depression, the gloom, the solemnity that reigned over the banquet from that time forth will be a lasting memory with many that were there. By that one thoughtless remark General Schenck lost forty-four of the best friends he had in England. More than one said that night, 'And this is the sort of person that is sent to represent us in a great sister empire!'"

⚡ 9 ⚡

I could find no information about the occasions for the next two speeches, "Cigars" and "Boggs." Paine includes them in his edition of 1910 and indicates that each was given "about 1874."

CIGARS

My friends for some years now have remarked that I am an inveterate consumer of tobacco. That is true but my habits with regard to tobacco have changed. I have no doubt that you will say, when I have explained to you what my present purpose is, that my taste has deteriorated. But I do not so regard it.

Whenever I held a smoking party at my house I found that my guests had always just taken the pledge.

Let me tell you briefly the history of my personal relation to tobacco. It began, I think, when I was a lad and took the form of a quid, which I became expert in tucking under my tongue. Afterward I learned the delights of the pipe, and I suppose there was no other youngster of my age who could more deftly cut plug tobacco so as to make it available for pipe smoking.

Well, time ran on and there came a time when I was able to gratify one of my youthful ambitions. I could buy the choicest Havana cigars without seriously interfering with my income. I smoked a good many, changing off from the Havana cigars to the pipe in the course of a day's smoking.

At last it occurred to me that something was lacking in the Havana cigar. It did not quite fulfil my youthful anticipations. I experimented. I bought what was called a seed-leaf cigar with a Connecticut wrapper. After a while I became satiated of these and I searched for something else. The Pittsburgh stogy was recommended to me.

[35]

It certainly had the merit of cheapness, if that be a merit in tobacco, and I experimented with the stogy.

Then once more I changed off, so that I might acquire the subtler flavor of the Wheeling toby. Now that palled, and I looked around New York in the hope of finding cigars which would seem to most people vile, but which, I am sure, would be ambrosial to me. I couldn't find any. They put into my hands some of those little things that cost ten cents a box. But they are a delusion.

I said to a friend, "I want to know if you can direct me to an honest tobacco merchant who will tell me what is the worst cigar in the New York market, excepting those made for Chinese consumption. I want real tobacco. If you will do this and I find the man is as good as his word I will guarantee him a regular market for a fair amount of his cigars."

We found a tobacco dealer who would tell the truth, who, if a cigar was bad, would boldly say so. He produced what he called the very worst cigars he had ever had in his shop. He let me experiment with one then and there. The test was satisfactory.

This was, after all, the real thing. I negotiated for a box of them and took them away with me so that I might be sure of having them handy when I wanted them.

I discovered that the "worst cigars," so called, are the best for me, after all.

about 1874

✆ **10** ✆

BOGGS

I can assure you, ladies and gentlemen, that Nevada had lively
newspapers in those days. My great competitor among the reporters was Boggs, of the *Union*, an excellent reporter. Once in
three or four months he would get a little intoxicated. But as a general thing he was a wary and cautious drinker, although always ready
to damp himself a little with the enemy. He had the advantage of
me in one thing: he could get the monthly public school report and I
could not, because the principal hated my sheet, the *Enterprise*.

One snowy night when the report was due I started out, sadly
wondering how I was to get it. Presently, a few steps up the almost
deserted street, I stumbled on Boggs and asked him where he was
going.

"After the school report."

"I'll go along with you."

"No, sir. I'll excuse you."

"Have it your own way."

A saloon keeper's boy passed by with a steaming pitcher of hot
punch, and Boggs snuffed the fragrance gratefully. He gazed fondly
after the boy, and saw him start up the *Enterprise* stairs.

I said, "I wish you could help me get that school business. But
since you can't I must run up to the *Union* office and see if I can get
a proof of it after it's set up, though I don't begin to suppose I can.
Good night."

"Hold on a minute. I don't mind getting the report and sitting
around with the boys a little while you copy it if you're willing to
drop down to the principal's with me."

[37]

"Now you talk like a human being. Come along."

We ploughed a couple of blocks through the snow, got the report (a short document) and soon copied it in our office. Meantime, Boggs helped himself to the punch.

I gave the manuscript back to him and we started back to get an inquest.

At four o'clock in the morning, when we had gone to press and were having a relaxing concert as usual (for some of the printers were good singers and others good performers on the guitar and on that atrocity the accordion), the proprietor of the *Union* strode in and asked if anybody had heard anything of Boggs or the school report.

We stated the case, and all turned out to help hunt for the delinquent. We found him standing on a table in a saloon, with an old tin lantern in one hand and the school report in the other, haranguing a gang of "corned" miners on the iniquity of squandering the public money on education "when hundreds and hundreds of honest, hardworking men were literally starving for whiskey."

He had been assisting in a regal spree with those parties for hours. We dragged him away and put him into bed. Of course there was no school report in the *Union*, and Boggs held me accountable though I was innocent of any intention or desire to compass its absence from that paper, and was as sorry as any one that the misfortune had occurred. But we were perfectly friendly.

The day the next school report was due the proprietor of the Tennessee Mine furnished us a buggy and asked us to go down and write something about the property—a very common request and one always gladly acceded to when people furnished buggies, for we were as fond of pleasure excursions as other people. The "mine" was a hole in the ground ninety feet deep, and no way of getting down into it but by holding on to a rope and being lowered with a windlass.

The workmen had just gone off somewhere to dinner. I was not strong enough to lower Boggs's bulk, so I took an unlighted candle in my teeth, made a loop for my foot in the end of the rope, implored Boggs not to go to sleep or let the windlass get the start of him, and then swung out over the shaft.

I reached the bottom muddy and bruised about the elbows, but safe. I lit the candle, made an examination of the rock, selected some specimens and shouted to Boggs to hoist away.

No answer.

Presently a head appeared in the circle of daylight away aloft, and a voice came down.

"Are you all set?"

"All set. Hoist away!"

"Are you comfortable?"

"Perfectly."

"Could you wait a little?"

"Oh, certainly. No particular hurry."

"Well—good-bye."

"Why, where are you going?"

"After the school report!"

And he did.

I stayed down there an hour and surprised the workmen when they hauled up and found a man on the rope instead of a bucket of rock.

I walked home, too—five miles—up-hill.

We had no school report next morning. But the *Union* had.

about 1874

~ 11 ~

In December of 1876 Clemens attended the seventy-first annual dinner of the New England Society of New York. The toast to which Clemens responded was "The oldest inhabitant—the weather of New England. 'Who can lose it and forget it?/Who can have it and regret it?/Be interposer 'twixt us Twain.'" The last sentence is from *The Merchant of Venice*.

NEW ENGLAND WEATHER

I reverently believe that the Maker who made us all makes everything in New England but the weather. I don't know who makes that, but I think it must be raw apprentices in the weather clerk's factory who experiment and learn how, in New England, for board and clothes, and then are promoted to make weather for countries that require a good article and will take their custom elsewhere if they don't get it.

There is a sumptuous variety about the New England weather that compels the stranger's admiration—and regret. The weather is always doing something there, always attending strictly to business, always getting up new designs and trying them on the people to see how they will go. But it gets through more business in spring than any other season.

In the spring I have counted one hundred and thirty-six different kinds of weather inside of four-and-twenty hours. It was I that made the fame and fortune of that man that had that marvelous collection of weather on exhibition at the Centennial, that so astounded the foreigners. He was going to travel all over the world and get specimens from all the climes.

I said, "Don't you do it. You come to New England on a favorable spring day."

I told him what we could do in the way of style, variety and quantity.

Well, he came and he made his collection in four days. As to variety, why, he confessed that he got hundreds of kinds of weather that he had never heard of before. And as to quantity—well, after he had picked out and discarded all that was blemished in any way, he not only had weather enough but weather to spare, weather to hire out, weather to sell, to deposit, weather to invest, weather to give to the poor.

The people of New England are by nature patient and forbearing but there are some things which they will not stand. Every year they kill a lot of poets for writing about "Beautiful Spring." These are generally casual visitors who bring their notions of spring from somewhere else and cannot, of course, know how the natives feel about spring. And so the first thing they know the opportunity to inquire how they feel has permanently gone by.

Old Probabilities has a mighty reputation for accurate prophecy and thoroughly well deserves it. You take up the paper and observe how crisply and confidently he checks off what today's weather is going to be on the Pacific, down South, in the Middle States, in the Wisconsin region. See him sail along in the joy and pride of his power till he gets to New England, and then see his tail drop. *He* doesn't know what the weather is going to be in New England. Well, he mulls over it, and by-and-by he gets out something about like this: Probably northeast to southwest winds, varying to the southward and westward and eastward, and points between, high and low barometer swapping around from place to place; probable areas of rain, snow, hail and drought, succeeded or preceded by earthquakes, with thunder and lightning.

Then he jots down his postscript from his wandering mind, to cover accidents.

"But it is possible that the programme may be wholly changed in the mean time."

Yes, one of the brightest gems in the New England weather is the dazzling uncertainty of it. There is only one thing certain about it. You are certain there is going to be plenty of it—a perfect grand review. But you never can tell which end of the procession is going to move first. You fix up for the drought, you leave your umbrella in the house and sally out, and two to one you get drowned. You make up your mind that the earthquake is due, you stand from under and take hold of something to steady yourself, and the first thing you know you get struck by lightning.

These are great disappointments but they can't be helped.

The lightning there is peculiar. It is so convincing that when it strikes a thing it doesn't leave enough of that thing behind for you to tell whether—Well, you'd think it was something valuable, and a Congressman had been there.

And the thunder. When the thunder begins to merely tune up and scrape and saw, and key up the instruments for the performance, strangers say, "Why, what awful thunder you have here!" But when the baton is raised and the real concert begins you'll find that stranger down in the cellar with his head in the ash barrel.

Now as to the *size* of the weather in New England—lengthways, I mean. It is utterly disproportioned to the size of that little country. Half the time, when it is packed as full as it can stick, you will see that New England weather sticking out beyond the edges and projecting around hundreds and hundreds of miles over the neighboring States. She can't hold a tenth part of her weather. You can see cracks all about where she has strained herself trying to do it.

I could speak volumes about the inhuman perversity of the New England weather but I will give but a single specimen. I like to hear rain on a tin roof. So I covered part of my roof with tin, with an eye to that luxury. Well, sir, do you think it ever rains on that tin? No, sir. Skips it every time.

Mind, in this speech I have been trying merely to do honor to the New England weather—no language could do it justice. But after all there is at least one or two things about that weather (or, if you please, effects produced by it) which we residents would not like to part with. If we hadn't our bewitching autumn foliage we should still have to credit the weather with one feature which compensates for all its bullying vagaries—the ice-storm: when a leafless tree is clothed with ice from the bottom to the top. Ice that is as bright and clear as crystal. When every bough and twig is strung with ice beads, frozen dew-drops, and the whole tree sparkles cold and white like the Shah of Persia's diamond plume.

Then the wind waves the branches and the sun comes out and

turns all those myriads of beads and drops to prisms that glow and burn and flash with all manner of colored fires, which change and change again with inconceivable rapidity from blue to red, from red to green, and green to gold. The tree becomes a spraying fountain, a very explosion of dazzling jewels, and it stands there the acme, the climax, the supremest possibility in art or nature of bewildering, intoxicating, intolerable magnificence. One cannot make the words too strong.

December 1876

~ **12** ~

In October of 1877 Clemens attended the Putnam Phalanx dinner for the Ancient and Honorable Artillery Company of Massachusetts, held in Hartford, Connecticut.

THE STIRRING CAMPAIGN

I wouldn't have missed being here for a good deal. The last time I had the privilege of breaking bread with soldiers was some years ago with the oldest military organization in England, the Ancient and Honourable Artillery Company of London, somewhere about its six-hundredth anniversary. And now I have enjoyed this privilege with its oldest child, the oldest military organization in America, the Ancient and Honorable Artillery Company of Massachusetts, on this your two-hundred-and-fortieth anniversary. Fine old stock, both of you. And if you fight as well as you feed, God protect the enemy.

I did not assemble at the hotel parlors today to be received by a committee as a mere civilian guest. No, I assembled at the headquarters of the Putnam Phalanx and insisted upon my right to be escorted to this place as one of the military guests. For I too am a soldier! I am inured to war. I have a military history. I have been through a stirring campaign. And there is not even a mention of it in any history of the United States or of the Southern Confederacy. To such lengths can the envy and the malignity of the historian go. I will unbosom myself here, where I cannot but find sympathy. I will tell you about it and appeal through you to justice.

In the earliest summer days of the war I slipped out of Hannibal, Missouri by night with a friend and joined a detachment of the rebel General Tom Harris's army (I find myself in a great minority here) up a gorge behind an old barn in Ralls County. Colonel Ralls of

Mexican War celebrity swore us in. He made us swear to uphold the flag and Constitution of the United States and to destroy every other military organization that we caught doing the same thing, which, being interpreted, means that we were to repel invasion.

Well, you see, this mixed us. We couldn't really tell which side we were on. But we went into camp and left it to the God of Battles. For that was the term then. I was made Second Lieutenant and Chief Mogul of a company of eleven men who knew nothing about war—nor anything, for we had no captain. My friend, who was nineteen years old, six feet high, three feet wide and some distance through, and just out of the infant school, was made orderly sergeant.

His name was Ben Tupper. He had a hard time. When he was mounted and on the march he used to go to sleep, and his horse would reach around and bite him on the leg, and then he would wake up and cry and curse and want to go home. The other men pestered him a good deal, too. When they were dismounted they said they couldn't march in double file with him because his feet took up so much room.

One night, when we were around the camp fire, some fellow on the outside in the cold said, "Ben Tupper, put down that newspaper. It throws the whole place into twilight and casts a shadow like a blanket."

Ben said, "I ain't got any newspaper."

Then the other fellow said, "Oh, I see—'twas your ear!"

We all slept in a corn crib, on the corn, and the rats were very thick. Ben Tupper had been carefully and rightly reared, and when he was ready for bed he would start to pray, and a rat would bite him on the heel. And then he would sit up and swear all night and keep everybody awake. He was town-bred and did not seem to have any correct idea of military discipline. If I commanded him to shut up he would say, "Who was your nigger last year?"

One evening I ordered him to ride out about three miles on picket duty, to the beginning of a prairie.

Said he, "What! In the night! And them blamed Union soldiers likely to be prowling around there any time!"

So he wouldn't go, and the next morning I ordered him again.

Said he, "In the rain! I think I see myself!"

He didn't go.

Next day I ordered him on picket duty once more. This time he looked hurt.

Said he, "What! On Sunday? You must be a damn fool!"

Well, picketing might have been a very good thing but I saw it was impracticable, so I dropped it from my military system.

We had a good enough time there at that barn, barring the rats and the mosquitoes and the rain. We levied on both parties impartially, and both parties hated us impartially. But one day we heard that the invader was approaching, so we had to pack up and move, of course, and within twenty-four hours he was coming again. So we moved again. Next day he was after us once more. Well, we didn't like it much, but we moved rather than make trouble. This went on for a week or ten days more, and we saw considerable scenery. Then Ben Tupper lost patience.

Said he, "War ain't what it's cracked up to be. I'm going home if I can't even git a chance to sit down a minute. Why do these people keep us a-humpin' around so? Blame their skins, do they think this is an excursion?"

Some of the other boys got to grumbling. They complained that there was an insufficiency of umbrellas. So I sent around to the farmers and borrowed what I could. Then they complained that the Worcestershire sauce was out. There was mutiny and dissatisfaction all around. And of course here came the enemy pestering us again—as much as two hours before breakfast, too, when nobody wanted to turn out, of course. This was carrying the thing too far. The whole command felt insulted.

I detached one of my aides and sent him to the brigadier and asked him to assign us a district where there wasn't so much bother going on. The history of our campaign was laid before him. But instead of being touched by it, what did he do? He sent back an indignant message and said, "You have had a dozen chances inside of two weeks to capture the enemy, and he is still at large. [Well, we knew that!] Stay where you are this time or I will courtmartial and hang the whole lot of you."

Well, I submitted this brutal message to my battalion and asked their advice.

Said the orderly sergeant, "If Tom Harris wants the enemy, let him come and get him. I ain't got any use for my share. And who's Tom Harris anyway, I'd like to know, that's putting on so many frills? Why, I knew him when he wasn't nothing but a darn telegraph operator. Gentlemen, you can do as you choose. As for me, I've got enough of this sashaying around so's you can't get a chance to pray, because the time's all required for cussing. So off goes my war paint. You hear me!"

The whole regiment said with one voice, "That's the talk for me."

So there and then, on the spot, my brigade disbanded itself and tramped off home, with me at the tail of it. I hung up my own sword and returned to the arts of peace. And there were people who said I hadn't been absent from them yet. We were the first men that went into the service in Missouri. We were the first that went out of it anywhere.

This, gentlemen, is the history of the part which my division took in the great rebellion, and such is the military record of its commander-in-chief, and this is the first time that the deeds of those warriors have been brought officially to the notice of humanity. Treasure these things in your hearts. And so shall the detected and truculent historians of this land be brought to shame and confusion.

I ask you to fill your glasses and drink with me to the reverent memory of the orderly sergeant and those other neglected and forgotten heroes, my footsore and travel-stained paladins, who were first in war, first in peace, and were not idle during the interval that lay between.

October 1877

13

This address, known as the Whittier birthday speech, fell dreadfully flat at the time, in Clemens's opinion, and as a result he feared he had badly damaged his reputation in New England literary circles. The following account of the dinner is from the *Boston Advertiser* of December 18, 1877. It offers a vivid social context of the occasion.

"The gathering of gentlemen at the Brunswick Hotel last evening was of a rare kind. December 17 was the twentieth anniversary of the founding of the Atlantic Monthly, and was also the day which rounded out the life of the poet Whittier to seventy full years. To celebrate these events the publishers of the Atlantic, Messrs. H. O. Houghton & Co., invited the contributors to the magazine, both the present and past, to meet in a never before attempted gathering. No heartier response could have been wished. Contributors of 1877 and 1857 were present, and the company was without doubt the most notable that has ever been seen in this country within four walls. The oldest and best known poets of our country were there, and the absent Bryant sent a letter of regret.

"About six o'clock the contributors began to gather in one of the reception rooms of the Brunswick, and, after a social union and friendly acquaintance-making for an hour, the doors of the east dining hall were opened, and the real interest of the evening from then onward was in that room. It had been tastefully prepared for the testimonial. Most marked of its decorations was the new portrait of Whittier issued by the Atlantic proprietors, which, set in a luxurious gilt frame and wreathed with a wealth of ivy, hung from the wall over the centre of the table. At the left, and facing it upon the opposite wall, was a beautiful country scene, with an old-fashioned New England dwelling—Whittier's birthplace. At the head of the table was a rich vase of flowers, and the table ornaments down the whole length were fitting to this decoration.

"If a painter could have caught for his canvas the picture presented when the hosts and guests were all seated, the scene would, as reality, have rivalled the imaginary one of Shakespeare and his friends. At the head of the table sat the chief host, Mr. H. O. Houghton. At his right was the honored guest and centre of loyal, loving interest, Mr. Whittier. Next to him sat the Concord philosopher, and at Mr. Emerson's right was Mr.

[48]

Longfellow. The trio—Whittier, Emerson, Longfellow—gave a reverend, almost holy air to the place, and their gray hairs and expressive, joyful faces formed a beautiful group. On Mr. Houghton's left was Dr. Oliver Wendell Holmes; next to him Mr. William D. Howells, the editor of the magazine, and at the extreme left Mr. Charles Dudley Warner."

The writer then gave the arrangement of the guests, adding, "How this list of guests compares with the invitations accepted and what persons were compelled to decline the invitation may be seen from the following." Then he presented a list of fifty-two acceptances and another list of forty-one regrets, after which he offered the menu.

"MENU. OYSTERS ON SHELL. *Sauterne.* SOUP. Purée of Tomatoes au Croutons. Consommé Printanier Royal. *Sherry.* FISH. Broiled Chicken Halibut à la Navarin. Potatoes à la Hollandaise. Smelts Panne, Sauce Tartare. *Chablis.* REMOVES. Capon à l'Anglaise. Rice. Cauliflower. *Champagne. Mumm's Dry Verzenay. Roederer Imperial.* Saddle of English Mutton à la Pontoise. String Beans. Turnips. ENTREES. Filet of Beef, larded, Sauce Financière. Epinards Veloutés. Vol au Vent of Oysters à l'Americaine. *Claret.* Squabs en compote à la Française, Tomatoes Sautées. Terrapin Stewed, Maryland Style. Sorbet au Kirsch. GAME. Broiled Partridges on Toast. Canvasback Ducks. Water Cresses. Sweet Potatoes. Dressed Lettuce. *Burgundy.* PASTRY. Charlotte Russe. Gelée au Champagne. Gâteaux Variés. Confectionery. FRUIT. DESSERT. COFFEE.

"Dinner was leisurely served, and the social part was by far the most prominent element. Each item on the bill of fare was served as a separate course, and the intervals between them were occupied by the guests in rising from their seats and circulating about, laughing and joking. Were there space and time for the detail it would be most interesting to sketch the noteworthy and constantly changing groups. Here was Mr. Longfellow talking with Mr. Emerson and Mr. Whittier; Colonel Higginson drawing his chair around for a tête-à-tête with Mr. Longfellow; Mr. E. P. Whipple and Mr. Whittier conversing earnestly; Mr. Houghton mingling with his guests; Dr. Holmes sparking with vivacity for all who greeted him; and so on, down both sides of the room; all through the evening the scenes were most rare, attractive and memorable.

"At quarter past ten Mr. Houghton called the tables to order for the after-dinner speaking to begin. By this time the company was enlarged by the presence of ladies, who had not before appeared upon the scene. The doors at the sides of the hall were opened, and the women who were staying in the hotel filled the entrances and were favored with seats even between the tables. In the rear was the cloud of black faces—for the waiters took a keen interest in all the proceedings."

There followed a speech by H. O. Houghton.

"Mr. Houghton's allusions to Mr. Whittier were applauded most rapturously. The tables rose to their feet and gave cheer upon cheer. Mr.

Whittier bore his welcome with characteristic modesty and spoke a few words in reply. Mr. Whittier was received with prolonged applause, and the entire company rose to do him honor."

Whittier spoke, then Longfellow read a note which Whittier had sent him when he did not expect to be present, and then "an exquisite little poem which Mr. Whittier had sent to be read." Next Houghton introduced Howells, who introduced Emerson. Emerson read Whittier's poem, "Ichabod," and then Howells made a speech. Holmes read a poem, after which Howells introduced Charles Eliot Norton and then read extracts from a few letters of regret, among them one from John J. Piatt, whose poem he carefully read aloud.

"The humorist of the evening was next introduced and the amusement was intense, while the subjects of the wit, Longfellow, Emerson and Holmes, enjoyed it as much as any."

Clemens's speech followed, and then there were a poem by R. H. Stoddard, remarks by Charles Dudley Warner, and a summary of other addresses as well as a presentation in print of some of the letters of regret. Clearly the *Advertiser* writer was having none of the implied scandal of irreverence. Perhaps he was whitewashing Clemens's gaffe by treating him as a sort of court jester or fool, who because of his special condition and role was allowed to say things forbidden to saner mortals.

The quotations in Clemens's speech are from the works of Holmes, Emerson and Longfellow. Of course, Clemens was kidding when he ascribed "Barbara Frietchie" (by Whittier) to Emerson, "The Biglow Papers" (by Lowell) to Longfellow and "Thanatopsis" (by Bryant) to Holmes.

WHITTIER'S BIRTHDAY

This is an occasion peculiarly meet for the digging up of pleasant reminiscences concerning literary folk. Therefore I will drop lightly into history myself.

Standing here on the shore of the Atlantic and contemplating certain of its largest literary billows, I am reminded of a thing which happened to me thirteen years ago when I had just succeeded in stirring up a little Nevadian literary puddle myself, whose spume flakes were beginning to blow thinly Californiaward. I started an inspection tramp through the southern mines of California. I was callow and conceited, and I resolved to try the virtue of my *nom de guerre*.

I very soon had an opportunity. I knocked at a miner's lonely log cabin in the foothills of the Sierras just at nightfall. It was snowing at the time. A jaded, melancholy man of fifty, barefooted, opened the door to me. When he heard my *nom de guerre* he looked more dejected than before. He let me in—pretty reluctantly, I thought— and after the customary bacon and beans, black coffee and hot whisky, I took a pipe. This sorrowful man had not said three words up to this time.

Now he spoke up and said in the voice of one who is secretly suffering, "You're the fourth. I'm going to move."

"The fourth what?" said I.

"The fourth literary man that has been here in twenty-four hours. I'm going to move."

"You don't tell me!" said I. "Who were the others?"

"Mr. Longfellow, Mr. Emerson and Mr. Oliver Wendell Holmes. Consound the lot!"

You can easily believe I was interested. I supplicated. Three hot whiskies did the rest. And finally the melancholy miner began. Said he:

"They came here just at dark yesterday evening and I let them in, of course. Said they were going to the Yosemite. They were a rough lot but that's nothing. Everybody looks rough that travels afoot. Mr. Emerson was a seedy little bit of a chap, red-headed. Mr. Holmes was as fat as a balloon. He weighed as much as three hundred and had double chins all the way down to his stomach. Mr. Longfellow was built like a prizefighter. His head was cropped and bristly, like as if he had a wig made of hair brushes. His nose lay straight down his face like a finger with the end joint tilted up. They had been drinking, I could see that. And what queer talk they used! Mr. Holmes inspected this cabin, then he took me by the buttonhole, and says he:

"'Through the deep caves of thought
I hear a voice that sings,
Build thee more stately mansions,
O my soul!'*

"Says I, 'I can't afford it, Mr. Holmes. And moreover I don't want to.' Blamed if I liked it pretty well, either, coming from a stranger that way. However, I started to get out my bacon and beans, when

Mr. Emerson came and looked on awhile. And then *he* takes me aside by the buttonhole and says:

"'Gives me agates for my meat;
Gives me cantharids to eat;
From air and ocean bring me foods,
From all zones and altitudes.'

"Says I, 'Mr. Emerson, if you'll excuse me, this ain't no hotel.' You see it sort of riled me. I warn't used to the ways of littery swells. But I went on a-sweating over my work. And next comes Mr. Longfellow and buttonholes me and interrupts me. Says he:

"'Honor be to Mudjekeewis!
You shall hear how Pau-Puk-Keewis—'

"But I broke in, and says I, 'Beg your pardon, Mr. Longfellow. If you'll be so kind as to hold your yawp for about five minutes and let me get this grub ready, you'll do me proud.' Well sir, after they'd filled up I set out the jug. Mr. Holmes looks at it and then he fires up all of a sudden and yells:

"'Flash out a stream of blood-red wine!
For I would drink to other days.'

"By George, I was getting kind of worked up. I don't deny it, I was getting kind of worked up. I turns to Mr. Holmes, and says I, 'Looky here, my fat friend, I'm a-running this shanty, and if the court knows herself, you'll take whisky straight or you'll go dry.' Them's the very words I said to him.

"Now I don't want to sass such famous littery people. But you see they kind of forced me. There ain't nothing onreasonable 'bout me. I don't mind a passel of guests a-treadin' on my tail three or four times. But when it comes to *standing* on it it's different. 'And if the court knows herself,' I says, 'you'll take whisky straight or you'll go dry.'

"Well, between drinks they'd swell around the cabin and strike attitudes and spout. And pretty soon they got out a greasy old deck and went to playing euchre at ten cents a corner—on trust. I began to notice some pretty suspicious things. Mr. Emerson dealt, looked at his hand, shook his head, says:

"'I am the doubter and the doubt—'

and ca'mly bunched the hands and went to shuffling for a new layout. Says he:

"'They reckon ill who leave me out;
They know not well the subtle ways I keep
I pass and deal again!'

"Hang'd if he didn't go ahead and do it, too! Oh, he was a cool one! Well, in about a minute things were running pretty tight. But all of a sudden I see by Mr. Emerson's eye he judged he had 'em. He had already corralled two tricks, and each of the others one. So now he kind of lifts a little in his chair and says:

"'I tire of globes and aces!—
Too long the game is played!'

and down he fetched a right bower.

"Mr. Longfellow smiles as sweet as pie and says:

"'Thanks thanks to thee, my worthy friend,
For the lesson thou hast taught,'

and blamed if he didn't down with *another* right bower!

"Emerson claps his hand on his bowie. Longfellow claps his on his revolver. And I went under a bunk. There was going to be trouble. But that monstrous Holmes rose up, wobbling his double chins, and says he, 'Order, gentlemen. The first man that draws, I'll lay down on him and smother him!'

"All quiet on the Potomac, you bet!

"They were pretty how-come-you-so by now. And they begun to blow. Emerson says, 'The nobbiest thing I ever wrote was "Barbara Frietchie."' Says Longfellow, 'It don't begin with my "Biglow Papers."' Says Holmes, 'My "Thanatopsis" lays over 'em both.'

"They mighty near ended in a fight. Then they wished they had some more company. And Mr. Emerson pointed to me and says:

> *"'Is yonder squalid peasant all*
> *That this proud nursery could breed?'*

"He was a-whetting his bowie on his boot so I let it pass. Well sir, next they took it into their heads that they would like some music. So they made me stand up and sing 'When Johnny Comes Marching Home' till I dropped—at thirteen minutes past four this morning. That's what I've been through, my friend. When I woke at seven they were leaving, thank goodness, and Mr. Longfellow had my only boots on, and his'n under his arm.

"Says I, 'Hold on there, Evangeline, what are you going to do with *them?'*

"He says, 'Going to make tracks with 'em. Because:

> *"'Lives of great men all remind us*
> *We can make our lives sublime;*
> *And, departing, leave behind us*
> *Footprints on the sands of time.'*

"As I said, Mr. Twain, you are the fourth in twenty-four hours. And I'm going to move. I ain't suited to a littery atmosphere."

I said to the miner, "Why, my dear sir, *these* were not the gracious singers to whom we and the world pay loving reverence and homage. These were impostors."

The miner investigated me with a calm eye for awhile. Then said he, "Ah! Impostors, were they? Are *you* ?"

I did not pursue the subject. And since then I have not traveled on my *nom de guerre* enough to hurt.

Such was the reminiscence I was moved to contribute, Mr. Chairman. In my enthusiasm I may have exaggerated the details a little but you will easily forgive me that fault since I believe it is the first time I have ever deflected from perpendicular fact on an occasion like this.

December 1877

There is an epilogue to this event which is very interesting. In January 1906 Clemens answered a letter he had received from a correspondent identified as "Mrs. H" by Albert Bigelow Paine.

"I am forever in your debt for reminding me of that curious passage in my life," he wrote, referring to the Whittier birthday speech. "During the first year or two after it happened I could not bear to think of it. My pain and shame were so intense and my sense of having been an imbecile so settled, established and confirmed, that I drove the episode entirely from my mind. And so all these twenty-eight or twenty-nine years I have lived in the conviction that my performance of that time was coarse, vulgar and destitute of humor. But your suggestion that you and your family found humor in it twenty-eight years ago moved me to look into the matter. So I commissioned a Boston typewriter to delve among the Boston papers of that bygone time and send me a copy of it.

"It came this morning, and if there is any vulgarity about it I am not able to discover it. If it isn't innocently and ridiculously funny, I am no judge. I will see to it that you get a copy."

Clemens then proceeded to reminisce in Paine's presence about the speech, producing one of his autobiographical dictations.

"What I have said to Mrs. H is true. I did suffer during a year or two from the deep humiliations of the episode. But at last in 1888 in Venice my wife and I came across Mr. and Mrs. A.P.C. of Concord, Massachusetts, and a friendship began then of the sort which nothing but death terminates. The C's were very bright people and in every way charming and companionable.

"We were together a month or two in Venice and several months in Rome afterward. And one day that lamented break of mine was mentioned. And when I was on the point of lathering those people for bringing it to my mind when I had gotten the memory of it almost squelched, I perceived with joy that the C's were indignant about the way that my performance had been received in Boston. They poured out their opinions most freely and frankly about the frosty attitude of the people who were present at that performance, and about the Boston newspapers for the position they had taken in regard to the matter. That position was that I had been irreverent beyond belief, beyond imagination.

"Very well. I had accepted that as a fact for a year or two and had been thoroughly miserable about it whenever I thought of it, which was not frequently if I could help it. Whenever I thought of it I wondered how I ever could have been inspired to do so unholy a thing. Well, the C's comforted me. But they did not persuade me to continue to think about the unhappy episode. I resisted that. I tried to get it out of my mind and let it die. And I succeeded. Until Mrs. H's letter came it had been a good twenty-five years since I had thought of that matter. And when she said that the thing was funny I wondered if possibly she might be right. At any rate my curiosity was aroused and I wrote to Boston and got the whole thing copied, as above set forth.

"I vaguely remember some of the details of that gathering. Dimly I can see a hundred people—no, perhaps fifty. Shadowy figures sitting at tables, feeding. Ghosts now to me and nameless forevermore. I don't know who they were but I can very distinctly see, seated at the grand table and facing the rest of us, Mr. Emerson supernaturally grave, unsmiling. Mr. Whittier grave, lovely, his beautiful spirit shining out of his face. Mr. Longfellow with his silken white hair and his benignant face. Dr. Oliver Wendell Holmes flashing smiles and affection and all good fellowship everywhere like a rose diamond whose facets are being turned toward the light first one way and then another—a charming man and always fascinating whether he was talking or whether he was sitting still (what *he* would call still but what would be more or less motion to other people). I can see those figures with entire distinctness across this abyss of time.

"One other feature is clear. Willie Winter (for these past thousand years dramatic editor of the *New York Tribune* and still occupying that high post in his old age) was there. He was much younger then than he is now and he showed it. It was always a pleasure to me to see Willie Winter at a banquet. During a matter of twenty years I was seldom at a banquet where Willie Winter was not also present and where he did not read a charming poem written for the occasion. He did it this time and it was up to standard: dainty, happy, choicely phrased, and as good to listen to as music, and sounding exactly as if it was pouring unprepared out of heart and brain.

"Now at that point ends all that was pleasurable about that notable celebration of Mr. Whittier's seventieth birthday. Because *I* got up at that point and followed Winter with what I have no doubt I supposed would be the gem of the evening—the gay oration above quoted from the Boston paper. I had written it all out the day before and had perfectly memorized it, and I stood up there at my genial and happy and self-satisfied ease and began to deliver it. Those majestic guests, that row of venerable and still active volcanoes, listened, as did everybody else in the house, with attentive interest.

"Well, I delivered myself of—we'll say the first two hundred words of my speech. I was expecting no returns from that part of the speech but this was not the case as regarded the rest of it. I arrived now at the dialogue. 'The old miner said, "You are the fourth, I'm going to move." "The fourth what?" said I. He answered, "The fourth littery man that has been here in twenty-four hours. I am going to move." "Why, you don't tell me," said I. "Who were the others?" "Mr. Longfellow, Mr. Emerson, Mr. Oliver Wendell Holmes, consound the lot—"'

"Now then, the house's *attention* continued but the expression of interest in the faces turned to a sort of black frost. I wondered what the trouble was. I didn't know. I went on but with difficulty. I struggled along and entered upon that miner's fearful description of the bogus Emerson, the bogus Holmes, the bogus Longfellow, always hoping, but with a gradually perishing hope, that somebody would laugh or that somebody would at least smile.

"But nobody did.

"I didn't know enough to give it up and sit down. I was too new to public speaking. And so I went on with this awful performance and carried it clear through to the end in front of a body of people who seemed turned to stone with horror. It was the sort of expression their faces would have worn if I had been making these remarks about the Deity and the rest of the Trinity. There is no milder way in which to describe the petrified condition and the ghastly expression of those people.

"When I sat down it was with a heart which had long ceased to beat. I shall never be as dead again as I was then. I shall never be as miserable again as I was then. I speak now as one who doesn't know what the conditions of things may be in the next world. But in this one I shall never be as wretched again as I was then. Howells, who was near me, tried to say a comforting word but couldn't get beyond a gasp. There was no use. He understood the whole size of the disaster. He had good intentions but the words froze before they could get out. It was an atmosphere that would freeze anything. If Benvenuto Cellini's salamander had been in that place he would not have survived to be put into Cellini's autobiography.

"There was a frightful pause. There was an awful silence. A desolating silence.

"Then the next man on the list had to get up. There was no help for it. That was Bishop. Bishop had just burst handsomely upon the world with a most acceptable novel which had appeared in the *Atlantic Monthly*, a place which would make any novel respectable and any author noteworthy. In this case the novel itself was recognized as being, without extraneous help, respectable. Bishop was away up in the public favor and he was an object of high interest, consequently there was a sort of national expectancy in the air. We may say our American millions were standing from Maine to Texas and from Alaska to Florida, holding their breath, their lips parted, their hands ready to applaud, when Bishop should get up on that occasion and for the first time in his life speak in public. It was under these damaging conditions that he got up to 'make good,' as the vulgar say.

"I had spoken several times before and that is the reason why I was able to go on without dying in my tracks as I ought to have done. But Bishop had had no experience. He was up facing those awful deities, facing those other people, those strangers, facing human beings for the first time in his life, with a speech to utter. No doubt it was well packed away in his memory, no doubt it was fresh and usable until I had been heard from. I suppose that after that, and under the smothering pall of that dreary silence, it began to waste away and disappear out of his head like the rags breaking from the edge of a fog. And presently there wasn't any fog left.

"He didn't go on. He didn't last long. It was not many sentences after his first before he began to hesitate and break and lose his grip and totter and wobble. And at last he slumped down in a limp and mushy pile.

"Well, the program for the occasion was probably not more than one-third finished. But it ended there. Nobody rose. The next man hadn't strength enough to get up. And everybody looked so dazed, so stupefied, paralyzed, it was impossible for anybody to do anything. Or even try. Nothing could go on in that strange atmosphere.

"Howells mournfully and without words hitched himself to Bishop and me and supported us out of the room. It was very kind, he was most generous. He towed us tottering away into some room in that building and we sat down there.

"I don't know what my remark was now but I know the nature of it. It was the kind of remark you make when you know that nothing in the world can help your case.

"But Howells was honest. He had to say the heart-breaking things he did say. That there was no help for this calamity, this shipwreck, this cataclysm. That this was the most disastrous thing that had ever happened in anybody's history.

"And then he added, 'That is, for *you*. And consider what you have done for Bishop. It is bad enough in your case, you deserve to suffer. You have committed this crime, and you deserve to have all you are going to get. But here is an innocent man. Bishop had never done you any harm, and see what you have done to him. He can never hold his head up again. The world can never look upon Bishop as being a live person. He is a corpse.'

"That is the history of that episode of twenty-eight years ago, which pretty nearly killed me with shame during that first year or two whenever it forced its way into my mind.

"Now then, I take that speech up and examine it. As I said, it arrived this morning from Boston. I have read it twice, and unless I am an idiot it hasn't a single defect in it from the first word to the last. It is just as good as good can be. It is smart. It is saturated with humor. There isn't a suggestion of coarseness or vulgarity in it anywhere.

"What could have been the matter with that house? It is amazing, it is incredible, that they didn't shout with laughter, and those deities the loudest of them all.

"Could the fault have been with me? Did I lose courage when I saw those great men up there whom I was going to describe in such a strange fashion? If that happened, if I showed doubt, that can account for it, for you can't be successfully funny if you show that you are afraid of it.

"Well, I can't account for it. But if I had those beloved and revered old literary immortals back here now on the platform at Carnegie Hall I would take that same old speech, deliver it word for word and melt them till they'd run all over that stage.

"Oh, the fault must have been with me, it is not in the speech at all."

14

Bayard Taylor (1825–1878) was an American poet, dramatist, author of travel books and translator of Goethe's *Faust*. Clemens spoke at a banquet given in New York early in April 1878 for Taylor shortly before the latter sailed for Germany to be the American ambassador there. Taylor died soon after taking up his duties. Moody and Sankey were prominent American revivalists.

NINETEENTH-CENTURY PROGRESS

I have been warned, as no doubt have all among you that are inexperienced, that a dinner to our Ambassador is an occasion which demands and even requires a peculiar caution and delicacy in the handling of the dangerous weapon of speech. I have been warned to avoid all mention of international politics and all criticisms, however mild, of countries with which we are at peace lest such utterances embarrass our minister and our government in their dealings with foreign states. In a word, I have been cautioned to talk but be careful not to say anything. I do not consider this a difficult task.

Now, it has often occurred to me that the conditions under which we live at the present day, with the revelations of geology all about us, viewing upon the one hand the majestic configurations of the silurian, oolitic, old red sandstone periods, and upon the other the affiliations and stratifications and ramifications of the prehistoric, post-pliocene, antepenultimate epochs, we are stricken dumb with amazed surprise and can only lift up our hands and say with that wise but odious Frenchman, "It was a slip of the tongue, sir, and wholly unintentional—entirely unintentional."

It would ill become me, upon an occasion like this, purposely to speak slightingly of a citizen of a country with whom we are at

peace, and especially great and gracious France, whom God preserve! The subject, however, is a delicate one and I will not pursue
it.

But, as I was about to remark, cast your eye abroad, sir, for one
pregnant moment over the vista which looms before you in the
mighty domain of intellectual progression and contemplate the awe-
compelling theory of the descent of man! Development, sir! Development! Natural selection! Correlation of the sexes! Spontaneous
combustion! What gulfs and whirlwinds of intellectual stimulus
these magic words fling upon the burning canvas of the material
universe of soul!

Across the chasm of the ages we take the oyster by the hand and
call him brother. And back and still further back we go, and breathe
the germ we cannot see, and know in him our truer Adam! And as
we stand, dazed, transfixed, exalted, and gaze down the long procession of life, marking how steadily, how symmetrically we have
ascended step by step to our sublime estate and dignity of humanity—out of one lowly form into a little higher and a little higher
forms—adding grace after every change—developing from tadpoles
into frogs, frogs into fishes, fishes into birds, birds into reptiles, reptiles into Russians—I beg a million pardons, sir and gentlemen—it
was a wholly innocent slip of the tongue, and due only to the excitement of debate—for far be it from me, on such an occasion as this,
to cast a seeming slur upon a great nation with which we are at
peace—a great and noble and Christian nation—whom God expand!

But, as I was about to remark, I maintain (and nothing can ever
drive me from that position) that the contributions of the nineteenth
century to science and the industrial arts are—are—but of course
they are. There is no need to dwell upon that.

You look at it yourself. Look at steam! Look at the steamboat, look
at the railway, look at the steamship! Look at the telegraph, which
enables you to flash your thoughts from world to world, ignoring
intervening seas. Look at the telephone, which enables you to speak
into affection's remote ear the word that cheers, and into the ear of
the foe the opinion which you ought not to risk at shorter range.

Look at the sewing machine, look at the foghorn, look at the bell
punch, look at the book agent. And, more than all, a thousand
times, look at the last and greatest, the aerophone, which will en-

able Moody and Sankey to stand on the tallest summit of the Rocky Mountains and deliver their message to listening America! And necessarily it will annul and do away with the pernicious custom of taking up a collection.

Look at all these things, sir, and say if it is not a far prouder and more precious boon to have been born in the nineteenth century than in any century that went before it. Ah, sir, clothed with the all-sufficient grandeur of citizenship in the nineteenth century, even the wild and arid New Jerseyman might—a mistake, sir, a mistake, and entirely unintentional. Of all the kingdoms, principalities and countries with which it is our privilege to hold peaceful relations, I regard New Jersey as dearest to our admiration, nearest to our heart, the wisest and the purest among the nations. I retire the undiplomatic language and beg your sympathy and indulgence.

But, as I was about to remark, it has always seemed to me (that is, of course, since I reached a reasoning age) that this much agitated question of future rewards and punishments was one upon which honest and sincere differences of opinion might exist—one individual, with more or less justice, leaning to the radical side of it, whilst another individual, with apparently equal justice but with infinitely more common sense, more intelligence, more justification, leans to a bitter and remorseless detestation of the pitiless Prince of Perdition—a slip of the tongue, I do sincerely assure you—I beg you to let me withdraw that unintentional slur upon the character of that great and excellent personage with whom and whose country we are upon the closest and warmest terms, and who—it is no use, sir, I will sit down. I don't seem to have any knack at a diplomatic speech. I have probably compromised the country enough for the present.

Nonsense aside, sir, I am most sincerely glad to assist at this public expression of appreciation of Mr. Taylor's character, scholarship and distinguished literary service. I am sure he was not merely one of the fittest men we had for the place but the fittest. In so honoring him, our country has conspicuously honored herself.

April 1878

⤟ **15** ⤠

In April 1879 Clemens spoke at a dinner of the Stanley Club, Paris. There is no additional information about the Stanley Club or the occasion from either Fatout or Paine.

THE CORPSE

Mr. Ryan said to me just now that I'd got to make a speech. I said to Mr. Ryan, "The news came too late to save Roger McPherson."

It is sad to know that some things always come too late. And when I look around upon this brilliant assembly I feel disappointed to think what a nice speech I might have made, what fine topic I might have found in Paris to speak about among these historic monuments, the architecture of Paris, the towers of Notre Dame, the caves and other ancient things. Then I might have said something about the objects of which Paris folks are fond—literature, art, medicine and adultery.

But the news came too late to save Roger McPherson! Perhaps you are not as well acquainted with McPherson as I am? Well, I'll explain who McPherson was.

When we sailed from New York there came on board a man all haggard, a mere skeleton. He wasn't much of a man, he wasn't, and on the voyage we often heard him say to himself, "The news came too late to save Roger McPherson."

I got interested, and I wanted to know about the man, so I asked him who was McPherson.

And he said, "I'm McPherson. But the news came too late to save Roger McPherson."

"How too late?" I asked.

"About three weeks too late," he replied. "I'll tell you how it happened. A friend of mine died, and they told me I must take his body on the cars to his parents in Illinois. I said I'd do it. And they gave me a card with the address and told me to go down to the depot and put it on a box I'd find there, have the box put on the baggage car and go right along with it to Illinois. I found the box all right and nailed the card on it, and put it on the cars. Then I went in the depot and got a sandwich.

"I was walking around, eating my sandwich, and I passed by the baggage room and there was my box, with a young man walking around, looking at it, and he had a card in his hand. I felt like going up to that young man, and saying, 'Stranger, that's my corpse.' But I didn't. I walked on, ate my sandwich, and when I looked in again the young man was gone. But there was that card nailed right on that box.

"I went and looked at that card. It was directed to Colonel Jenkins, Cleveland, Ohio. So I looked in the car, and there was my box, all right.

"Just before the train started a man came into the baggage car and laid a lot of limburger cheese down on my box. He didn't know what was in my box, you know, and I didn't know what was in his paper. But I found out later.

"It was an awful cold night, and after we started, the baggage master came in. He was a nice fellow, Johnson was, and he said, 'A man would freeze to death, out there. I'll make it all right.'

"So he shut all the doors and all the windows, built a roaring coal fire in the stove. Then he took turns fixing the car and poking the fire till I began to smell something and feel uncomfortable, so I moved as far away from my corpse as I could, and Johnson says to me, 'A friend of yours? Did he die lately? This year, I mean.'

"Says I, 'I'll fix it.'

"So I opened a window and we took turns breathing the fresh air.

"After a while Johnson said, 'Let's smoke. I think that'll fix it.'

"So we lit our cigars and puffed a bit. But we got so sick that we let 'em go out again. It didn't do any good. We tried the air again.

"Says Johnson, 'He's in no trance, is he? There's doubt about some people being dead. But there's no doubt about him, is there? What did he die of?'

"We stopped at a station, and when we started off again Johnson came in with a bottle of disinfector and says, 'I've got something now that'll fix it.'

"So he sprinkled it all around, over the box, the limburger and over everything. But it wouldn't do. The smells didn't mix well.

"Johnson said, 'Just think of it. We've all got to die, all got to come to this.'

"Then we thought we'd move the box to one end of the car, so we stooped over it. I took one end and he took the other but we couldn't get it far.

"Johnson says, 'We'll freeze to death if we stay out on the platform. We'll die if we stay in here.'

"So we took hold of it again. But Johnson, he couldn't stand it, he fell right over. I dragged him out on the platform, and the cold air soon brought him to, and we went in the car to get warm.

"'What are we going to do?' asked Johnson, and he looked ill. 'We are sure to have typhoid fever and half a dozen other fevers. We're pizened, we are!'

"At last we thought it was better to go out on the platform. In an hour and a half I was taken off that platform stiff, nearly frozen to death. They put me to bed, and I had all them fevers that Johnson spoke about. You see the thing worked on my mind. It didn't do me no good to learn, three weeks later, that there had been a mistake— that my corpse had gone to Colonel Jenkins, Cleveland, and that I'd taken his box of rifles for decent burial to Illinois. The news came too late to save Roger McPherson—about three weeks too late."

When I'm not prepared to speak I always apologize. And that's the reason I've told you so much about Roger McPherson.

April 1879

~ 16 ~

During a Paris sojourn some time in the spring of 1879, Clemens attended a dinner given by the Stomach Club, a sub rosa organization that enjoyed earthy humor. A typescript of the speech he gave there survives in the Mark Twain Papers. It is not known whether the original manuscript is still extant. Presumably it was this manuscript that was the basis of the first (and private) publication of the speech in January 1952. The speech was again privately printed in 1964, in which year it also appeared in *Fact* magazine. It was later republished by *Playboy*.

SCIENCE OF ONANISM

My gifted predecessor has warned you against the "social evil—adultery." In his able paper he exhausted that subject. He left absolutely nothing more to be said on it. But I will continue his good work in the cause of morality by cautioning you against that species of recreation called self-abuse, to which I perceive that you are too much addicted.

All great writers upon health and morals, both ancient and modern, have struggled with this stately subject. This shows its dignity and importance. Some of these writers have taken one side, some the other.

Homer, in the second book of the *Iliad*, says with fine enthusiasm, "Give me masturbation or give me death!" Caesar, in his *Commentaries*, says, "To the lonely it is company. To the forsaken it is a friend. To the aged and impotent it is a benefactor. They that be penniless are yet rich in that they still have this majestic diversion." In another place this excellent observer has said, "There are times when I perfer it to sodomy."

Robinson Crusoe says, "I cannot describe what I owe to this gentle art." Queen Elizabeth said, "It is the bulwark of virginity."

Cetewayo, the Zulu hero, remarked that "a jerk in the hand is worth two in the bush." The immortal Franklin has said, "Masturbation is the mother of invention." He also said, "Masturbation is the best policy."

Michelangelo and all the other Old Masters—Old Masters, I will remark, is an abbreviation, a contraction—have used similar language. Michelangelo said to Pope Julius II, "Self-negation is noble. Self-culture is beneficent. Self-possession is manly. But to the truly great and inspiring soul they are poor and tame compared to self-abuse."

Mr. Brown, here, in one of his latest and most graceful poems refers to it in an eloquent line which is destined to live to the end of time—"None know it but to love it, None name it but to praise."

Such are the utterances of the most illustrious of the masters of this renowned science and apologists for it. The name of those who decry it and oppose it is legion. They have made strong arguments and uttered bitter speeches against it. But there is not room to repeat them here in much detail.

Brigham Young, an expert of incontestable authority, said, "As compared with the other thing, it is the difference between the lightning bug and the lightning."

Solomon said, "There is nothing to recommend it but its cheapness."

Galen said, "It is shameful to degrade to such bestial use that grand limb, that formidable member, which we votaries of science dub the 'Major Maxillary'—when they dub it at all—which is seldom. It would be better to decapitate the Major than to use him so. It would be better to amputate the *os frontis* than to put it to such a use."

The great statistician, Smith, in his report to Parliament says, "In my opinion more children have been wasted in this way than in any other."

It cannot be denied that the high authority of this art entitles it to our respect. But at the same time I think that its harmfulness demands our condemnation. Mr. Darwin was grieved to feel obliged to give up his theory that the monkey was the connecting link between man and the lower animals. I think he was too hasty. The monkey is the only animal except man that practices this science. Hence he is our brother. There is a bond of sympathy and relationship between us. Give this ingenious animal an audience of the proper kind and he will straightway put aside his other affairs and take a whet. And you will see by the contortions and his ecstatic expression that he takes an intelligent and human interest in his performance.

The signs of excessive indulgence in this destructive pastime are easily detectable. They are these. A disposition to eat, to drink, to smoke, to meet together convivially, to laugh, to joke and tell indelicate stories—and mainly a yearning to paint pictures. The results of the habit are: loss of memory, loss of virility, loss of cheerfulness, loss of hopefulness, loss of character and loss of progeny. Of all the various kinds of sexual intercourse this has least to recommend it.

As an amusement it is too fleeting. As an occupation it is too wearing. As a public exhibition there is no money in it. It is unsuited to the drawing room. And in the most cultured society it has long since been banished from the social board. It has at last, in our day of progress and improvement, been degraded to brotherhood with flatulence. Among the best bred these two arts are now indulged only in private. Though by consent of the whole company, when only males are present, it is still permissible in good society to remove the embargo upon the fundamental sigh.

My illustrious predecessor has taught you that all forms of the "social evil" are bad. I would teach you that some of those forms are more to be avoided than others. So in concluding I say, "If you *must* gamble away your lives sexually, don't play a Lone Hand too much." When you feel a revolutionary uprising in your system get your Vendôme Column down some other way—don't jerk it down.

Spring 1879

⤳ 17 ⤳

The thirteenth reunion banquet of the Army of the Tennessee was held in Chicago in November 1879. It was a tremendous affair, attended by Generals Grant, Sheridan, Sherman and others, and six hundred veterans, with a fancy dinner including oysters, venison and buffalo steaks. There were fireworks both actual and oratorical. At about 3:30 A.M. Clemens responded to the fifteenth toast, which was "The Babies—as they comfort us in our sorrows, let us not forget them in our festivities." His speech cracked up the usually stone-faced Grant.

GENERAL GRANT AND THE BABIES

I like that. We have not all had the good fortune to be ladies. We have not all been generals or poets or statesmen. But when the toast works down to the babies we stand on common ground.

It is a shame that for a thousand years the world's banquets have utterly ignored the baby as if he didn't amount to anything. If you will stop and think a minute, if you will go back fifty or one hundred years to your early married life and recontemplate your first baby, you will remember that he amounted to a good deal, and even something over. You soldiers all know that when that little fellow arrived at family headquarters you had to hand in your resignation. He took entire command.

You became his lackey, his mere body servant, and you had to stand around, too. He was not a commander who made allowances for time, distance, weather or anything else. You had to execute his order whether it was possible or not. And there was only one form of marching in his manual of tactics, and that was the double-quick. He treated you with every sort of insolence and disrespect, and the bravest of you didn't dare to say a word. You could face the death storm at Donelson and Vicksburg and give back blow for blow. But when he clawed your whiskers and pulled your hair and twisted your nose you had to take it.

When the thunders of war were sounding in your ears you set your faces toward the batteries and advanced with steady tread. But when he turned on the terrors of his war whoop you advanced in the other direction, and mighty glad of the chance, too. When he called for soothing syrup did you venture to throw out any side remarks about certain services being unbecoming an officer and a gentleman? No. You got up and got it. When he ordered his pap bottle and it was not warm did you talk back? Not you. You went to work and warmed it.

You even descended so far in your menial office as to take a suck at that warm insipid stuff yourself to see if it was right—three parts water to one of milk, a touch of sugar to modify the colic, and a drop of peppermint to kill those immortal hiccoughs. I can taste that stuff yet.

And how many things you learned as you went along! Sentimental young folks still take stock in that beautiful old saying that when the baby smiles in his sleep it is because the angels are whispering to him. Very pretty but too thin. Simply wind on the stomach, my friend. If the baby proposed to take a walk at his usual hour, two o'clock in the morning, didn't you rise up promptly and remark, with a mental addition which would not improve a Sunday school book much, that that was the very thing you were about to propose yourself? Oh, you were under good discipline, and as you went fluttering up and down the room in your undress uniform, you not only prattled undignified baby talk but even tuned up your martial voices and tried to sing!—*Rock-a-by Baby in the Tree-top*, for instance. What a spectacle for an Army of the Tennessee!

And what an affliction for the neighbors, too. For it is not everybody within a mile around that likes military music at three in the morning. And when you had been keeping this sort of thing up two or three hours, and your little velvet head intimated that nothing suited him like exercise and noise, what did you do? You simply went on until you dropped in the last ditch.

The idea that a baby doesn't amount to anything! Why, one baby is just a house and a front yard full by itself. One baby can furnish more business than you and your whole Interior Department can attend to. He is enterprising, irrepressible, brimful of lawless activities. Do what you please, you can't make him stay on the reservation. Sufficient unto the day is one baby. As long as you are in your right mind don't you ever pray for twins. Twins amount to a permanent riot. And there ain't any real difference between triplets and an insurrection.

Yes, it was high time for a toastmaster to recognize the importance of the babies. Think what is in store for the present crop! Fifty years from now we shall all be dead, I trust, and then this flag, if it still survive (and let us hope it may), will be floating over a republic numbering 200,000,000 souls, according to the settled laws of our increase. Our present schooner of state will have grown into a political leviathan, a Great Eastern.

The cradled babies of today will be on deck. Let them be well trained, for we are going to leave a big contract on their hands. Among the three or four million cradles now rocking in the land are some which this nation would preserve for ages as sacred things if we could know which ones they are.

In one of these cradles the unconscious Farragut of the future is at this moment teething—think of it!—and putting in a world of dead earnest, unarticulated but perfectly justifiable profanity over it, too. In another the future renowned astronomer is blinking at the shining Milky Way with but a languid interest, poor little chap, and wondering what has become of that other one they call the wet nurse. In another the future great historian is lying, and doubtless will continue to lie until his earthly mission is ended.

In another the future President is busying himself with no profounder problem of state than what the mischief has become of his hair so early. And in a mighty array of other cradles there are now some 60,000 future office seekers getting ready to furnish him occasion to grapple with that same old problem a second time.

And in still one more cradle somewhere under the flag the future illustrious commander-in-chief of the American armies is so little burdened with his approaching grandeurs and responsibilities as to be giving his whole strategic mind at this moment to trying to find out some way to get his big toe into his mouth—an achievement which, meaning no disrespect, the illustrious guest of this evening turned *his* entire attention to some fifty-six years ago. And if the child is but a prophecy of the man, there are mighty few who will doubt that he succeeded.

November 1879

๛ **18** ๛

When the publishers of the *Atlantic Monthly* celebrated Oliver Wendell Holmes's seventieth birthday in December 1879 with a splendid breakfast which various literary lights attended, including Emerson, Longfellow and Whittier, Clemens was intent on atoning for his gaffe of 1877.

INNOCENT PLAGIARISM

I would have traveled a much greater distance than I have come to witness the paying of honors to Doctor Holmes, for my feeling toward him has always been one of peculiar warmth. When one receives a letter from a great man for the first time in his life it is a large event to him, as all of you know by your own experience. You never can receive letters enough from famous men afterward to obliterate that one, or dim the memory of the pleasant surprise it was and the gratification it gave you. Lapse of time cannot make it commonplace or cheap.

Well, the first great man who ever wrote me a letter was our guest, Oliver Wendell Holmes. He was also the first great literary man I ever stole anything from, and that is how I came to write to him and he to me.

When my first book was new a friend of mine said to me, "The dedication is very neat."

Yes, I said, I thought it was.

My friend said, "I always admired it, even before I saw it in *The Innocents Abroad.*"

I naturally said, "What do you mean? Where did you ever see it before?"

"Well, I saw it first some years ago as Doctor Holmes's dedication to his *Songs in Many Keys.*"

Of course my first impulse was to prepare this man's remains for burial. But upon reflection I said I would reprieve him for a moment or two and give him a chance to prove his assertion if he could.

We stepped into a book store, and he did prove it. I had really stolen that dedication almost word for word. I could not imagine how this curious thing had happened, for I knew one thing, that a certain amount of pride always goes along with a teaspoonful of brains, and that this pride protects a man from deliberately stealing other people's ideas. That is what a teaspoonful of brains will do for a man. And admirers had often told me I had nearly a basketful though they were rather reserved as to the size of the basket.

However, I thought the thing out and solved the mystery. Two years before, I had been laid up a couple of weeks in the Sandwich Islands and had read and re-read Doctor Holmes's poems till my mental reservoir was filled up with them to the brim. The dedication lay on the top, and handy, so by and by I unconsciously stole it. Perhaps I unconsciously stole the rest of the volume too, for many people have told me that my book was pretty poetical in one way or another.

Well, of course I wrote Doctor Holmes and told him I hadn't meant to steal. And he wrote back and said in the kindest way that it was all right and no harm done, and added that he believed we all unconsciously worked over ideas gathered in reading and hearing, imagining they were original with ourselves. He stated a truth and did it in such a pleasant way and salved over my sore spot so gently and so healingly that I was rather glad I had committed the crime. For the sake of the letter.

I afterward called on him and told him to make perfectly free with any ideas of mine that struck him as being good protoplasm for poetry. He could see by that that there wasn't anything mean about me, so we got along right from the start. I have not met Doctor Holmes many times since. And lately he said—

However, I am wandering wildly away from the one thing which I got on my feet to do. That is, to make my compliments to you, my fellow teachers of the great public, and likewise to say that I am right glad to see that Doctor Holmes is still in his prime and full of generous life.

And as age is not determined by years, but by trouble and infirmities of mind and body, I hope it may be a very long time yet before any one can truthfully say, "He is growing old."

December 1879

✎ **19** ✎

In October of 1880, during the last week of the presidential campaign, Clemens attended a rally in the opera house in Hartford, Connecticut. William Wallace Eaton was the Republican senator from Connecticut. James Edward English was the former governor of Connecticut and former senator from that state. William Hayden English was an Indiana Congressman.

REPUBLICAN RALLY

Friends say to me, "What do you mean by this? You swore off from lecturing years ago."

Well, that is true. I did reform. And I reformed permanently, too. But this ain't a lecture, it is only a speech, nothing but a mere old cut-and-dried impromptu speech. And there's a great moral difference between a lecture and a speech, I can tell you, for when you deliver a lecture you get good pay, but when you make a speech you don't get a cent. You don't get anything at all from your own party, and you don't get anything out of the opposition but a noble, good supply of infamous episodes in your own private life which you hadn't heard of before—a scorching lot of facts about your private rascalities and scoundrelisms which is brand-new to you, and good enough stuff for by and by when you get ready to write your autobiography but of no immediate use to you further than to show you what you *could* have become if you had attended strictly to business.

I have never made but one political speech before this. That was years ago. I made a logical, closely reasoned, compact, powerful argument against a discriminating and iniquitous tax which was about to be imposed by the opposition. I may say I made a most thoughtful, symmetrical and admirable argument. But a Michigan newspaper editor answered it, refuted it, utterly demolished it by saying I was in the constant habit of horsewhipping my great-grand-mother. I should not have minded it so much. Well, I don't know that I should have minded it at all, a little thing like that, if he had said I did it for her good. But when he said I merely did it for exercise I felt that such a statement as that was almost sure to cast a shadow over my character.

However, I don't mind these things particularly. It is the only intelligent and patriotic way of conducting a campaign. I don't mind what the opposition say of me so long as they don't tell the truth about me. But when they descend to telling the truth about me I consider that that is taking an unfair advantage. Why should we be bitter against each other—such of us of both parties as are not ashamed of being Americans? But perhaps I have said enough by way of preface.

I am going to vote the Republican ticket, myself, from old habit. But what I am here for is to try to persuade you to vote the Democratic ticket. Because if you throw the government of this country into the hands of the Republicans they will unquestionably kill that Wood tariff project. But if you throw this government into the hands of the Democrats, the Wood tariff project will become the law of the land, and every one of us will reap his share of the enormous benefits resulting from it. There will be nothing sectional about it, its wholesome generosities are as all-embracing as the broad and general atmosphere. The North, the South, the East, the West will all have their portion of those benefactions.

Consider the South's share, for instance. With a tariff "for revenue only," and no tariff for "protection," she will not be obliged to carry on a trade with us of the North and pay northern prices. No! She can buy of England duty free at far cheaper rates. The price of her cotton will remain as before but the cost of producing will be vastly diminished and the profit vastly increased. Wealth will pour in on her in such a deluge that she will not know what to do with the money. In time she will be able to buy and sell the North. Will the South cast a solid vote for the Wood tariff bill? I am glad to believe—yes, to know—that the South will stand by our Senator Eaton to a man in this great and good cause.

And think of our share in the benefits of the Wood tariff. Some of our people sit up and cry all night for joy when they think of them. They've raised the rivers here with their tears, joyful tears, and dissipated the malaria. And I wish they'd keep on crying. It is the only efficient sewerage we've ever had. Our first and chiefest benefit from the Wood tariff will be that we shan't have any more factory smoke. Statistics on file in the War Department show that more people's eyes are injured by factory smoke in a year than by any other agent.

Statistics. I've come loaded with statistics, for I've noticed that a man can't prove anything without statistics. No man can. Senator Eaton himself can't prove anything without statistics—or with them, whichever it is. I don't remember which it is now, but I know it is one or the other of them, for I had it all thought out, once. Statistics—statistics—why, statistics are more precious and useful than any other one thing in this world except whisky—I mean hymnbooks. This comes of trusting to inspiration instead of sticking to the cold text. A man can ruin himself that way making a public speech.

Statistics in the Navy Department show that if the factory smoke were done away with, there would be a saving to the North every year of over $200,000 in diminished wash bills alone, and that the washerwoman who is today able to support her husband and children in free-handed plenty at the tub would have to come down to wages that would not only benefit her health and strength by requiring her to work nights as well as days but would enable you and me to fairly wallow in dissipations which are denied to us now by the grinding tyranny of the weekly wash bill. Statistics in the Interior Department show that factory smoke causes more profanity to the square mile than any other known agent except the book agent.

Statistics in the Department of Justice show that with the departure of factory smoke the factory workmen would depart also, of necessity, they and their wives and children, and get what they need and what their honest hard work has earned for them, a good, long, soul-satisfying holiday. Nothing in the world to do but lie around in comfort and enjoy themselves. And while they were having holidays and a good time the rest of the people would be vastly benefited too, for occasionally when you needed a capable man to do some work for you you could get him for half a dollar a day. You could have your pick and choice then but you can't now, for there is more work and money than men. So they are in a position to come or not, just as they please. For a man can be as independent and as much his own master, free and untrammeled on enough, as he can be on fifty thousand times enough. It is only when you cut him below enough that he ceases to be independent and can neither ante nor pass the buck, as the prophet says. And so of course you raise him and raise him and raise him till you raise him out, as the poet says. And it's no trick for you to do it, because you hold a flush against his two pair and a jack. I trust I make myself understood.

Yes, you can get men exceeding cheap, then, in the good time that is coming, when the Democratic tariff bill goes through. And our architecture will improve too, for we shall have the stateliest kind of poorhouses all around and everywhere. They'll be so thick that the worst marksman here couldn't miss them with an old-fashioned Allen's revolver. And ten percent of the population will be in them, and just as comfortable and contented as angels. Why, you can even save on pew rent then. Pew rent will go down to next to nothing, and the poorest sinner can have a place to sleep.

And real estate—think of that. You can buy a corner lot then for less than it costs you to buy a grave now. Of course you'll need the grave more then, but never mind that, that's a matter of detail. You'll take which you please. I'm not trying to dictate. I'm only using the thing as an illustration. And you can build a house then cheaper than you can bury a man today, and there's more satisfaction in it, too, unless you can pick your man. You can keep a carriage then for less than it costs you to keep a wheelbarrow now. And bigamy—think of that! Bigamy will be cheaper then than monogamy is now. There's a million arguments—but I've only got all night to talk in, so I must leave most of them out.

The tyrannous unequal values of today will disappear, and real estate on the ground and real estate in a cart will be the same price—fifteen cents a cubic yard. And that is right—that is just. Try to make me believe there's differences in dirt, with my familiarity with it, that one kind of dirt is worth more than another kind, that even the best dirt is worth more than fifteen cents a yard? No, sir, I think it's *high*.

And in place of the confusion and noise of today and the unsightly mud the streets of the North will slumber in a soothing Sabbath calm, restful to the weary spirit, and be adorned with soft, rich carpets of grass, a solace to the eye and a satisfaction to the foot. The odious law which today deprives us of the improving, elevating, humanizing society of the tramp will be swept from the statute book by the tramp himself. For we shall all be tramps then and can outvote anything that can be devised to hamper us, and give the opposition long odds, too. Once more we shall see our old ragged tourists moving in eternal procession from house to house disdaining bread and demanding pie at the butt end of the club. Immigration will cease and emigration will take its place. And we shall all be benefited, because we shall pack up and go to countries where we can get fifty-five cents a day and feed on meat four times a month.

And we can stretch forth a helping hand to revered old England in this her time of heavy distress. She was our enemy in the war days and did all she could to injure us and cripple us and insult us. But she stands ready to be our friend now, and it is our duty and should be our pleasure to forgive and forget and meet her with the kiss of love and peace. She is ready to be our friend. Yes, more than ready. She is eager, she is anxious, to be our friend. And all she asks for this is that we shall pass the Wood tariff bill and so give her famishing factories a magnificent new lease of life and her whole people a rousing prosperity such as they have not known for years, a prosperity which will amply make up for all she is losing through her land troubles in Ireland. And by the generous might of the great Democratic party we will pass this bill and fall weeping upon the grateful bosom of our old suffering mother land.

We will say, "You fitted out pirates against us but we forgive you. You cheated us out of one pirate after we had thrashed him in fair fight and had a just and righteous mortgage on him. But we forgive you. You connived secretly with Louis Napoleon for our overthrow but we forgive you. You feasted and honored and sheltered our enemies and obstructed our friends and sneered at them but we forgive you. You have been the Irishman's hard master at home for seven hundred years and you will be his hard master now in America, but no matter, he forgives you and we forgive you—all and everything—and you shall have your Wood tariff bill which you urge upon us with an eloquence which moves even the unsentimental among us to say. 'Take our forges, take our factories, take our prosperities, take all we have, only say we are the one utterly loving, generous, forgiving, forgetting, magnanimous nation that graces the earth.'"

Yes, let her say that to us and remove the troublesome factory smoke, and it is all we ask. For the one great central idea of this presidential battle is not which is the better man of the two. It is not war or peace. It is not religion. It is not sectional supremacy. It is not national honor, national glory. No, it is none of these. It is factory smoke. It all turns on factory smoke. Other matters are trifling, they are nothing. The supreme and only question is, who will rid us of the factory smoke? Only rid us of the factory smoke and you rid us of everything else. And on top of it we win England's imperishable gratitude.

Now, I beseech you, lay aside all private selfishness, and mere considerations of bread and high wages, and go to the polls, vote the good old Democratic ticket and clear this murky northern atmosphere of its all-pervading clouds of suffocating factory smoke. Then we will all knock off and have a good permanent holiday and a general good time. Vote your full strength for our three great and good Democratic standard bearers—English of Connecticut, English of Indiana and the English on the other side of the water. For this fight is an English fight pure and simple (all the family are in it), and there's nothing else to it. I would vote that ticket myself, but I have grown old in Republican sin and it is too late to reform.

Now, I have spoken somewhat fantastically, but no matter, these fantastic trappings are hung around as solid and real a truth as anyone can utter. And it is a truth which not any of us can afford to whistle down the wind or scoff at or ignore or banish out of our minds unexamined and undigested, for in plain simple terms it involves our actual *bread and meat*, and no amount of fine talk and cooked-up statistics can take away from it that stern and ominous fact.

October 1880

20

In February of 1881 Clemens spoke at the Papyrus Club of Boston on "Ladies Night."

SPEECHLESS

I am perfectly astonished—a-s-t-o-n-i-s-h-e-d, ladies and gentlemen—astonished at the way history repeats itself.

I find myself situated at this moment exactly and precisely as I was once before, years ago, to a jot, to a tittle, to a very hair. There isn't a shade of difference. It is the most astonishing coincidence that ever—but wait. I will tell you the former instance, and then you will see it for yourself.

Years ago I arrived one day at Salamanca, New York, eastward bound. Must change cars there and take the sleeper train. There were crowds of people there, and they were swarming into the long sleeper train and packing it full, and it was a perfect purgatory of dust and confusion and gritting of teeth and soft, sweet and low profanity.

I asked the young man in the ticket office if I could have a sleeping section. And he answered, "No," with a snarl that shrivelled me up like burned leather.

I went off smarting under this insult to my dignity, and asked another local official, supplicatingly, if I couldn't have some poor little corner somewhere in a sleeping car. But he cut me short with a venomous, "No, you can't. Every corner is full. Now, don't bother me any more."

And he turned his back and walked off.

My dignity was in a state now which cannot be described. I was so ruffled that—well, I said to my companion, "If these people knew who I am they . . ."

But my companion cut me short there.

"Don't talk such folly," he said. "If they did know who you are, do you suppose it would help your high mightiness to a vacancy in a train which has no vacancies in it?"

This did not improve my condition any to speak of, but just then I observed that the colored porter of a sleeping car had his eye on me. I saw his dark countenance light up. He whispered to the uniformed conductor, punctuating with nods and jerks toward me, and straightway this conductor came forward, oozing politeness from every pore.

"Can I be of any service to you?" he asked. "Will you have a place in the sleeper?"

"Yes," I said, "and much oblige me, too. Give me anything—anything will answer."

"We have nothing left but the big family stateroom," he continued, "with two berths and a couple of armchairs in it, but it is entirely at your disposal. Here, Tom, take these satchels aboard!"

Then he touched his hat and we and the colored Tom moved along. I was bursting to drop just one little remark to my companion but I held in and waited.

Tom made us comfortable in that sumptuous great apartment and then said with many bows and a perfect affluence of smiles, "Now, is dey anything you want, sah? Case you kin have jes' anything you wants. It don't make no difference what it is."

"Can I have some hot water and a tumbler at nine tonight—blazing hot?" I asked. "You know about the right temperature for a hot Scotch punch?"

"Yes, sah, dat you kin. You kin pen on it. I'll get it myself."

"Good! Now, that lamp is hung too high. Can I have a big coach candle fixed up just at the head of my bed, so that I can read comfortably?"

"Yes, sah, you kin. I'll fix her up myself. An' I'll fix her so she'll burn all night. Yes, sah. An' you can jes' call for anything you want, and dish yer whole railroad 'll be turned wrong end up an' inside out for to get it for you. Dat's so."

And he disappeared.

Well, I tilted my head back, hooked my thumbs in my armholes, smiled a smile on my companion and said gently, "Well, what do you say now?"

My companion was not in the humor to respond, and didn't. The next moment that smiling black face was thrust in at the crack of the door, and this speech followed.

"Laws bless you, sah, I knowed you in a minute. I told de conductah so. Laws! I knowed you de minute I sot eyes on you."

"Is that so, my boy?" (Handing him a quadruple fee.) "Who am I?"

"Jenuel McClellan," and he disappeared again.

My companion said vinegarishly, "Well, well! What do you say now?"

Right there comes in the marvelous coincidence I mentioned a while ago—to wit, I was speechless, and that is my condition now.

Perceive it?

February 1881

ᘒ 21 ᘓ

In June of 1881 the Army of the Potomac held its twelfth annual reunion in Hartford, Connecticut, Mark Twain's home. Responding to the toast "The benefit of judicious training," Clemens said, "Let but the thoughtful civilian instruct the soldier in his duties, and the victory is sure." He was quoting Martin Farquhar Tupper, an uninspired but popular English poet, on the Art of War.

THE ART OF WAR

I gladly join with my fellow townsmen in extending a hearty welcome to these illustrious generals and war-scarred soldiers of the Republic. This is a proud day for us, and if the sincere desire of our hearts has been fulfilled it has not been an unpleasant day for them.

I am in full accord, sir, with the sentiment of the toast, for I have always maintained with enthusiasm that the only wise and true way is for the soldier to fight the battle and the unprejudiced civilian to tell him how to do it. Yet when I was invited to respond to this toast and furnish this advice and instruction I was almost as embarrassed as I was gratified, for I could bring to this great service but the one virtue of absence of prejudice and set opinion.

Still, but one other qualification was needed, and it was of only minor importance. I mean knowledge of the subject. Therefore I was not disheartened, for I could acquire that, there being two weeks to spare. A general of high rank in this Army of the Potomac said two weeks was really more than I would need for the purpose. He had known people of my style who had learned enough in forty-eight hours to enable them to advise an army. Aside from the compliment, this was gratifying because it confirmed the impression I had had before.

He told me to go to the United States Military Academy at West Point. Said in his flowery professional way that the cadets would "load me up."

I went there and stayed two days and his prediction proved correct. I make no boast on my own account—none. All I know about military matters I got from the gentlemen at West Point, and to them belongs the credit. They treated me with courtesy from the first. But when my mission was revealed this mere courtesy blossomed into the warmest zeal. Everybody, officers and all, put down their work and turned their whole attention to giving me military information. Every question I asked was promptly and exhaustively answered. Therefore I feel proud to state that in the advice which I am about to give you as soldiers, I am backed up by the highest military authority in the land, yes, in the world, if an American does say it—West Point!

To begin, gentlemen. When an engagement is meditated it is best to feel the enemy first. That is, if it is night. For, as one of the cadets explained to me, you do not need to feel him in the daytime, because you can see him then. I never should have thought of that but it is true, perfectly true. In the daytime the methods of procedure are various. But the best, it seems to me, is one which was introduced by General Grant. General Grant always sent an active young redoubt to reconnoiter and get the enemy's bearings. I got this from a high officer at the Point, who told me he used to be a redoubt on General Grant's staff and had done it often.

When the hour for the battle is come, move to the field with celerity. Fool away no time. Under this head I was told of a favorite maxim of General Sheridan's.

General Sheridan always said, "If the siege train isn't ready, don't wait. Go by any train that is handy. To get there is the main thing."

Now that is the correct idea. As you approach the field it is best to get out and walk. This gives you a better chance to dispose your forces judiciously for the assault. Get your artillery in position and throw out stragglers to right and left to hold your lines of communication against surprise. See that every hodcarrier connected with the mortar battery is at his post. They told me at the Point that Napoleon despised mortar batteries and never would use them. He said that for real efficiency he wouldn't give a hatful of brickbats for a ton of mortar. However, that is all *he* knew about it.

Everything being ready for the assault, you want to enter the field with your baggage to the front. This idea was invented by our renowned guest, General Sherman. They told me General Sherman said the trunks and steamer chairs make a good protection for the soldiers but that chiefly they attract the attention and rivet the interest of the enemy, and this gives you an opportunity to whirl the other end of the column around and attack him in the rear. I have given a good deal of study to this tactic since I learned about it, and it appears to me it is a rattling good idea.

Never fetch on your reserves at the start. This was Napoleon's first mistake at Waterloo. Next he assaulted with his bomb proofs and embrasures and ambulances when he ought to have used a heavier artillery. Thirdly, he retired his right by ricochet, which uncovered his pickets, when his only possibility of success lay in doubling up his center flank by flank and throwing out his chevaux-de-frise by the left oblique to relieve the skirmish line and confuse the enemy. And at West Point they said it would.

It was about this time that the emperor had two horses shot under him. How often you see the remark that General So-and-So in such and such a battle had two or three horses shot under him. General Burnside and many great European military men, as I was informed by a high artillery officer at West Point, has justly characterized this as a wanton waste of projectiles. And he impressed upon me a conversation held in the tent of the Prussian chiefs at Gravelotte, in the course of which our honored guest just referred to, General Burnside, observed that if you can't aim a horse so as to hit the general with it shoot it over him and you may bag somebody on the other side, whereas a horse shot under a general does no sort of damage. I agree cordially with General Burnside, and Heaven knows I shall rejoice to see the artillerists of this land and all lands cease from this wicked and idiotic custom.

At West Point they told me of another mistake at Waterloo, to wit, that the French were under fire from the beginning of the fight until the end of it, which was plainly a most effeminate and ill-timed attention to comfort and a fatal and foolish division of military strength. For it probably took as many men to keep up the fires as it did to do the fighting. It would have been much better to have a small fire in the rear and let the men go there by detachments and get warm, and not try to warm up the whole army at once. All the cadets said that.

An assault along the whole line was the one thing which could have restored Napoleon's advantages at this juncture. And he was actually rising in his stirrups to order it when a sutler burst at his side and covered him with dirt and debris. And before he could recover his lost opportunity Wellington opened a tremendous and devastating fire upon him from a monster battery of vivandières, and the star of the great captain's glory set, to rise no more. The cadet wept while he told me these mournful particulars.

When you leave a battlefield always leave it in good order. Remove the wreck and rubbish and tidy up the place. However, in the case of a drawn battle it is neither party's business to tidy up anything. You can leave the field looking as if the city government of New York had bossed the fight.

When you are traversing in the enemy's country in order to destroy his supplies and cripple his resources, you want to take along plenty of camp followers. The more the better. They are a tremendously effective arm of the service and they inspire in the foe the liveliest dread. A West Point professor told me that the wisdom of this was recognized as far back as Scripture times. He quoted the verse. He said it was from the new revision and was a little different from the way it reads in the old one. I do not recollect the exact wording of it now but I remember that it wound up with something about such and such a devastating agent being as "terrible as an army with bummers."

I believe I have nothing further to add but this. The West Pointer said a private should preserve a respectful attitude toward his superiors and should seldom or never proceed so far as to offer suggestions to his general in the field. If the battle is not being conducted to suit him it is better for him to resign. By the etiquette of war, it is permitted to none below the rank of newspaper correspondent to dictate to the general in the field.

June 1881

⚕ 22 ⚕

When Clemens traveled to Canada to apply for copyright on *The Prince and the Pauper* he was given a dinner, an occasion which the *New York Times* described, reprinting an article from the *Montreal Gazette*. The headlines in the *Times* declared, "Mark Twain in Montreal/His Speech at the Banquet in/His Honor/An Explanation How He Came to Be/in an Ostensibly Foreign Land—/Looking Forward to the Good Time/Coming When Literary Property/Will Be as Sacred as Whisky."

The article said, "There was a very pleasant gathering of gentlemen at the banquet given Mr. Samuel L. Clemens (Mark Twain) at the Windsor Hotel, in Montreal, on Thursday evening. The *Gazette* says of it: 'The assembly was essentially a gathering of the devoted admirers of a great genius, who sought in a peculiarly English way to evince their appreciation of his literary peerage. The gathering was thoroughly representative of the intellectual and commercial greatness of Canada.'"

A fellow craftsman—Louis Honoré Fréchette, known as the Poet Laureate of Canada. Wolfe—James Wolfe, British major general, killed while trying to take Quebec. Champlain—Samuel de Champlain, French explorer who founded Quebec.

VISIT TO CANADA

That a banquet should be given to me in this ostensibly foreign land and in this great city, and that my ears should be greeted by such complimentary words from such distinguished lips are eminent surprises to me. And I will not conceal the fact that they are also deeply gratifying. I thank you one and all, gentlemen, for these marks of favor and friendliness, and even if I have not really or sufficiently deserved them, I assure you that I do not any the less keenly enjoy and esteem them on that account.

When a stranger appears abruptly in a country without any apparent business there and at an unusual season of the year the judicious thing for him to do is to explain. This seems peculiarly necessary in my case on account of a series of unfortunate happenings here which followed my arrival and which I suppose the public have felt compelled to connect with that circumstance. I would most gladly explain if I could, but I have nothing for my defense but my bare word, so I simply declare in all my sincerity and with my hand on my heart that I never heard of that diamond robbery till I saw it in the morning paper. And I can say with perfect truth that I never saw that box of dynamite till the police came to inquire of me if I had any more of it.

These are mere assertions, I grant you, but they come from the lips of one who was never known to utter an untruth except for practice, and who certainly would not so stultify the traditions of an upright life as to utter one now in a strange land and in such a presence as this, when there is nothing to be gained by it and he does not need any practice. I brought with me to this city a friend, a Boston publisher. But alas even this does not sufficiently explain these sinister mysteries. If I had brought a Toronto publisher along, the case would have been different. But no, possibly not. The burglar took the diamond studs but left the shirt. Only a *reformed* Toronto publisher would have left the shirt.

To continue my explanation. I did not come to Canada to commit crime—this time—but to prevent it. I came here to place myself under the protection of the Canadian law and secure a copyright. I have complied with the requirements of the law. I have followed the instructions of some of the best legal minds in the city, including my own, and so my errand is accomplished, at least so far as any exertions of mine can aid that accomplishment. This is rather a cumbersome way to fence and fortify one's property against the literary buccaneer, it is true. Still, if it is effective it is a great advance upon past conditions and one to be correspondingly welcomed.

It makes one hope and believe that a day will come when in the eye of the law literary property will be as sacred as whisky or any other of the necessaries of life. In this age of ours if you steal another man's label to advertise your own brand of whisky with you will be heavily fined and otherwise punished for violating that trademark. If you steal the whisky without the trademark you go to jail. But if you could prove that the whisky was literature you can steal them both and the law wouldn't say a word. It grieves me to think how far more profound and reverent a respect the law would have for literature if a body could only get drunk on it. Still the world moves. The interests of literature upon our continent are improving. Let us be content and wait.

We have with us here a fellow craftsman, born on our own side of the Atlantic, who has created an epoch in this continent's literary history, an author who has earned and worthily earned and received the vast distinction of being crowned by the Academy of France. This is honor and achievement enough for the cause and the craft for one decade, assuredly.

If one may have the privilege of throwing in a personal impression or two, I may remark that my stay in Montreal and Quebec has been exceedingly pleasant. But the weather has been a good deal of a disappointment. Canada has a reputation for magnificent winter weather and has a prophet who is bound by every sentiment of honor and duty to furnish it, but the result this time has been a mess of characterless weather which all right-feeling Canadians are probably ashamed of. Still, only the country is to blame. Nobody has a right to blame the prophet, for this wasn't the kind of weather he promised.

Well, never mind, what you lack in weather you make up in the means of grace. This is the first time I was ever in a city where you couldn't throw a brick without breaking a church window. Yet I was told that you were going to build one more. I said the scheme is good, but where are you going to find room? They said, we will build it on top of another church and use an elevator. This shows that the gift of lying is not yet dead in the land.

I suppose one must come in the summer to get the advantages of the Canadian scenery. A cabman drove me two miles up a perpendicular hill in a sleigh and showed me an admirable snowstorm from the heights of Quebec. The man was an ass. I could have seen the snowstorm as well from the hotel window and saved my money. Still, I may have been the ass myself. There is no telling. The thing is all mixed up in my mind.

But anyway there was an ass in the party, and I do suppose that wherever a mercenary cabman and a gifted literary character are gathered together for business there is bound to be an ass in the combination somewhere. It has always been so in my experience, and I have usually been elected, too. But it is no matter. I would rather be an ass than a cabman any time except in summer time. Then, with my advantages, I could be both.

I saw the Plains of Abraham, and the spot where the lamented Wolfe stood when he made the memorable remark that he would rather be the author of Gray's "Elegy" than take Quebec. But why did he say so rash a thing? It was because he supposed there was going to be international copyright. Otherwise there would be no money in it. I was also shown the spot where Sir William Phipps stood when he said he would rather take a walk than take two Quebecs. And he took the walk.

I have looked with emotion, here in your city, upon the monument which makes forever memorable the spot where Horatio Nelson did not stand when he fell. I have seen the cab which Champlain employed when he arrived overland at Quebec. I have seen the horse which Jacques Cartier rode when he discovered Montreal. I have used them both. I will never do it again.

Yes, I have seen all the historical places. The localities have been pointed out to me where the scenery is warehoused for the season. My sojourn has been to my moral and intellectual profit. I have behaved with propriety and discretion, I have meddled nowhere but in the election. But I am used to voting, for I live in a town where, if you may judge by local prints, there are only two conspicuous industries—committing burglaries and holding elections. And I like to keep my hand in, so I voted a good deal here.

Where so many of the guests are French the propriety will be recognized of my making a portion of my speech in the beautiful language in order that I may be partly understood. I speak French with timidity and not flowingly except when excited. When using that language I have often noticed that I have hardly ever been mistaken for a Frenchman, except perhaps by horses. Never, I believe, by people. I had hoped that mere French construction, with English words, would answer but this is not the case.

I tried it at a gentleman's house in Quebec and it would not work. The maid servant asked, "What would Monsieur?"

I said, "Monsieur So and So, is he with himself?"

She did not understand that either.

I said, "He will desolate himself when he learns that his friend American was arrived, and he not with himself to shake him at the hand."

She did not even understand that. I don't know why, but she didn't and she lost her temper besides. Somebody in the rear called out, "Qui est donc la?" or words to that effect.

She said, "C'est un fou" and shut the door on me.

Perhaps she was right. But how did she ever find that out? For she had never seen me before till that moment.

But, as I have already intimated, I will close this oration with a few sentiments in the French language. I have not ornamented them, I have not burdened them with flowers or rhetoric, for to my mind that literature is best and most enduring which is characterized by a noble simplicity.

J'ai belle bouton d'or de mon oncle, mais je n'ai pas celui du charpentier. Si vous avez le fromage du brave menuisier, c'est bon. Mais si vous ne l'avez pas, ne se desole pas, prenez le chapeau de drap noir de son beau frere malade. Tout a l'heure! Savoir faire! Qu'est ce que vous dit! Pate de fois gras! Revenons a nos moutons! Pardon, messieurs, pardonnez moi. Essayant a parler la belle langue d'Ollendorf strains me more than you can possibly imagine.

But I mean well, and I've done the best I could.

December 1881

❧ 23 ❧

In December of 1881 Clemens attended the first annual dinner of the New England Society of Philadelphia.

PLYMOUTH ROCK AND THE PILGRIMS

I rise to protest. I have kept still for years, but really I think there is no sufficient justification for this sort of thing. What do you want to celebrate those people for? Those ancestors of yours of 1620. The *Mayflower* tribe, I mean. What do you want to celebrate *them* for? Your pardon: the gentleman at my left assures me that you are not celebrating the Pilgrims themselves but the landing of the Pilgrims at Plymouth Rock on the 22d of December.

So you are celebrating their landing. Why, the other pretext was thin enough but this is thinner than ever. The other was tissue, tinfoil, fish-bladder, but this is gold-leaf.

Celebrating their landing! What was there remarkable about it, I would like to know? What can you be thinking of? Why, those Pilgrims had been at sea three or four months. It was the very middle of winter. It was as cold as death off Cape Cod there. Why shouldn't they come ashore? If they *hadn't* landed there would be some reason for celebrating the fact. It would have been a case of monumental leatherheadedness which the world would not willingly let die. If it had been *you*, gentlemen, you probably wouldn't have landed. But you have no shadow of right to be celebrating in your ancestors gifts which they did not exercise but only transmitted. Why, to be celebrating the mere landing of the Pilgrims, to be trying to make out that this most natural and simple and customary procedure was an extraordinary circumstance, a circumstance to be amazed at and admired, aggrandized and glorified at orgies like this for two hundred and sixty years—hang it, a horse would have known enough to land. A horse—

Pardon again, the gentleman on my right assures me that it was not merely the landing of the Pilgrims that we are celebrating but the Pilgrims themselves. So we have struck an inconsistency here, one says it was the landing, the other says it was the Pilgrims. It is an inconsistency characteristic of your intractable and disputatious tribe, for you never agree about anything but Boston.

Well then, what do you want to celebrate those Pilgrims for? They were a mighty hard lot—you know it. I grant you without the slightest unwillingness that they were a deal more gentle and merciful and just than were the people of Europe of that day. I grant you that they are better than their predecessors. But what of that? That is nothing. People always progress. You are better than your fathers and grandfathers were. (This is the first time I have ever aimed a measureless slander at the departed, for I consider such things improper.) Yes, those among you who have not been in the penitentiary, if such there be, are better than your fathers and grandfathers were, but is that any sufficient reason for getting up annual dinners and celebrating you? No, by no means—by no means.

Well, I repeat, those Pilgrims were a hard lot. They took good care of themselves but they abolished everybody else's ancestors. I am a border ruffian from the State of Missouri. I am a Connecticut Yankee by adoption. In me, you have Missouri morals, Connecticut culture. This, gentlemen, is the combination which makes the perfect man. But where are my ancestors? Whom shall I celebrate? Where shall I find the raw material?

My first American ancestor, gentlemen, was an Indian—an early Indian. Your ancestors skinned him alive, and I am an orphan. Not one drop of my blood flows in that Indian's veins today. I stand here lone and forlorn, without an ancestor. They skinned him! I do not object to that if they needed his fur. But alive, gentlemen—alive! They skinned him alive—and before company! That is what rankles. Think how he must have felt. For he was a sensitive person and easily embarrassed. If he had been a bird it would have been all right and no violence done to his feelings, because he would have been considered "dressed." But he was not a bird, gentlemen, he was a man, and probably one of the most undressed men that ever was.

I ask you to put yourselves in his place. I ask it as a favor. I ask it as a tardy act of justice. I ask it in the interest of fidelity to the traditions of your ancestors. I ask it that the world may contemplate, with vision unobstructed by disguising swallow-tails and white cravats, the spectacle which the true New England Society ought to present. Cease to come to these annual orgies in this hollow modern mockery, the surplusage of raiment. Come in character. Come in the summer grace. Come in the unadorned simplicity. Come in the free and joyous costume which your sainted ancestors provided for mine.

Later ancestors of mine were the Quakers William Robinson, Marmaduke Stevenson, *et al.* Your tribe chased them out of the country for their religion's sake. Promised them death if they came back. For your ancestors had forsaken the homes they loved and braved the perils of the sea, the implacable climate and the savage wilderness to acquire that highest and most precious of boons, freedom for every man on this broad continent to worship according to the dictates of his own conscience—and they were not going to allow a lot of pestiferous Quakers to interfere with it. Your ancestors broke forever the chains of political slavery and gave the vote to every man in this wide land, excluding none! None except those who did not belong to the orthodox church. Your ancestors—yes, they were a hard lot but nevertheless they gave us religious liberty to worship as they required us to worship, and political liberty to vote as the church required. And so I the bereft one, I the forlorn one, am here to do my best to help you celebrate them right.

The Quaker woman Elizabeth Hooton was an ancestress of mine. Your people were pretty severe with her—you will confess that. But poor thing! I believe they changed her opinions before she died, and took her into their fold. And so we have every reason to presume that when she died she went to the same place which your ancestors went to. It is a great pity, for she was a good woman. Roger Williams was an ancestor of mine. I don't really remember what your people did with him. But they banished him to Rhode Island, anyway. And then, I believe, recognizing that this was really carrying harshness to an unjustifiable extreme, they took pity on him and burned him. They were a hard lot.

All those Salem witches were ancestors of mine. Your people made it tropical for them. Yes, they did. By pressure and the gallows they made such a clean deal with them that there hasn't been a witch and hardly a halter in our family from that day to this, and that is one hundred and eighty-nine years.

The first slave brought into New England out of Africa by your progenitors was an ancestor of mine—for I am a mixed breed, an infinitely shaded and exquisite Mongrel. I'm not one of your sham meerschaums that you can color in a week. No, my complexion is the patient art of eight generations.

Well, in my own time I had acquired a lot of my kin—by purchase, and swapping around, and one way and another—and was getting along very well. Then, with the inborn perversity of your lineage, you got up a war and took them all away from me. And so, again am I bereft, again am I forlorn. No drop of my blood flows in the veins of any living being who is marketable.

O my friends, hear me and reform! I seek your good, not mine. You have heard the speeches. Disband these New England societies—nurseries of a system of steadily augmenting laudation and hosannaing which, if persisted in uncurbed, may some day in the remote future beguile you into prevaricating and bragging. Oh, stop, stop, while you are still temperate in your appreciation of your ancestors! Hear me, I beseech you. Get up an auction and sell Plymouth Rock. The Pilgrims were a simple and ignorant race. They never had seen any good rocks before, or at least any that were not watched, and so they were excusable for hopping ashore in frantic delight and clapping an iron fence around this one. But you, gentlemen, are educated. You are enlightened. You know that in the rich land of your nativity, opulent New England, overflowing with rocks, this one isn't worth, at the outside, more than thirty-five cents. Therefore sell it before it is injured by exposure, or at least throw it open to the patent-medicine advertisements and let it earn its taxes.

Yes, hear your true friend, your only true friend, list to his voice. Disband these societies, hotbeds of vice, of moral decay, perpetuators of ancestral superstition. Here on this board I see water, I see milk, I see the wild and deadly lemonade. These are but steps upon the downward path. Next we shall see tea, then chocolate, then coffee—hotel coffee. A few more years—all too few, I fear— mark my words, we shall have cider. Gentlemen, pause ere it be too late. You are on the broad road which leads to dissipation, physical ruin, moral decay, gory crime and the gallows.

I beseech you, I implore you in the name of your anxious friends, in the name of your suffering families, in the name of your impending widows and orphans, stop ere it be too late. Disband these New England societies, renounce these soul-blistering saturnalia, cease from varnishing the rusty reputations of your long-vanished ancestors—the super-high-moral old iron-clads of Cape Cod, the pious buccaneers of Plymouth Rock. Go home and try to learn to behave.

However, chaff and nonsense aside, I think I honor and appreciate your Pilgrim stock as much as you do yourselves, perhaps. And I endorse and adopt a sentiment uttered by a grandfather of mine once, a man of sturdy opinions, of sincere make of mind, and not given to flattery. He said, "People may talk as they like about that Pilgrim stock but, after all's said and done, it would be pretty hard to improve on these people. And as for me, I don't mind coming out flatfooted and saying there ain't any way to improve on them—except having them born in Missouri!"

December 1881

24

In January of 1882 there was a dinner for Louis Honoré Fréchette, a Canadian poet, in Holyoke, Massachusetts. Petroleum Vesuvius Nasby was the pen name of the American humorist David Ross Locke, who like Clemens was popular on the lecture platform.

A RAGGED RAMSHACKLE VOW

I have broken a vow in order that I might give myself the pleasure of meeting my friend Fréchette again. But that is nothing to brag about. A person who is rightly constructed will break a vow any time to meet a friend.

Before I last met Monsieur Fréchette he had become the child of good fortune. That is to say, his poems had been crowned by the Academy of France. Since I last met him he has become the child of good fortune once more. That is to say, I have translated his poems into English and written a eulogy of them in the French language to preface the work.

He possessed a single-barrelled fame before. He will possess a double-barrelled fame now. For this reason: translations always reverse a thing and bring an entirely new side of it into view, thus doubling the property and making two things out of what was only one thing before. So in my translation his pathetic poems have naturally become humorous, his humorous poems have become sad. Anybody who knows even the rudiments of arithmetic will know that Monsieur Fréchette's poems are now worth exactly twice as much as they were before.

I am glad to help welcome the laureate of Quebec to our soil. And I assure him that we will do our best to leave him no room to regret that he came.

Yes, as I was saying, I broke a vow. If it had been a trig, shiny, brand-new one I should be sorry, of course, for it is always wrong and a pity to mistreat and injure good new property. But this was different. I don't regret this one, because it was an old ragged ramshackle vow that had seen so much service and been broken so often and patched and spliced together in so many places that it was become a disgraceful object, and so rotten that I could never venture to put any strain worth mentioning upon it. This vow was a vow which I first made eleven years ago, on a New Year's Day, that I would never make another after-dinner speech as long as I lived. It was as good a vow then as I ever saw. But I have broken it in sixty-four places since, and mended it up fresh every New Year's.

Seven years ago I reformed in another way. I made a vow that I would lead an upright life, meaning by that that I would never deliver another lecture. I believe I have never broken that one. I think I can be true to it always and thus disprove the Rev. Petroleum V. Nasby's maxim that "burglars and lecturers never reform."

But this other vow has always been beyond my strength. I mean I have always been beyond its strength. The reason is simple. It lies in the fact that the average man likes to hear himself talk when he is not under criticism. The very man who sneers at your after-dinner speech when he reads it in next morning's paper would have been powerfully moved to make just as poor a one himself if he had been present with the encouraging champagne in him and the friendly, uncritical faces all about him.

But that discourteous man doesn't do all the sneering that is done over your speech. No, he does only a tenth of it. You do the other nine-tenths yourself. Your little talk, which sounded so fine and warbly and nice when you were delivering it in the mellow light of the lamps and in an enchanted atmosphere of applause and all-pervading good fellowship, looks miserably pale and vapid and lifeless in the cold print of a damp newspaper next morning, with obituaries and cast-iron politics all around it and the hard gray light of day shining upon it and mocking at it.

You do not recognize the corpse. You wonder if this is really that gay and handsome creature of the evening before. You look him over and find he certainly is those very remains. Then you want to bury him. You wish you could bury him privately.

January 1882

~ 25 ~

The occasion and the exact date of the following speech are not known. Paine dates it "about 1882." It may have been delivered in the spring of that year, when Clemens made a long-deferred trip down the Mississippi so he could finish his river book. He boarded the steamer *Gold Dust* in St. Louis, hoping to travel under an assumed name. He was recognized both in the city and on the boat. In New Orleans he met Horace Bixby, who had taught him the river and who was now captain of the *City of Baton Rouge*, a new Anchor Line steamer. He returned upriver with Bixby and spent some time in Hannibal, Missouri, the village in which he had spent his boyhood.

ADVICE TO YOUTH

Being told I would be expected to talk here, I inquired what sort of a talk I ought to make. They said it should be something suitable to youth, something didactic, instructive, or something in the nature of good advice.

Very well. I have a few things in my mind which I have often longed to say for the instruction of the young. For it is in one's tender early years that such things will best take root and be most enduring and most valuable.

First then I will say to you, my young friends, and I say it be-seechingly, urgingly—

Always obey your parents. When they are present. This is the best policy in the long run. Because if you don't they will make you. Most parents think they know better than you do, and you can generally make more by humoring that superstition than you can by acting on your own better judgment.

Be respectful to your superiors, if you have any. Also to strangers. And sometimes to others. If a person offend you and you are in doubt as to whether it was intentional or not, do not resort to extreme measures. Simply watch your chance and hit him with a brick. That will be sufficient. If you shall find that he had not intended any offense, come out frankly and confess yourself in the wrong when you struck him. Acknowledge it like a man and say you didn't mean to. Yes, always avoid violence. In this age of charity and kindliness the time has gone by for such things. Leave dynamite to the low and unrefined.

Go to bed early, get up early. This is wise. Some authorities say get up with the sun. Some others say get up with one thing, some with another. But a lark is really the best thing to get up with. It gives you a splendid reputation with everybody to know that you get up with the lark. And if you get the right kind of a lark and work at him right you can easily train him to get up at half past nine every time. It is no trick at all.

Now as to the matter of lying. You want to be very careful about lying, otherwise you are nearly sure to get caught. Once caught you can never again be in the eyes of the good and the pure what you were before. Many a young person has injured himself permanently through a single clumsy and ill-finished lie, the result of carelessness born of incomplete training.

Some authorities hold that the young ought not to lie at all. That of course is putting it rather stronger than necessary. Still, while I cannot go quite so far as that I do maintain, and I believe I am right, that the young ought to be temperate in the use of this great art until practice and experience shall give them that confidence, elegance and precision which alone can make the accomplishment graceful and profitable.

Patience, diligence, painstaking attention to detail—these are the requirements. These in time will make the student perfect. Upon these and upon these only may he rely as the sure foundation for future eminence. Think what tedious years of study, thought, practice, experience went to the equipment of that peerless old master who was able to impose upon the whole world the lofty and sounding maxim that "truth is mighty and will prevail"—the most majestic compound fracture of fact which any of woman born has yet achieved. For the history of our race, and each individual's experience, are sown thick with evidence that a truth is not hard to kill and that a lie told well is immortal.

There in Boston is a monument of the man who discovered anaesthesia. Many people are aware, in these latter days, that that man didn't discover it at all but stole the discovery from another man. Is this truth mighty and will it prevail? Ah no, my hearers, the monument is made of hardy material but the lie it tells will outlast it a million years.

An awkward, feeble, leaky lie is a thing which you ought to make it your unceasing study to avoid. Such a lie as that has no more real permanence than an average truth. Why, you might as well tell the truth at once and be done with it. A feeble, stupid, preposterous lie will not live two years—except it be a slander upon somebody. It is indestructible then, of course, but that is no merit of yours. A final word. Begin your practice of this gracious and beautiful art early. Begin now. If I had begun earlier I could have learned how.

Never handle firearms carelessly. The sorrow and suffering that have been caused through the innocent but heedless handling of firearms by the young! Only four days ago, right in the next farmhouse to the one where I am spending the summer, a grandmother, old and gray and sweet, one of the loveliest spirits in the land, was sitting at her work, when her young grandson crept in and got down an old, battered, rusty gun which had not been touched for many years and was supposed not to be loaded, and pointed it at her, laughing and threatening to shoot. In her fright she ran screaming and pleading toward the door on the other side of the room. But as she passed him he placed the gun almost against her very breast and pulled the trigger.

He had supposed it was not loaded. And he was right, it wasn't. So there wasn't any harm done. It is the only case of that kind I ever heard of.

Therefore, just the same, don't you meddle with old unloaded firearms. They are the most deadly and unerring things that have ever been created by man. You don't have to take any pains at all with them. You don't have to have a rest. You don't have to have any sights on the gun. You don't have to take aim, even. No, you just pick out a relative and bang away, and you are sure to get him.

A youth who can't hit a cathedral at thirty yards with a Gatling gun in three-quarters of an hour can take up an old empty musket and bag his grandmother every time at a hundred. Think what Waterloo would have been if one of the armies had been boys armed with old muskets supposed not to be loaded, and the other army had been composed of their female relations. The very thought of it makes one shudder.

There are many sorts of books. But good ones are the sort for the young to read. Remember that. They are a great, an inestimable, an unspeakable means of improvement. Therefore be careful in your selection, my young friends. Be very careful. Confine yourselves exclusively to Robertson's Sermons, Baxter's *Saint's Rest, The Innocents Abroad* and works of that kind.

But I have said enough. I hope you will treasure up the instructions which I have given you and make them a guide to your feet and a light to your understanding. Build your character thoughtfully and painstakingly upon these precepts, and by and by, when you have got it built, you will be surprised and gratified to see how nicely and sharply it resembles everybody else's.

about 1882

✆ 26 ✆

In December of 1882 Clemens spoke at the seventy-seventh annual dinner of the New England Society of New York. Among the guests were many celebrities.

WOMAN, GOD BLESS HER!

The toast includes the sex, universally. It is to Woman comprehensively, wheresoever she may be found. Let us consider her ways.

First comes the matter of dress. This is a most important consideration and must be disposed of before we can intelligently proceed to examine the profounder depths of the theme. For text let us take the dress of two antipodal types—the savage woman of Central Africa and the cultivated daughter of our high modern civilization.

Among the Fans, a great Negro tribe, a woman when dressed for home or to go out shopping or calling doesn't wear anything at all but just her complexion. That is all. It is her entire outfit. It is the lightest costume in the world but is made of the darkest material. It has often been mistaken for mourning. It is the trimmest and neatest and gracefulest costume that is now in fashion. It wears well, is fast colors, doesn't show dirt, you don't have to send it downtown to wash and have some of it come back scorched with the flatiron and some of it with the buttons ironed off and some of it petrified with starch and some of it chewed by the calf and some of it rotted with acids and some of it exchanged for other customers' things that haven't any virtue but holiness, and ten-twelfths of the pieces overcharged for the rest of the dozen "mislaid."

And it always fits. It is the perfection of a fit. And it is the handiest dress in the whole realm of fashion. It is always ready, always "done up."

When you call on a Fan lady and send up your card the hired girl never says, "Please take a seat, madame is dressing. She'll be down in three-quarters of an hour." No, madame is always dressed, always ready to receive. And before you can get the doormat before your eyes she is in your midst. Then again the Fan ladies don't go to church to see what each other has got on, and they don't go back home and describe it and slander it.

Such is the dark child of savagery as to everyday toilet. And thus, curiously enough, she finds a point of contact with the fair daughter of civilization and high fashion—who often has "nothing to wear." And thus these widely separated types of the sex meet upon common ground.

Yes, such is the Fan woman as she appears in her simple, unostentatious, everyday toilet. But on state occasions she is more dressy. At a banquet she wears bracelets. At a lecture she wears earrings and a belt. At a ball she wears stockings—and, with true feminine fondness for display, she wears them on her arms. At a funeral she wears a jacket of tar and ashes. At a wedding the bride who can afford it puts on pantaloons.

Thus the dark child of savagery and the fair daughter of civilization meet once more upon common ground, and these two touches of nature make their whole world kin.

Now we will consider the dress of our other type. A large part of the daughter of civilization is her dress—as it should be. Some civilized women would lose half their charm without dress and some would lose all of it. The daughter of modern civilization dressed at her utmost best is a marvel of exquisite and beautiful art and expense. All the lands, all the climes and all the arts are laid under tribute to furnish her forth. Her linen is from Belfast, her robe is from Paris, her lace is from Venice or Spain or France. Her feathers are from the remote regions of Southern Africa, her furs from the remoter home of the iceberg and the aurora, her fan from Japan, her diamonds from Brazil, her bracelets from California, her pearls from Ceylon, her cameos from Rome. She has gems and trinkets from buried Pompeii, and others that graced comely Egyptian forms that have been dust and ashes now for forty centuries. Her watch is from Geneva, her cardcase is from China, her hair is from—from—I don't know where her hair is from. I never could find out.

That is, her other hair—her public hair, her Sunday hair. I don't mean the hair she goes to bed with. Why, you ought to know the hair I mean. It's that thing which she calls a switch and which resembles a switch as much as it resembles a brickbat or a shotgun or any other thing which you correct people with. It's that thing which she twists and then coils round and round her head beehive fashion and then tucks the end in under the hive and harpoons it with a hairpin.

And that reminds me of a trifle: any time you want to, you can glance around the carpet of a Pullman car and go and pick up a hairpin. But not to save your life can you get any woman in that car to acknowledge that hairpin. Now, isn't that strange? But it's true. The woman who has never swerved from castiron veracity and fidelity in her whole life will, when confronted with this crucial test, deny her hairpin. She will deny that hairpin before a hundred witnesses. I have stupidly got into more trouble and more hot water trying to hunt up the owner of a hairpin in a Pullman car than by any other indiscretion of my life.

Well, you see what the daughter of civilization is when she is dressed, and you have seen what the daughter of savagery is when she isn't. Such is woman as to costume. I come now to consider her in her higher and nobler aspects—as mother, wife, widow, grass widow, mother-in-law, hired girl, telegraph operator, telephone helloer, queen, book-agent, wet nurse, stepmother, boss, professional fat woman, professional double-headed woman, professional beauty, and so forth and so on.

We will simply discuss these few—let the rest of the sex tarry in Jericho till we come again. First in the list of right and first in our gratitude comes a woman who—why, dear me, I've been talking three-quarters of an hour! I beg a thousand pardons. But you see yourselves that I had a large contract. I have accomplished something, anyway. I have introduced my subject. And if I had till next Forefathers' Day I am satisfied that I could discuss it as adequately and appreciatively as so gracious and noble a theme deserves.

But as the matter stands now, let us finish as we began—and say, without jesting but with all sincerity, "Woman—God bless her!"

December 1882

ॐ 27 ॐ

Neither the exact time nor the occasion of this speech is known. Paine has conjectured that it was delivered "about 1880–85." In his study in Elmira, New York, during the summer of 1876 Clemens had worked on a tale which he believed to be a continuation of *Tom Sawyer*. By mid-August he had written several hundred manuscript pages of the new work, which we would know as *Huckleberry Finn*. But his interest had flagged and he put the manuscript aside. In Elmira again, now in the summer of 1883, with the Mississippi book behind him and with the trip down the river to inspire him, he picked up *Huck Finn* and it ran away with him.

ADAM

I never feel wholly at home and equal to the occasion except when I am to respond for the royal family or the President of the United States. But I am full of serenity, courage and confidence then because I know by experience that I can drink standing "in silence" just as long as anybody wants me to. Sometimes I have gone on responding to those toasts with mute and diligent enthusiasm until I have become an embarrassment, and people have requested me to sit down and rest myself.

But responding by speech is a sore trial to me. The list of toasts being always the same, one is always so apt to forget and say something that has already been said at some other banquet some time or other. For instance, you take the toast to—well, take any toast in the regulation lot, and you won't get far in your speech before you notice that everything you are saying is old. Not only old, but stale. And not only stale, but rancid. At any rate that is my experience.

There are gifted men who have the faculty of saying an old thing in a new and happy way. They rub the old Aladdin lamp and bring forth the smoke and thunder, the giants and genii, the pomp and pageantry of all the wide and secret realms of enchantment. And these men are the saviors of the banquet. But for them it must have gone silent, as Carlyle would say, generations ago, and ceased from among the world's occasions and industries. But I cannot borrow their trick. I do not know the mystery of how to rub the old lamp the right way.

And so it has seemed to me that for the behoof of my sort and kind the toast list ought to be reconstructed. We ought to have some of the old themes knocked out of it and a new one or two inserted in their places. There are plenty of new subjects, if we would only look around. And plenty of old ones, too, that have not been touched.

There is Adam, for instance. Whoever talks about Adam at a banquet? All sorts of recent and ephemeral celebrities are held up and glorified on such occasions. But who ever says a good word for Adam? Yet why is he neglected, why is he ignored in this offensive way? Can you tell me that? What has he done that we let banquet after banquet go on and never give him a lift? Considering what we and the whole world owe him, he ought to be in the list, too.

He ought to take precedence of the Press. Yes and the Army and Navy. And Literature. And the Day We Celebrate. And pretty much everything else. In the United States he ought to be at the very top. He ought to take precedence of the President. And even in the loyalist monarchy he ought at least to come right after the royal family. And be "drunk in silence and standing," too. It is his right. And, for one, I propose to stick here and drink in silence and standing till I can't tell a ministering angel from a tax collector.

This neglect has been going on too long. You always place Woman at the bottom of the toast list. It is but simple justice to place Adam at the top of it, for if it had not been for the help of these two, where would you and your banquets be? Answer me that. You must excuse me for losing my temper and carrying on in this way. And in truth I would not do it if it were almost anybody but Adam. But I am of a narrow and clannish disposition, and I never can see a relative of mine misused without going into a passion.

It is no trick for people with plenty of celebrated kin to keep cool when their folk are misused. But Adam is the only solitary celebrity in our family. And that man that misuses him has got to walk over my dead body or go around, that is all there is to that. That is the way I feel about Adam.

Years ago when I went around trying to collect subscriptions to build a monument to him there wasn't a man that would give a cent. And generally they lost their temper because I interrupted their business, and they drove me away and said they didn't care A-dam for Adam. And in ninety-nine cases out of a hundred they got the emphasis on the wrong end of the word. Such is the influence of passion on a man's pronunciation.

I tried Congress. Congress wouldn't build the monument. They wouldn't sell me the Washington monument. They wouldn't lend it to me temporarily while I could look around for another. I am negotiating for that Bastille yonder by the public square in Montreal. But they say they want to finish it first. Of course that ends the project, because there couldn't be any use of a monument after the man was forgotten. It is a pity, because I thought Adam might have pleasant associations with that building. He must have seen it in his time.

But he shall have a monument yet, even if it be only a grateful place in the list of toasts. For to him we owe the two things which are most precious, Life and Death. Life, which the young, the hopeful, the undefeated hold above all wealth and all honors. And Death, the refuge, the solace, the best and kindliest and most prized friend and benefactor of the erring, the forsaken, the old and weary and broken of heart, whose burdens be heavy upon them and who would lie down and be at rest.

I would like to see the toast list reconstructed, for it seems to me a needed reform. And as a beginning in this direction, if I can meet with a second, I beg to nominate Adam. I am not actuated by family considerations. It is a thing which I would do for any other member of our family, or anybody else's if I could honestly feel that he deserved it. But I do not. If I seem to be always trying to shove Adam into prominence, I can say sincerely that it is solely because of my admiration of him as a man who was a good citizen. A good husband at a time when he was not married. A good father at a time when he had to guess his way, having never been young himself. And would have been a good son if he had had the chance.

He could have been governor if he had wanted to. He could have been postmaster-general, speaker of the house, he could have been anything he chose if he had been willing to put himself up and stand a canvass. Yet he lived and died a private citizen without a handle to his name, and he comes down to us as plain simple Adam and nothing more, a man who could have elected himself Major General Adam or anything else as easy as rolling off a log. A man who comes down to us without a stain upon his name unless it was a stain to take one apple when most of us would have taken the whole crop.

I stand up for him on account of his sterling private virtues and not because he happens to be a connection of mine.

about 1880–85

28

During the presidential campaign of 1884 Clemens, a Republican, joined an independent movement in support of Grover Cleveland, a Democrat, against the Republican nominee, James G. Blaine. The independents were known as Mugwumps. The occasion and exact date of the following speech are not known. The "Mulligan letters" were written by Blaine. When they were widely referred to by the press, Blaine's already clouded reputation for political probity became even more susceptible to attack.

In the spring of that year Clemens wrote to his friend William Dean Howells, "My days are given up to cursings, both loud and deep, for I am reading the *Huck Finn* proofs. They don't make a great many mistakes but those that do occur are of a nature that make a man swear his teeth loose."

Howells was for Blaine. Cleveland was to become the first Democratic president since the Civil War.

TURNCOATS

IT seems to me that there are things about this campaign which almost amount to inconsistencies. The language may sound violent. If it does, it is traitor to my mood. The Mugwumps are contemptuously called turncoats by the Republican speakers and journals. The charge is true. We have turned our coats. We have no denials to make as to that.

But does a man become of a necessity base because he turns his coat? And are there no Republican turncoats except the Mugwumps? Please look at the facts in the case candidly and fairly before sending us to political perdition without company.

Why are we called turncoats? Because we have changed our opinion. Changed it about what? About the greatness and righteousness of the principles of the Republican party? No, that is not changed. We believe in those principles yet. No one doubts this. What, then, is it that we have changed our opinion about?

Why, about Mr. Blaine. That is the whole change. There is no other. Decidedly, we have done that, and do by no means wish to deny it.

But when did we change it? Yesterday? Last week? Last summer? No. We changed it years and years ago, as far back as 1876. The vast bulk of the Republican party changed its opinion of him at the same time and in the same way.

Will anybody be hardy enough to deny this? Was there more than a handful of really respectable and respect-worthy Republicans on the north Atlantic seaboard who did not change their opinion of Mr. Blaine at that time? Was not the Republican atmosphere, both private and journalistic, so charged with this fact that none could fail to perceive it?

Very well. Was this multitude called turncoats at that time? Of course not. That would have been an absurdity. Was any of this multitude held in contempt at that time and derided and execrated, for turning his Blaine coat? No one thought of such a thing. Now then, we who are called the Mugwumps turned our coats at that time and they have remained so turned to this day.

If it is shameful to turn one's coat once, what measure of scorn can adequately describe the man who turns it twice? If to turn one's coat once makes one a dude, a Pharisee, a Mugwump and fool, where shall you find language rancid enough to describe a double turncoat? If to turn your coat, at a time when no one can impeach either the sincerity of the act or the cleanliness of your motives in doing it, is held to be a pathetic spectacle, what sort of spectacle is it when such a coat-turned turner turns his coat again, and this time under quite suggestively different circumstances? That is to say, after a nomination.

Do these double turncoats exist? And who are they? They are the bulk of the Republican party. And it is hardly venturing too far to say that neither you nor I can put his finger upon a respectable member of that great multitude who can put a denial of it instantly into words and without blush or stammer. Here in Hartford they do not deny. They confess that they are double turncoats. They say they are convinced that when they formerly changed their opinion about Mr. Blaine they were wrong, and so they have changed back again. Which would seem to be an admission that to change one's opinion and turn one's coat is not necessarily a base thing to do, after all.

Yet they call my tribe customary hard names in their next campaign speeches just the same, without seeming to see any inconsistency or impropriety in it. Well, it is all a muddle to me. I cannot make out how it is or why it is that a single turncoat is a reptile and a double turncoat a bird of paradise.

I easily perceive that the Republican party has deserted us and deserted itself, but I am not able to see that *we* have deserted anything or anybody. As for me, I have not deserted the Republican code of principles, for I propose to vote its ticket—with the presidential exception. And I have not deserted Mr. Blaine, for as regards him I got my free papers before he bought the property.

Personally I know that two of the best known of the Hartford campaigners for Blaine did six months ago hold as uncomplimentary opinions about him as I did then and as I do today. I am told, upon what I conceive to be good authority, that the two or three other Connecticut campaigners of prominence of that ilk held opinions concerning him of that same uncomplimentary breed up to the day of the nomination. These gentlemen have turned their coats and they now admire Blaine, and not calmly, temperately, but with a sort of ferocious rapture. In a speech the other night one of them spoke of the author of the Mulligan letters—these strange Vassarlike exhibitions of eagerness, gushingness, timidity, secretiveness, frankness, naïveté, unsagacity, and almost incredible and impossible indiscretion—as the "first statesman of the age."

Another of them spoke of "the three great statesmen of the age, Gladstone, Bismarck and Blaine." Doubtless this profound remark was received with applause.

But suppose the gentlemen had had the daring to read some of those letters first, appending the names of Bismarck and Gladstone to them. Do not you candidly believe that the applause would have been missing and that in its place there would have been a smile which you could have heard to Springfield? For no one has ever seen a Republican mass meeting that was devoid of the perception of the ludicrous.

October 1884

29

Of the following address, Paine has written, "This mock speech on the dead partisan written after the election of Grover Cleveland in 1884 was probably never delivered in public."

Huckleberry Finn was officially published in the United States and England in December 1884 but it was not ready for delivery to purchasers until February, by which time some 40,000 copies had been ordered, and 50,000 a few weeks later. The novel, parts of which had appeared in two issues of the *Century* magazine, was a success both critically and financially from the beginning.

THE DEAD PARTISAN

That is a noble and beautiful ancient sentiment which admonishes us to speak well of the dead. Therefore let us try to do this for our late friend who is mentioned in the text.

How full of life and strength and confidence and pride he was but a few short months ago. And alas how dead he is today! We that are gathered at these obsequies, we that are here to bury this dust and sing the parting hymn and say the comforting word to the widow and the orphan now left destitute and sorrowing by him, their support and stay in the post office, the consulship, the navy yard and the Indian reservation—we knew him, right well and familiarly we knew him, and so it is meet that we and not strangers should take upon ourselves these last offices lest his reputation suffer through explanations of him which might not explain him happily, and justifications of him which might not justify him conclusively.

First it is right and well that we censure him in those few minor details wherein some slight censure may seem to be demanded—to the end that when we come to speak his praises the good he did may shine with all the more intolerable brightness by the contrast.

To begin then with the twilight side of his character: He was a slave. Not a turbulent and troublesome, but a meek and docile, cringing and fawning, dirt-eating and dirt-preferring slave. And Party was his lord and master. He had no mind of his own, no will of his own, no opinion of his own. Body and soul he was the property and chattel of that master, to be bought and sold, bartered, traded, *given* away at his nod and beck—branded, mutilated, boiled in oil if need were.

And the desire of his heart was to make of a nation of freemen a nation of slaves like to himself. To bring to pass a time when it might be said that "all are for the Party and none are for the State." And the labors of his diligent hand and brain did finally compass his desire. For he fooled the people with plausible new readings of familiar old principles and beguiled them to the degradation of their manhood and the destruction of their liberties.

He taught them that the only true freedom of thought is to think as the party thinks. That the only true freedom of speech is to speak as the party dictates. That the only righteous toleration is toleration of what the party approves. That patriotism, duty, citizenship, devotion to country, loyalty to the flag are all summed up in loyalty to party. Save the party, uphold the party, make the party victorious though all things else go to ruin and the grave.

In these few little things he who lies here cold in death was faulty. Say we no more concerning them, but over them draw the veil of a charitable oblivion, for the good which he did far overpasses this little evil. With grateful hearts we may unite in praises and thanksgivings to him for one majestic fact of his life—that in his zeal for his cause he finally overdid it. The precious result was that a change came.

And that change remains and will endure. And on its banner is written, "Not all are for the Party. *Now* some are for the State."

November 1884

~ 30 ~

Paine has dated this address "about 1884." The exact date and occasion are unknown. The next year was Clemens's fiftieth. During it he launched himself fully, although without at first intending to, into the publishing business, a venture which would eventually bankrupt him.

PLETHORA OF SPEECHES

Like many another well-intentioned man, I have made too many speeches. And like other transgressors of this sort, I have from time to time reformed, binding myself by oath on New Year's Days to never make another speech. I found that a new oath holds pretty well, but that when it is become old and frayed out and damaged by a dozen annual retyings of its remains, it ceases to be serviceable. Any little strain will snap it. So, last New Year's Day I strengthened my reform with a money penalty and made that penalty so heavy that it has enabled me to remain pure from that day to this.

Although I am falling once more now, I think I can behave myself from this out because the penalty is going to be doubled ten days hence. I see before me and about me the familiar faces of many poor, sorrowing fellow sufferers, victims of the passion for speech making—poor, sad-eyed brothers in affliction, who, fast in the grip of this fell, degrading, demoralizing vice, have grown weak with struggling, as the years drifted by, and at last have all but given up hope. To them I say in this last final obituary of mine, don't give up. Don't do it. There is still hope for you. I beseech you, swear one more oath and back it up with cash.

I do not say this to all, of course, for there are some among you who are past reform, some who, being long accustomed to success and to the delicious intoxication of the applause which follows it, are too wedded to their dissipation to be capable now or hereafter of abandoning it. They have thoroughly learned the deep art of speech making and they suffer no longer from those misgivings and embarrassments and apprehensions which are really the only things that ever make a speech maker want to reform. They have learned their art by long observation and slowly compacted experience.

So now they know what they did not know at first, that the best and most telling speech is not the actual impromptu one but the counterfeit of it. They know that that speech is most worth listening to which has been carefully prepared in private and tried on a plaster case or an empty chair or any other appreciative object that will keep quiet until the speaker has got his matter and his delivery limbered up so that they will seem impromptu to an audience. The expert knows that. A touch of indifferent grammar flung in here and there, apparently at random, has a good effect, often restores the confidence of a suspicious audience.

He arranges these errors in private. For a really random error wouldn't do any good. It would be sure to fall in the wrong place. He also leaves blanks here and there, leaves them where genuine impromptu remarks can be dropped in of a sort that will add to the natural aspect of the speech without breaking its line of march. At the banquet he listens to the other speakers, invents happy turns upon remarks of theirs and sticks these happy turns into his blanks for impromptu use by and by when he shall be called up. When this expert rises to his feet he looks around over the house with the air of a man who has just been strongly impressed by something. The uninitiated cannot interpret his aspect. But the initiated can.

They know what is coming. When the noise of the clapping and stamping has subsided this veteran says, "Aware that the hour is late, Mr. Chairman, it was my intention to abide by a purpose which I framed in the beginning of the evening—to simply rise and return my duty and thanks in case I should be called upon, and then make way for men more able and who have come with something to say. But, sir, I was so struck by General Smith's remark concerning the proneness of evil to fly upward that"—etc., etc., etc., and before you know it he has slidden smoothly along on his compliment to the general and out of it and into his set speech, and you can't tell, to save you, where it was nor when it was that he made the connection.

And that man will soar along in the most beautiful way on the wings of a practiced memory, heaving in a little decayed grammar here and a little wise tautology there and a little neatly counterfeited embarrassment yonder and a little finely acted stumbling and stammering for a word, rejecting this word and that, and finally getting the right one, and fetching it out with ripping effect and with the glad look of a man who has got out of a bad hobble entirely by accident—and wouldn't take a hundred dollars down for that accident. And every now and then he will sprinkle you in one of those happy turns on something that has previously been said. And at last, with supreme art he will catch himself when in the very act of sitting down, and lean over the table and fire a parting rocket in the way of an afterthought, which makes everybody stretch his mouth as it goes up, and dims the very stars in heaven when it explodes. And yet that man has been practicing that afterthought and that attitude for about a week.

Well, you can't reform that kind of a man. It's a case of Eli joined to his idols. Let him alone.

But there is one sort that can be reformed. That is the genuine impromptu speaker. I mean the man who "didn't expect to be called upon and isn't prepared," and yet goes waddling and warbling along just as if he thought it wasn't any harm to commit a crime so long as it wasn't premeditated.

Now and then he says, "But I must not detain you longer." Every little while he says, "Just one word more and I am done." But at these times he always happens to think of two or three more unnecessary things and so he stops to say them.

Now that man has no way of finding out how long his windmill is going. He likes to hear it creak, and so he goes on creaking and listening to it and enjoying it, never thinking of the flight of time. And when he comes to sit down at last and look under his hopper he is the most surprised person in the house to see what a little bit of a grist he has ground and how unconscionably long he has been grinding it. As a rule he finds that he hasn't said anything (a discovery which the unprepared man ought always to make and does usually make), and has the added grief of making it at second hand, too.

This is a man who can be reformed. And so can his near relative, who now rises out of my reconstructed past: the man who provisions himself with a single prepared bite of a sentence or so and trusts to luck to catch quails and manna as he goes along. This person frequently gets left. You can easily tell when he has finished his prepared bit and begun on the impromptu part. Often the prepared portion has been built during the banquet. It may consist of ten sentences but it oftener consists of two. Oftenest of all it is but a single sentence. And it has seemed so happy and pat and bright and good that the creator of it, the person that laid it, has been sitting there cackling privately over it and admiring it and petting it and shining it up and imagining how fine it is going to "go," when, of course, he ought to have been laying another one and still another one and maybe a basketful if it's a fruitful day.

Yes, and he is thinking that when he comes to hurl that egg at the house there is going to be such electric explosion of applause that the inspiration of it will fill him instantly with ideas and clothe the ideas in brilliant language, and that an impromptu speech will result which will be infinitely finer than anything he could have deliberately prepared.

But there are two damaging things which he is leaving out of the calculation. One is the historical fact that a man is never called up as soon as he thinks he is going to be called up, and that every speech that is injected into the proceedings ahead of him gives his fires an added chance to cool. And the other thing which he is forgetting is that he can't sit there and keep saying that fine sentence of his over and over to himself for three quarters of an hour without by and by getting a trifle tired of it and losing somewhat of confidence in it.

When at last his chance comes and he touches off his pet sentence it makes him sick to see how shame-facedly and apologetically he has done it, and how compassionate the applause is and how sorry everybody feels. And then he bitterly thinks what a lie it is to call this a free country, where none but the unworthy and the undeserving may swear. And at this point, naked and blind and empty, he swallows off into his *real* impromptu speech. Stammers out three or four incredibly flat things. Then collapses into his seat, murmuring, "I wish I was in _____"

He doesn't say where, because he doesn't.

The stranger at his left says, "Your opening was very good." Stranger at his right says, "I liked your opening." Man opposite says, "Opening very good indeed—*very* good." Two or three other people mumble something about his opening.

People always feel obliged to pour some healing thing on a crippled man that way. They mean it for oil. They think it *is* oil. But the sufferer recognizes it for aquafortis.

about 1884

⧼ 31 ⧽

In January of 1886 the Typothetae dinner was held in New York to commemorate Benjamin Franklin's birthday. The Typothetae was a printers' association whose members venerated Franklin as the master American printer. Clemens's speech is sprinkled with terms belonging to the era of printing by hand.

THE COMPOSITOR

The chairman's historical reminiscences of Gutenberg have caused me to fall into reminiscences, for I myself am something of an antiquity. All things change in the procession of years, and it may be that I am among strangers. It may be that the printer of today is not the printer of thirty-five years ago.

I was no stranger to him. I knew him well. I built his fire for him in the winter mornings. I brought his water from the village pump. I swept out his office. I picked up his type from under his stand. And, if he were there to see, I put the good type in his case and the broken ones among the "hell matter." And if he wasn't there to see, I dumped it all with the "pi" on the imposing-stone—for that was the furtive fashion of the cub, and I was a cub.

I wetted down the paper Saturdays, I turned it Sundays—for this was a country weekly. I rolled, I washed the rollers, I washed the forms, I folded the papers, I carried them around at dawn Thursday mornings. The carrier was then an object of interest to all the dogs in town. If I had saved up all the bites I ever received I could keep M. Pasteur busy for a year.

I enveloped the papers that were for the mail. We had a hundred town subscribers and three hundred and fifty country ones. The town subscribers paid in groceries and the country ones in cabbages

and cord wood—when they paid at all, which was merely sometimes, and then we always stated the fact in the paper and gave
them a puff. And if we forgot it they stopped the paper.

Every man on the town list helped edit the thing. That is, he gave
orders as to how it was to be edited, dictated its opinions, marked
out its course for it, and every time the boss failed to connect he
stopped his paper. We were just infested with critics, and we tried
to satisfy them all over.

We had one subscriber who paid cash, and he was more trouble
than all the rest. He bought us once a year, body and soul, for two
dollars. He used to modify our politics every which way and he
made us change our religion four times in five years. If we ever tried
to reason with him he would threaten to stop his paper, and of
course that meant bankruptcy and destruction. That man used to
write articles a column and a half long, leaded long primer, and sign
them "Junius," or "Veritas," or "Vox Populi," or some other high-
sounding rot. And then after it was set up he would come in and say
he had changed his mind, which was a gilded figure of speech, because he hadn't any, and order it to be left out.

We couldn't afford "bogus" in that office, so we always took the
leads out, altered the signature, credited the article to the rival paper in the next village, and put it in. Well, we did have one or two
kinds of "bogus." Whenever there was a barbecue or a circus or a
baptizing we knocked off for half a day, and then to make up for
short matter we would "turn over ads"—turn over the whole page
and duplicate it. The other "bogus" was deep philosophical stuff,
which we judged nobody ever read, so we kept a galley of it standing, and kept on slapping the same old batches of it in every now
and then till it got dangerous.

Also, in the early days of the telegraph we used to economize on
the news. We picked out the items that were pointless and barren of
information and stood them on a galley and changed the dates and
localities and used them over and over again till the public interest
in them was worn to the bone. We marked the ads but we seldom
paid any attention to the marks afterward, so the life of a "td" ad and
a "tf" ad was equally eternal. I have seen a "td" notice of a sheriff's
sale still booming serenely along two years after the sale was over,
the sheriff dead, and the whole circumstance become ancient his-

tory. Most of the yearly ads were patent medicine stereotypes, and we used to fence with them.

I can see that printing office of prehistoric times yet, with its horse bills on the walls, its "d" boxes clogged with tallow, because we always stood the candle in the "k" box nights, its towel, which was not considered soiled until it could stand alone, and other signs and symbols that marked the establishment of that kind in the Mississippi Valley. And I can see also the tramping "jour," who flitted by in the summer and tarried a day, with his wallet stuffed with one shirt and a hatful of handbills. For if he couldn't get any type to set he would do a temperance lecture. His way of life was simple, his needs not complex. All he wanted was plate and bed and money enough to get drunk on, and he was satisfied.

But it may be, as I have said, that I am among strangers and sing the glories of a forgotten age to unfamiliar ears, so I will "make even" and stop.

January 1886

32

With the exception of the ending (beginning "In my capacity of publisher I recently received"), which Paine included in the 1910 edition of *Mark Twain's Speeches* but excluded from the 1923 edition, the following speech is reprinted here for the first time. I found the speech in the form of a clipping from the San Francisco *Examiner* of May 12, 1887, in the Documents File for that year in the Mark Twain Papers in Berkeley, California. The *Examiner* noted that it was reprinting the speech from the *New York World* of February 11, 1887.

The article noted that the occasion of the speech was the twelfth annual dinner of the Stationers' Board of Trade, given "the other night" at the Hotel Brunswick. There were about a hundred and fifty people present. The dinner was served in the hotel's ballroom. "There was no attempt at ornamentation except for the baskets of cut flowers and fancy cut pieces upon the tables. The president and guests sat at a table placed lengthwise on the east side of the room and the members at six tables placed across the hall." The Mr. Beaman mentioned by Clemens was probably the president of the Stationers' Board of Trade.

AUTHOR AND PUBLISHER

I find this an evening of surprises. I came here through an understanding with the chairman that I, having reformed, was not to break over pledges made and drift into an after-dinner speech unless I saw immoralities or crimes being committed. And lo, I have waited in constant expectation that something would be said and done that would compel me to speak. But concerning what has been said and done here, I am bound to say that thus far they have been mere misdemeanors.

I have been introduced to you as an example of the author and publisher. I am one of the latest publishers and I am one of the oldest authors, and certainly one of the best. When I came here I expected to remain in some humble capacity outside of the door and never dreamt of being made conspicuous by taking a seat high up among the distinguished guests. But then I am used to being made conspicuous.

As I say, I have found nothing really to attack. I expected Mr. Beaman to commit himself—lawyers are always committing themselves—but Mr. Beaman was—was—the fact is, his speech can actually be complimented. As to his attacking Ben, that is to say Ben Franklin, an old dead man, that can be explained. Franklin was sober because he lived in Philadelphia. Why, Philadelphia is a sober city today. What must it have been in Franklin's time. Why, it is as good as Sunday to be in Philadelphia now.

Franklin was frugal, and as he says himself, with becoming modesty, he had no vices, but though he little suspected it, he made a vice of frugality. You saw, as Mr. Beaman told you, how he did it, but when he mentions why he did it he gives himself away. And finally he wishes that at the last he may be shoved into a barrel of Madeira. But if he had lived here instead of in Philadelphia he would have wanted to get the barrel of Madeira into him.

I am here in the character of author and publisher but I think I will let that rest. Oh, I can tell you a great deal about publishing but I don't think I will. I am rather too fresh yet. I am at the honest stage now but after a while, when I graduate and grow rich, I will tell you all about it.

It is so common that an education is within the grasp of everyone. And if he does not want to pay for it, why here is the State ready to pay for it for him. But sometimes I want to inquire what an education is. I remember myself, and all of you old fellows probably remember the same of yourselves, that when I went to school I was told that an adjective is an adverb and it must be governed by the third person singular, and all that sort of thing, and when I got out of school I straightaway forgot all about it.

In my combined character of publisher and author I receive a great many manuscripts from people who say they want a candid opinion whether that is good literature or bad. That is all a lie. What they want is a compliment. But as to this matter of education. The first thing that strikes me is how much teaching has really been done and how much is worthless cramming. You have all seen a little book called *English as She is Spoke*. Now, in my capacity of publisher I recently received a manuscript from a teacher which embodied a number of answers given by her pupils to questions propounded. These answers show that the children had nothing but the sound to go by. The sense was perfectly empty.

Here are some of their answers to words they were asked to define. Auriferous—pertaining to an orifice. Ammonia—the food of the gods. Equestrian—one who asks questions. Parasite—a kind of umbrella. Ipecac—a man who likes a good dinner.

And here is the definition of an ancient word honored by a great party: Republican—a sinner mentioned in the Bible. And here is an innocent deliverance of a zoological kind: "There are a good many donkeys in the theological gardens." Here also is a definition which really isn't very bad in its way: Demagogue—a vessel containing beer and other liquids.

Here too is a sample of a boy's composition on girls, which I must say I rather like.

"Girls are very stuckup and dignified in their manner and behaveyour. They think more of dress than anything and like to play with dowls and rags. They cry if they see a cow in a far distance and are afraid of guns. They stay at home all the time and go to church every Sunday. They are al-ways sick. They are al-ways funy and making fun of boys hands and they say how dirty. They cant play marbles. I pity them poor things. They make fun of boys and then turn round and love them. I don't belave they ever kiled a cat or anything. They look out every nite and say, 'Oh, aint the moon lovely!' Thir is one thing I have not told and that is they al-ways now their lessons bettern boys."

about February 1887

~ **33** ~

In April of 1887 Clemens attended a reunion banquet of the Union Veterans Association of Maryland, which was given in Baltimore.

AN AUTHOR'S SOLDIERING

You Union veterans of Maryland have prepared your feast and offered to me, a rebel veteran of Missouri, the wound-healing bread and salt of a gracious hospitality. Do you realize all the vast significance of the situation? Do you sense the whole magnitude of this conjunction and perceive with what opulence of blessing for this nation it is freighted?

What is it we are doing? Reflect! Upon this stage tonight we play the closing scene of the mightiest drama of modern times and ring down for good and all the curtain raised at Sumter six-and-twenty years ago. The two grand divisions of the nation, which we name in general terms the North and the South, have shaken hands long ago and given and taken the kiss of peace.

Was anything lacking to make the reconciliation perfect, the fusion of feeling complete? Yes. The great border States attached to those grand divisions, but belonging to neither of them and independent of both, were silent, had made no forgiving sign to each other across the chasm left by the convulsion of war, and the world grieved that this was so. But tonight the Union veteran of Maryland clasps hands with the rebel veteran of Missouri and the gap is closed. In this supreme moment the imperfect welding of the broken Union is perfected at last, and from this hour the seam of the joining shall no more be visible. The long tragedy is ended—ring down the curtain!

When your secretary invited me to this reunion of the Union Veterans of Maryland he requested me to come prepared to clear up a matter which he said had long been a subject of dispute and bad blood in war circles in this country—to wit, the true dimensions of my military service in the Civil War, and the effect which they had upon the general result. I recognize the importance of this thing to history and I have come prepared. Here are the details.

I was in the Civil War two weeks. In that brief time I rose from private to second lieutenant. The monumental feature of my campaign was the one battle which my command fought—it was in the summer of '61. If I do say it, it was the bloodiest battle ever fought in human history. There is nothing approaching it for destruction of human life in the field, if you take in consideration the forces engaged and the proportion of death to survival.

And yet you do not even know the name of that battle. Neither do I. It had a name but I have forgotten it. It is no use to keep private information which you can't show off.

Now look at the way history does. It takes the battle of Boonville, fought near by about the date of our slaughter and shouts its teeth loose over it and yet never even mentions ours, doesn't even call it an "affair," doesn't call it anything at all, never even heard of it. Whereas what are the facts? Why, these.

In the battle of Boonville there were two thousand men engaged on the Union side and about as many on the other—supposed to be. The casualties all told were two men killed, and not all of these were killed outright but only half of them, for the other man died in hospital next day. I know that, because his great-uncle was second cousin to my grandfather, who spoke three languages and was perfectly honorable and upright though he had warts all over him, and used to—but never mind about that, the facts are just as I say and I can prove it. Two men killed in that battle of Boonville, that's the whole result. All the others got away—on both sides.

Now then, in our battle there were just fifteen men engaged on our side—all brigadier generals but me, and I was a second lieutenant. On the other side there was one man. He was a stranger. We killed him. It was night and we thought he was an army of observation. He looked like an army of observation—in fact he looked bigger than an army of observation would in the daytime. And some of us believed he was trying to surround us, and some thought he was going to try to turn our position, and so we shot him. Poor fellow, he probably wasn't an army of observation after all. But that wasn't our fault. As I say, he had all the look of it in that dim light.

It was a sorrowful circumstance, but he took the chances of war and he drew the wrong card. He overestimated his fighting strength and he suffered the likely result. But he fell as the brave should fall—with his face to the foe and feet to the field—so we buried him with the honors of war and took his things.

So began and ended the only battle in the history of the world where the opposing force was *utterly exterminated*, swept from the face of the earth—to the last man. And yet you don't know the name of that battle. You don't even know the name of that man.

Now then for the argument. Suppose I had continued in the war and gone on as I began and exterminated the opposing force every time—every two weeks—where would your war have been? Why, you see yourself the conflict would have been too one-sided. There was but one honorable course for me to pursue and I pursued it. I withdrew to private life and gave the Union cause a chance.

There, now, you have the whole thing in a nutshell. It was not my presence in the Civil War that determined that tremendous contest—it was my retirement from it that brought the crash. It left the Confederate side too weak.

And yet when I stop and think I cannot regret my course. No, when I look abroad over this happy land, with its wounds healed and its enmities forgotten; this reunited sisterhood of majestic States; this freest of free commonwealths the sun in his course shines upon; this one sole country nameable in history or tradition where a man is a man and manhood the only royalty; this people ruled by the justest and wholesomest laws and government yet devised by the wisdom of men; this mightiest of the civilized empires of the earth in numbers, in prosperity, in progress and in promise; and reflect that there is no North, no South any more, but that as in the old time it is now and will remain forever in the hearts and speech of Americans our land, our country, our giant empire, and the flag floating in its firmament our flag, I would not wish it otherwise.

No, when I look about me and contemplate these sublime results I feel deep down in my heart that I acted for the best when I took my shoulder out from under the Confederacy and let it come down.

April 1887

✍ **34** ✍

This speech was given at a dinner marking the hundredth performance of *The Taming of the Shrew*, produced in Daly's Theatre, New York, named after the American theatrical producer and proprietor, Augustin Daly.

BENCH SHOWS

I am glad to be here. This is the hardest theater in New York to get into, even at the front door. I never got in without hard work. I am glad we have got so far in at last.

Two or three years ago I had an appointment to meet Mr. Daly on the stage of this theater at eight o'clock in the evening. Well, I got on a train at Hartford to come to New York and keep the appointment. All I had to do was to come to the back door of the theater on Sixth Avenue. I did not believe that, I did not believe it could be on Sixth Avenue, but that is what Daly's note said—come to that door, walk right in and keep the appointment. It looked very easy. It looked easy enough but I had not much confidence in the Sixth Avenue door.

Well, I was kind of bored on the train and I bought some newspapers—New Haven newspapers—and there was not much news in them, so I read the advertisements. There was one advertisement of a bench show. I had heard of bench shows and I often wondered what there was about them to interest people. I had seen bench shows—lectured to bench shows, in fact—but I didn't want to advertise them or to brag about them.

Well, I read on a little and learned that a bench show was not a bench show—but dogs, not benches at all—only dogs. I began to be interested, and as there was nothing else to do I read every bit of the advertisement and learned that the biggest thing in this show was a St. Bernard dog that weighed one hundred and forty-five pounds. Before I got to New York I was so interested in the bench shows that I made up my mind to go to one the first chance I got.

Down on Sixth Avenue, near where that back door might be, I began to take things leisurely. I did not like to be in too much of a hurry. There was not anything in sight that looked like a back door. The nearest approach to it was a cigar store. So I went in and bought a cigar, not too expensive, but it cost enough to pay for any information I might get and leave the dealer a fair profit. Well, I did not like to be too abrupt, to make the man think me crazy, by asking him if that was the way to Daly's Theatre, so I started gradually to lead up to the subject, asking him first if that was the way to Castle Garden.

When I got to the real question and he said he would show me the way I was astonished. He sent me through a long hallway, and I found myself in a back yard. Then I went through a long passageway and into a little room, and there before my eyes was a big St. Bernard dog lying on a bench.

There was another door beyond and I went there and was met by a big, fierce man with a fur cap on and coat off, who remarked, "Phwat do yez want?"

I told him I wanted to see Mr. Daly.

"Yez can't see Mr. Daly this time of night," he responded.

I urged that I had an appointment with Mr. Daly, and gave him my card, which did not seem to impress him much.

"Yez can't get in and yez can't shmoke here. Throw away that cigar. If yez want to see Mr. Daly, yez'll have to be after going to the front door and buy a ticket, and then if yez have luck and he's around that way yez may see him."

I was getting discouraged but I had one resource left that had been of good service in similar emergencies. Firmly but kindly I told him my name was Mark Twain, and I awaited results. There was none. He was not fazed a bit.

"Phwere's your order to see Mr. Daly?" he asked.

I handed him the note and he examined it intently.

"My friend," I remarked, "you can read that better if you hold it the other side up."

But he took no notice of the suggestion and finally asked, "Where's Mr. Daly's name?"

"There it is," I told him, "on the top of the page."

"That's all right," he said, "that's where he always puts it. But I don't see the 'W' in his name," and he eyed me distrustfully.

Finally he asked, "Phwat do yez want to see Mr. Daly for?"

"Business."

"Business?"

"Yes."

It was my only hope.

"Phwat kind—theaters?"

That was too much.

"No."

"What kind of shows, then?"

"Bench shows."

It was risky but I was desperate.

"Bench shows, is it—where?"

The big man's face changed and he began to look interested.

"New Haven."

"New Haven, it is? Ah, that's going to be a fine show. I'm glad to see you. Did you see a big dog in the other room?"

"Yes."

"How much do you think that dog weighs?"

"One hundred and forty-five pounds."

"Look at that, now! He's a good judge of dogs and no mistake. He weighs all of one hundred and thirty-eight. Sit down and shmoke—go on and shmoke your cigar, I'll tell Mr. Daly you are here."

In a few minutes I was on the stage shaking hands with Mr. Daly, and the big man was standing around glowing with satisfaction.

"Come around in front," said Mr. Daly, "and see the performance. I will put you into my own box."

And as I moved away I heard my honest friend mutter, "Well, he desarves it."

April 1887

~ 35 ~

In April of 1887 Clemens attended a banquet of the Army and Navy Club, Hartford, Connecticut. Clemens's publishing firm, Charles L. Webster & Co., had published Grant's *Memoirs* by subscription. The book was a great success both critically and financially.

GENERAL GRANT'S ENGLISH

Lately a great and honored author, Matthew Arnold, has been finding fault with General Grant's English.

That would be fair enough, maybe, if the examples of imperfect English averaged more instances to the page in General Grant's book than they do in Arnold's criticism of the book. But they do not. It would be fair enough, maybe, if such instances were commoner in General Grant's book than they are in the works of the average standard author. But they are not. In fact, General Grant's derelictions in the matter of grammar and construction are not more frequent than such derelictions in the works of a majority of the professional authors of our time, and of all previous times, authors as exclusively and painstakingly trained to the literary trade as was General Grant to the trade of war.

This is not a random statement. It is a fact, and easily demonstrable. I have a book at home called *Modern English Literature: Its Blemishes and Defects,* by Henry H. Breen, a countryman of Mr. Arnold. In it I find examples of bad grammar and slovenly English from the pens of Sydney Smith, Sheridan, Hallam, Whately, Carlyle, Disraeli, Allison, Junius, Blair, Macaulay, Shakespeare, Milton, Gibbon, Southey, Lamb, Landor, Smollett, Walpole, Walker (of the dictionary), Christopher North, Kirk White, Benjamin Franklin, Sir Walter Scott and Mr. Lindley Murray (who made the grammar).

In Mr. Arnold's criticism of General Grant's book we find two grammatical crimes and more than several examples of very crude and slovenly English, enough of them to easily entitle him to a lofty place in the illustrious list of delinquents just named. The following passage all by itself ought to elect him.

"Meade suggested to Grant that he might wish to have immediately under him, Sherman, who had been serving with Grant in the West. He begged him not to hesitate if he thought it for the good of the service. Grant assured him that he had not thought of moving him, and in his memoirs, after relating what had passed, he adds," etc.

To read that passage a couple of times would make a man dizzy. To read it four times would make him drunk.

Mr. Breen makes this discriminating remark, "To suppose that because a man is a poet or an historian he must be correct in his grammar is to suppose that an architect must be a joiner, or a physician a compounder of medicine."

Mr. Breen's point is well taken. If you should climb the mighty Matterhorn to look out over the kingdoms of the earth it might be a pleasant incident to find strawberries up there. But great Scott, you don't climb the Matterhorn for strawberries.

People may hunt out what microscopic motes they please, but after all the fact remains and cannot be dislodged that General Grant's book is a great and in its peculiar department unique and unapproachable literary masterpiece. In their line there is no higher literature than those modest, simple memoirs. Their style is at least flawless and no man could improve upon it. And great books are weighed and measured by their style and matter, and not by the trimmings and shadings of their grammar.

There is that about the sun which makes us forget his spots. And when we think of General Grant our pulses quicken and his grammar vanishes. We only remember that this is the simple soldier who, all untaught of the silken phrase makers, linked words together with an art surpassing the art of the schools and put into them a something which will still bring to American ears, as long as America shall last, the roll of his vanished drums and the tread of his marching hosts. What do we care for grammar when we think of those thunderous phrases: "unconditional and immediate surrender," "I propose to move immediately upon your works," "I propose to fight it out on this line if it takes all summer."

Mr. Arnold would doubtless claim that that last phrase is not strictly grammatical. And yet it did certainly wake up this nation as a hundred million tons of A No.1, fourth-proof, hard-boiled, hidebound grammar from another mouth could not have done.

And finally we have that gentler phrase, that one which shows you another true side of the man, shows you that in his soldier heart there was room for other than glory war mottoes and in his tongue the gift to fitly phrase them—"Let us have peace."

April 1887

⚲ **36** ⚲

This talk was given at the Forefathers' Day dinner of the Congregational Club in Boston. The *Boston Daily Globe* of Wednesday, December 21, 1887, ran headlines and a long story about the affair. "Pilgrims./Their Deeds and Trials/Again Recalled./Forefathers' Day in the Con-/gregationalist Club./Speeches, Poems, Music and/a Big Dinner./Governor Ames and Lieutenant/Governor Bracket Present./Mark Twain Makes a 'Pat-/tent Adjustable Speech.'/Chauncey M. Depew on the/Meaning of Liberty./Collector Saltonstall, Rev. Dr. Gage/and Other Speakers."

"Ye Congregational Clubbe," the article began, "mette as aforetime in ye Musick Halle to think over and with ye savorie helpe of sundrie goodies of songe and soe forthe to talk about Ye Pilgrim Fathers and their getting ashoare at New Plimmoth two hundred sixty and seven years agone.

"Ye Pilgrim forefathers, could they have filed into Music Hall last night, would have found several things strange to them. First of all, they would have seen something less than a quarter of an acre of heavily laden tables, all ready for the feast which followed. Then they would have noted the crowd of something over 1000 guests. This would have excited their curiosity, and in answer to their query some one would have said it was the Congregational Club gathered to celebrate Forefathers' Day, an event among the descendants of the Pilgrims almost as sacredly commemorated as is Christmas itself.

"It was 'two hundred, sixty and seven years agone' yesterday that the Mayflower dropped her old-fashioned anchor off New Plymouth, and a little time thereafter the voyagers got ashore. There were not a great many of them, but there were enough to found this great Commonwealth. In conjunction with the Puritans they founded much of the good order, established many laws now considered as good enough to govern a people greater in numbers and more advanced than they were. More than all, they gave us institutions which have lived through all the years and are yet considered models.

"The hall was filled. There were 18 large tables, more than could be placed upon the main floor and stage, and so some were put into the first gallery. The guests began to assemble at about 5 o'clock, and spent the ensuing half hour in the usual conversation and in hunting for their seats.

Descendants of all the Pilgrims, the Congregationalists of course talked more or less about the brave men who had courage enough in their convictions to follow, even blindly, their consciences. The speeches of the evening, too, were loyal and loving tributes to the bravery and devotion of that little band. It was not a new experience for the people gathered together to commemorate the day, for they have done the same thing year after year since the organization of the club. The Pilgrims landed in 1620, the Congregational Club was founded in 1869. Surely the memory of the day has not grown gray nor been forgotten."

The president of the club introduced Clemens. The article reported, "Mr. Clemens was given quite an ovation, and his remarks which followed were so droll in their nature and the manner in which they were delivered that his hearers were kept upon a broad grin from the first to the last. It would be almost impossible to convey upon paper anything that would give more than an indication of their intense humor, which was derived largely from the peculiar gestures, inflections and actions which accompanied them. This was particularly so of his description of his 'patent adjustable speech.'"

A SPEECH FOR ALL OCCASIONS

In treating of this subject of post-prandial oratory, a subject which I have long been familiar with and may be called an expert in observing in others, I wish to say that a public dinner is the most delightful thing in the whole world—to the guest. That is one fact. And here is another. A public dinner is the most unendurable suffering in the whole world—to the guest.

These two facts don't seem to jibe. But I will explain. Now, at a public dinner when a man knows he is going to be called upon to speak and is thoroughly well prepared, got it all by heart and the pauses marked in his head where the applause is going to come in, that man is simply—is simply in heaven. He won't care to be anywhere else than just where he is. But when at a public dinner it is getting way along toward the end of things and a man is sitting over his glass of wine or his glass of milk, according to the kind of banquet it is, and sitting there not meditating the danger of it, with somebody at his ear bothering him to talk, talk, talk about nothing, why—well, that is just as nearly in the other place as he can be— that man is to be pitied. And the very worst of it is, he *is* pitied.

Now, he could stand the pity of ten people or a dozen but there is no misery in this world that is comparable to the mass of solidifying compassion of five hundred. Why, that wide Sahara of sympathizing faces completely takes the tuck out of him. He stands there in his misery and stammers out the usual stuff of not being prepared and not expecting, and all that kind of folly, and he is wandering and stumbling and getting further and further in, and all the time being unhappy, and at last he fetches out a poor, miserable, crippled joke, and in his grief and confusion he laughs at it himself, and the others look sick. And then he slumps into his chair and wishes he was dead. He knows he is a defeated man, and so do the others.

To a humane person that is a heartrending spectacle. It is indeed. That sort of sacrifice ought to be stopped. And there is only one way to accomplish it that I can think of, and that is for a man to go always prepared, always loaded, always ready, whether he is likely to be called on or not. You can't defeat that man, you can't pity him at all.

My scheme is this: that he shall carry in his head a connected and tried and thoroughly and glibly memorized speech that will fit every conceivable occasion in this life, fit it to a dot, and win success and applause every time. I have completed a speech of that kind and I have brought it along to exhibit here as an example.

We suppose that it is a granger gathering, and this man is suddenly called on. He comes up with some lively hesitancies and deferences and repetitions so as to give the idea that the speech is impromptu. Here, of course, after he has got used to delivering it, he can venture outside and make a genuine impromptu remark to start off with. For instance, if a distinguished person is present he can make a complimentary reference to him, say to Mr. Depew. He could speak about his great talent or his clothes. Such a thing gives him a sort of opening. And about the time that audience is getting to pity that man, he opens his throttle valve and goes for those grangers. That person wants to be gorgeously eloquent. You want to fire the farmer's heart and start him from his mansard down to his cellar.

Now this man is called up, and he says, "I'm called up suddenly, sir, and am indeed not, not prepared to—I was not expecting to be called up, sir, but I will, with what effect I may, add my shout to the jubilations of this spirited, stirring occasion. Agriculture, sir, is, after all, the palladium of our economic liberties. By it, approximately speaking, we may be said to live and move and have our being. All that we have been, all that we are, all that we hope to be, was, is and must continue to be profoundly influenced by that sublimest of the mighty interests of man, thrice glorious agriculture. While we have life, while we have soul, and in that soul the sweet and hallowed sentiment of gratitude, let us with generous accord attune our voices to songs of praise, perennial outpourings of thanksgiving, for that most precious boon whereby we physically thrive, and are made rich and strong and grand and inspiring, imbued with the mighty, far-reaching and all-embracing grace and beauty and purity and loveliness. The least of us knows, the least of us feels, the humblest of us will confess that, whereas—but the hour is late and I will not detain you."

Now then, supposing it is not a granger gathering at all but is a wedding breakfast. Now, of course, then that speech has got to be delivered in an airy, light fashion but it must terminate seriously. It is a mistake to make it any other way.

This person is called up by the minister of the feast and he says, "I am called up suddenly, sir, and am indeed not prepared to—I was not expecting to be called up, sir, but I will, with what effect I may, add my shout to the jubilations of this spirited, stirring occasion. Matrimony, sir, is, after all, the palladium of our domestic liberties. By it, approximately speaking, we may be said to live and move and acquire our being. All that we have been, all that we are, all that we hope to be, was, is and must continue to be profoundly influenced by that sublimest of the mighty interests of man, thrice glorious matrimony. While we have life, while we have soul, and in that soul the sweet and hallowed sentiment of gratitude, let us with generous accord attune our voices to songs of praise, perennial outpourings of thanksgiving for that most precious boon whereby our otherwise sterile existence is made rich and strong and grand and inspiring, and is imbued with a mighty, far-reaching grace and beauty and purity and loveliness. The least of us knows, the least of us feels, the humblest among us will confess that, whereas—but the hour is late and I do not wish to detain you."

Now then, supposing a man with his cut-and-dried speech, this patent adjustable speech, as you may call it, finds himself at a granger gathering or a wedding breakfast or a theological disturbance or a political blowout, an inquest, or funeral anywhere in the world you choose to mention, and be suddenly called up. All he has got to do is to change three or four words in that speech and make his delivery anguishing and tearful, or chippy and facetious, or luridly and thunderously eloquent just as the occasion happens to call for, and just turn himself loose, and he is all right.

Now then, supposing that the occasion—I will make one more illustration so that you will always be perfectly safe here or any-where—supposing that this is an occasion of an inquest. This is a most elastic speech in a matter of that kind. Where there are grades of men you must observe them. At a private funeral of some friend you want to be just as mournful as you can, but in the case where you don't know the person, grade it accordingly. You want simply to be impressive. That is all.

Now take a case halfway between, about No. 4½, somewhere about there—that is, an inquest on a second cousin, a wealthy second cousin. He has remembered you in the will. Of course all these things count. They all raise the grade a little, and—well, perhaps he hasn't remembered you. Perhaps he has left you a horse, an ordinary horse, a good enough horse, one that can go about three minutes, or perhaps a pair of horses. It may have been one pair of horses at hand, not two pair or two pair and a jack. I don't know whether you understand that, but there are people here.

Well now then, this is a second cousin and he knows all the circumstances. We will say that he has lost his life trying to save somebody from drowning. Well, he saved the mind-cure physician from drowning. He tried to save him but he didn't succeed. Of course he wouldn't succeed. Of course you wouldn't want him to succeed in that way and plan. A person must have some experience and aplomb and all that before he can save anybody from drowning of the mind-cure. I am just making these explanations here.

A person can get so glib in a delivery of this speech, why by the time he has delivered it fifteen or twenty times he could go to any intellectual gathering in Boston even and he would draw like a prizefight. Well, at the inquest of a second cousin under these circumstances a man gets up with graded emotion and he says:

"I am called up suddenly, sir, and am, indeed, not prepared. I was not expecting to be called up, sir, but I will, with what effect I may, add my shout—voice to the lamentations of this spirited, crushing grief. Death, death, sir, is, after all, the palladium of our spiritual liberties. By it, approximately speaking, we may be said to live and move and have ending. All that we may be here, all that we are, all that we hope to be, was, is and must continue to be profoundly influenced by that sublimest of the mighty interests of man, thrice-sorrowful desolation. While we have life, while we have soul, and in that soul the sweet and hallowed sentiment of gratitude, let us with generous accord attune our voices to songs of peace, perennial outpourings of thanksgiving for that most potent boon by which we spiritually save, by which our otherwise sterile existence is made rich and strong and is imbued with a mighty, far-reaching and all-embracing grace and beauty and loveliness. The least of us knows, the least of us feels, the humblest among us will confess— but the hour is late and I will not detain you."

December 1887

ᔕ 37 ᔓ

In June 1888 Clemens received his first honorary degree: Master of Arts, conferred by Yale. He was notified of this honor by his friend Charles H. Clarke, editor of the *Hartford Courant*, to whom he wrote, "I feel mighty proud of that degree. In fact, I could squeeze the truth a little closer and say vain of it. And why shouldn't I be? I am the only literary animal of my particular subspecies who has ever been given a degree by any College in any age of the world, as far as I know." Being busy in Elmira, he was unable to attend the award ceremony in June.

Although Paine has written, "Later in the year he made the following address to the students," it is uncertain whether Clemens actually delivered the speech.

REFORMING YALE

I was sincerely proud and grateful to be made a Master of Arts by this great and venerable university. And I would have come last June to testify this feeling, as I do now testify it, but that the sudden and unexpected notice of the honor done me found me at a distance from home and unable to discharge that duty and enjoy that privilege.

Along at first, say for the first month or so, I did not quite know how to proceed, because of my not knowing just what authorities and privileges belonged to the title which had been granted me. But after that I consulted some students of Trinity, in Hartford, and they made everything clear to me.

It was through them that I found out that my title made me head of the governing body of the university and lodged in me very broad and severely responsible powers. It is through trying to work these powers up to their maximum of efficiency that I have had such a checkered career this year.

I was told that it would be necessary for me to report to you at this time, and of course I comply though I would have preferred to put it off till I could make a better showing, for indeed I have been so pertinaciously hindered and obstructed at every turn by the faculty that it would be difficult to prove that the university is really in any better shape now than it was when I first took charge.

In submitting my report I am sorry to have to begin it with the remark that respect for authority seems to be at a quite low ebb in the college. It is true that this has caused me pain but it has not discouraged me.

By advice, I turned my earliest attention to the Greek department. I told the Greek professor I had concluded to drop the use of the Greek written character, because it is so hard to spell with and so impossible to read after you get it spelled. Let us draw the curtain there. I saw by what followed that nothing but early neglect saved him from being a very profane man.

I ordered the professor of mathematics to simplify the whole system, because the way it was I couldn't understand it, and I didn't want things going on in the college in what was practically a clandestine fashion. I told him to drop the conundrum system. It was not suited to the dignity of a college, which should deal in facts, not guesses and suppositions. We didn't want any more cases of *if* A and B stand at opposite poles of the earth's surface and C at the equator of Jupiter, at what variations of angle will the left link of the moon appear to these different parties?

I said you just let that thing alone. It's plenty time to get in a sweat about it when it happens. As like as not it ain't going to do any harm anyway.

His reception of these instructions bordered on insubordination, insomuch that I felt obliged to take his number and report him.

I found the astronomer of the university gadding around after comets and other such odds and ends—tramps and derelicts of the skies. I told him pretty plainly that we couldn't have that. I told him it was no economy to go on piling up and piling up raw material in the way of new stars and comets and asteroids that we couldn't ever have any use for till we had worked off the old stock. I said if I caught him strawberrying around after any more asteroids especially, I should have to fire him out.

Privately, prejudice got the best of me there, I ought to confess it. At bottom I don't really mind comets so much. But somehow I have always been down on asteroids. There is nothing mature about them. I wouldn't sit up nights, the way that man does, if I could get a basketful of them.

He said it was the best line of goods he had. He said he could trade them to Rochester for comets and trade the comets to Harvard for nebulae and trade the nebulae to the Smithsonian for flint hatchets.

I felt obliged to stop this thing on the spot. I said we couldn't have the university turned into an astronomical junk shop.

And while I was at it I thought I might as well make the reform complete. The astronomer is extraordinarily mutinous. And so with your approval I will transfer him to the law department and put one of the law students in his place. A boy will be more biddable, more tractable, also cheaper. It is true he cannot be entrusted with important work at first, but he can comb the skies for nebulae till he gets his hand in.

I have other changes in mind but as they are in the nature of surprises I judge it politic to leave them unspecified at this time.

about 1888

❦ **38** ❧

This speech was given in November of 1889 at a dinner of the Fellowcraft Club in New York, an association of magazine writers and illustrators. At around this time the Paige typesetting machine and Clemens's typesetting, get-rich fever were a constant financial drain on Clemens. James W. Paige was designing and building a machine which was intended to revolutionize type composition in an era when type was set entirely by hand. It would set, justify and distribute type at such a speed that it would do the work of half a dozen men. Unfortunately his product was too complicated and too delicate and had the disastrous habit of breaking type. Paige, the tinkerer who couldn't let well enough alone, was a persuasive talker. Clemens once said that Paige could persuade a fish to leave the water and go for a walk with him.

In the summer of 1889 Rudyard Kipling, a great admirer of Clemens's work, visited him in Elmira and described the visit in the *New York Herald*.

"You are a contemptible lot out there, over yonder. Some of you are Commissioners and some Lieutenant Governors and some have the V.C., and a few are privileged to walk about the Mall arm in arm with the Viceroy; but I have seen Mark Twain this golden morning, have shaken his hand and smoked a cigar—no, two cigars—with him, and talked with him for more than two hours! Understand clearly that I do not despise you, indeed I don't. I am only very sorry for you all, from the Viceroy downward. . . .

"Morning revealed Elmira, whose streets were desolated by railway tracks, and whose suburbs were given up to the manufacture of door sashes and window frames. It was surrounded by pleasant, fat little hills trimmed with timber and topped with cultivation. The Chemung River flowed generally up and down the town and had just finished flooding a few of the main streets. . . .

"It was a very pretty house, anything but Gothic, clothed with ivy, standing in a very big compound and fronted by a veranda full of all sorts of chairs and hammocks for lying in all sorts of positions. The roof of the veranda was a trellis work of creepers and the sun peeped through and moved on the shining boards below. . . .

"A big, darkened drawing room, a huge chair, a man with bright eyes, a mane of grizzled hair, a brown mustache covering a mouth as delicate as a woman's, a strong, square hand shaking mine, and the slowest, calmest, levellest voice in all the world saying:

"'Well, you think you owe me something and you've come to tell me so. That's what I call squaring a debt handsomely.' . . .

"The thing that struck me first was that he was an elderly man, yet after a minute's looking at me, I saw that the gray hair was an accident of the most trivial kind. He was quite young. I had shaken his hand. I was smoking his cigar, and I was hearing him talk—this man I had learned to love and admire fourteen thousand miles away. . . .

"He spoke always through his eyes, a light under the heavy eyebrows; anon crossing the room with a step as light as a girl's to show me some book or other; then resuming his walk up and down the room puffing at the cob pipe. I would have given much for nerve enough to demand the gift of that pipe, value five cents when new. . . .

"Once indeed he put his hand on my shoulder. It was an investiture of the Star of India, blue silk, trumpets and diamond studded jewel, all complete. If hereafter among the changes and chances of this mortal life I fall to cureless ruin I will tell the superintendent of the workhouse that Mark Twain once put his hand on my shoulder, and he shall give me a room to myself and a double allowance of paupers' tobacco."

FOOLPROOF SCHEME

I am Langhorne. That is my middle name. I am the inventor of the scheme which has been mentioned, and I think it is a good one and likely to be of great benefit to the world. Still, this hope may be disappointed and therefore I can't afford to use my real name lest in trying to acquire a new and possibly valuable reputation I destroy the valuable one which I already possess, and yet fail to replace it with a new one.

I propose to take classes and teach under this apparently fictitious name. I wish to describe my scheme to you and prove its value by illustration. The scheme is founded upon a certain fact, a fact which long experience has convinced me *is* a fact and not a fiction of my imagination. That fact is this. Those speakers who are called upon at a banquet after the regular toasts have been responded to are generally merely called upon by name and requested to get up and talk— that is all. No text is furnished them and they are in a difficult situation, apparently—but only apparently. The situation is not difficult at all, in fact, for they are usually men who know that they may be possibly called upon, therefore they go to the banquet prepared— after a certain fashion.

The speeches which these volunteers make are all of a pattern. They consist of three first-rate anecdotes, first-water jewels, so to speak, set in the midst of a lot of rambling and incoherent talk, where they flash and sparkle and delight the house. The speech is made solely for the sake of the ancedotes, whereas they shamelessly pretend that the ancedotes are introduced upon sudden inspiration to illustrate the reasonings advanced in the speech.

There *are* no reasonings in the speech. The speech wanders along in a random and purposeless way for a while. Then all of a sudden the speaker breaks out as with an unforeseen and happy inspiration and says, "How felicitously what I have just been saying is illustrated in the case of the man who"—then he explodes his first anecdote.

It's a good one, so good that a storm of delighted laughter sweeps the house and so disturbs its mental balance for the moment that it fails to notice that the ancedote didn't illustrate what the man had been saying—didn't illustrate anything at all, indeed, but was dragged in by the scruff of the neck and had no relation to the subject which the speaker was pretending to talk about.

He doesn't allow the laughter to entirely subside before he is off and hammering away at his speech again. He doesn't wait, because that would be dangerous. It would give the house time to reflect. Then it would see that the anecdote did not illustrate anything. He goes flitting airily along in his speech in the same random way as before, and presently has another of those inspirations and breaks out again with his "How felicitously what I have just been saying is illustrated in the case of the man who"—then he lets fly his second anecdote and again the house goes down with a crash.

Before it can recover its senses he is away again and cantering gaily toward the home stretch, filling the air with a stream of empty words that have no connection with anything.

And finally he has his third inspiration, introduced with the same set form, "How felicitously what I have just been saying is illustrated in the case of the man who"—then he lets fly his last and best anecdote and sits down under tempests and earthquakes of laughter. And everybody in his neighborhood seizes his hand and shakes it cordially and tells him it was a splended speech, splendid.

That is my scheme. I hope to get classes. I shall charge a high rate because the pupil will need but one lesson. By grace of a single lesson I will make it possible for the novice who has never faced an audience in his life to rise to his feet upon call, without trepidation or embarrassment, and make an impromptu speech upon any subject that can be mentioned, without preparation of any kind, and also without even any knowledge of the subject which may be chosen for him. He shall always be ready, for he shall always have his three anecdotes in his pocket, written on a card, and thus equipped he shall never fail. I beg you to give me a text and let me prove what I have been saying. Any text, any subject, will do. All subjects are alike under my system. Give me a text.

[The text of "Portrait Painting" was selected by lot among the audience.]

It is a good enough text. I want no better. I've already told you that all texts are alike under this noble system. All that I need to do now is to talk a straight and uninterrupted stream of irrelevancies which shall ostensibly deal learnedly and instructively with the subject of portrait painting. The stream must not break anywhere. I must never hesitate for a word, because under this scheme the orator that hesitates is lost. It can give the house a chance to collect its reasoning faculties, and that is a thing which must not happen.

Portrait painting? That's a good subject for a speech, a very good subject indeed. Portrait painting is an ancient and honorable art, and there are many interesting things to say about it. Yes, it's an ancient and honorable art, although I don't really know how ancient it is. I never heard that Adam ever sat for his portrait but maybe he did. Maybe he did. But I don't know. And how felicitously what I have just been saying is illustrated in the case of the man who reached home at two o'clock in the morning and his wife said plaintively, "Oh, John, when you've had whisky enough why don't you ask for sarsaparilla?" And he said, "Why, Maria, when I have had whisky enough I can't *say* sarsaparilla."

And how felicitously what I have just been saying is illustrated in the case of the man who arrived at his home at that unusual unfortunate hour in the super-early morning and stood there and watched his portico rising and sinking and swaying and reeling. And at last, when it swung around into his neighborhood he made a plunge and scrambled up the steps and got safely onto the portico, stood there watching his dim house rise and fall and swing and sway until the front door came his way and he made a plunge and got it, and scrambled up the long flight of stairs. But at the topmost step instead of planting his foot upon it he only caught it with his toe. And down he tumbled, and rolled and thundered all the way down the stairs, fetched up in a sitting posture on the bottom step with his arm braced around the friendly newel post and said, "God pity the poor sailors out at sea on such a night as this."

November 1889

✤ 39 ✤

This talk was given at a dinner in Boston in April 1890. Sir Lepel Griffin was a British government official who had published disparaging remarks about American life and culture.

FOREIGN CRITICS

If I look harried and worn it is not from an ill conscience. It is from sitting up nights to worry about the foreign critic. He won't concede that we have a civilization, a "real" civilization. Five years ago he said we had never contributed anything to the betterment of the world. And now comes Sir Lepel Griffin, whom I had not suspected of being in the world at all, and says, "There is no country calling itself civilized where one would not rather live than in America, except Russia."

That settles it. That is, it settles it for Europe. But it doesn't make me any more comfortable than I was before.

What is a "real" civilization? Nobody can answer that conundrum. They have all tried. Then suppose we try to get at what it is not and then subtract the what it is not from the general sum and call the remainder "real" civilization so as to have a place to stand on while we throw bricks at these people. Let us say then in broad terms that any system which has in it any one of these things—to wit, human slavery, despotic government, inequality, numerous and brutal punishments for crime, superstition almost universal, ignorance almost universal, and dirt and poverty almost universal—is not a real civilization, and any system which has none of them is.

If you grant these terms, one may then consider this conundrum: how old is real civilization? The answer is easy and unassailable. A century ago it had not appeared anywhere in the world during a single instant since the world was made. If you grant these terms (and I don't see why it shouldn't be fair, since civilization must surely be fair, since civilization must surely mean the humanizing of a people, not a class) there is today but one real civilization in the world, and it is not yet thirty years old. We made the trip and hoisted its flag when we disposed of our slavery.

However, there are some partial civilizations scattered around over Europe. Pretty lofty civilizations they are, too. But who begot them? What is the seed from which they sprang? Liberty and intelligence. What planted that seed? There are dates and statistics which suggest that it was the American Revolution that planted it. When that revolution began, monarchy had been on trial some thousands of years over there and was a distinct and convicted failure every time. It had never produced anything but a vast, a nearly universal savagery, with a thin skim of civilization on top, and the main part of that was nickel plate and tinsel.

The French, imbruted and improverished by centuries of oppression and official robbery, were a starving nation clothed in rags, slaves of an aristocracy and smirking dandies clad in unearned silks and velvet. It makes one's cheek burn to read of the laws of the time and realize that they were for human beings; realize that they originated in this world and not in hell. Germany was unspeakable. In the Scotch lowlands the people lived in sties and were human swine. In the highlands drunkenness was general and it hardly smirched a young girl to have a family of her own. In England there was a sham liberty and not much of that. Crime was general. Ignorance the same. Poverty and misery were widespread. London fed a tenth of her population by charity. The law awarded the death penalty to almost every conceivable offense. What was called medical science by courtesy stood where it had stood for two thousand years. Tom Jones and Squire Western were gentlemen.

The printer's art had been known in Germany and France three and a quarter centuries, and in England three. In all that time there had not been a newspaper in Europe that was worthy of the name. Monarchies had no use for that sort of dynamite. When we hoisted the banner of revolution and raised the first genuine shout for human liberty that had ever been heard, this was a newspaperless globe. Eight years later there were six daily journals in London to proclaim to all the nations the greatest birth this world had ever seen.

Who woke that printing press out of its trance of three hundred years? Let us be permitted to consider that we did it. Who summoned the French slaves to rise and set the nation free? We did it. What resulted in England and on the Continent? Crippled liberty took up its bed and walked. From that day to this its march has not halted, and please God it never will.

We are called the nation of inventors. And we are. We could still claim that title and wear its loftiest honors if we had stopped with the first thing we ever invented, which was human liberty. Out of that invention has come the Christian world's great civilization. Without it it was impossible, as the history of all the centuries has proved. Well, then, who invented civilization?

Even Sir Lepel Griffin ought to be able to answer that question. It looks easy enough. *We* have contributed *nothing*! Nothing hurts me like ingratitude.

April 1890

✑ **40** ✑

This address was given at a banquet of the National Wholesale Druggists Association in Washington, D.C., in the early fall of 1890.

THE DRUGGIST

About a thousand years ago, approximately, I was apprenticed as a printer's devil to learn the trade in common with three other boys of about my own age. There came to the village a long-legged individual of about nineteen from one of the interior counties. Fish-eyed, no expression and without the suggestion of a smile—couldn't have smiled for a salary.

We took him for a fool and thought we would try to scare him to death. We went to the village druggist and borrowed a skeleton. The skeleton didn't belong to the druggist, but he had imported it for the village doctor because the doctor thought he would send away for it, having some delicacy about using—The price of a skeleton at that time was fifty dollars. I don't know how high they go now but probably higher on account of the tariff.

We borrowed the skeleton about nine o'clock at night and we got this man—Nicodemus Dodge was his name—we got him downtown, out of the way, and then we put the skeleton in his bed. He lived in a little one-storied log cabin in the middle of a vacant lot. We left him to get home by himself. We enjoyed the result in the light of anticipation. But by and by we began to drop into silence. The possible consequences were preying upon us. Suppose that it frightens him into madness, overturns his reason and sends him screeching through the streets! We shall spend sleepless nights the rest of our days. Everybody was afraid.

By and by it was forced to the lips of one of us that we had better go at once and see what had happened. Loaded down with crime, we approached that hut and peeped through the window. That long-legged critter was sitting on his bed with a hunk of gingerbread in his hand, and between the bites he played a tune on a jew's harp. There he sat perfectly happy, and all around him on the bed were toys and gimcracks and striped candy. The darned cuss, he had gone and sold that skeleton for five dollars.

The druggist's fifty-dollar skeleton was gone. We went in tears to the druggist and explained the matter. We couldn't have raised that fifty dollars in two hundred and fifty years. We were getting board and clothing for the first year, clothing and board for the second year, and both of them for the third year. The druggist forgave us on the spot but he said he would like us to let him have our skeletons when we were done with them. There couldn't be anything fairer than that. We spouted our skeletons and went away comfortable.

But from that time the druggist's prosperity ceased. This was one of the most unfortunate speculations he ever went into. After some years one of the boys went and got drowned. That was one skeleton gone, and I tell you the druggist felt pretty badly about it. A few years after, another of the boys went up in a balloon. He was to get five dollars an hour for it. When he gets back they will be owing him one million dollars. The druggist's property was decreasing right along.

After a few more years the third boy tried an experiment to see if a dynamite charge would go. It went all right. They found some of him, perhaps a vest pocketful. Still, it was enough to show that some more of that estate had gone.

The druggist was getting along in years and he commenced to correspond with me. I have been the best correspondent he has. He is the sweetest-natured man I ever saw—always mild and polite and never wants to hurry me at all.

I get a letter from him every now and then, and he never refers to my form as a skeleton. Says, "Well, how is it getting along. Is it in good repair?"

I got a night-rate message from him recently. Said he was getting old and the property was depreciating in value, and if I could let him have a part of it now he would give time on the balance.

Think of the graceful way in which he does everything, the generosity of it all. You cannot find a finer character than that. It is the gracious characteristic of all druggists. So, out of my heart, I wish you all prosperity and every happiness.

about September 1890

~ 41 ~

In the spring of 1891 Livy, Clemens's wife, was complaining about her health. Several doctors, agreeing she had a heart disturbance, recommended a European stay. Also, Clemens was plagued by rheumatism in his writing arm. The simpler and vastly cheaper life of Europe beckoned. After closing the Hartford house, in which they had lived seventeen years (closing it permanently, as it would turn out), the Clemens family sailed on June 6 for France. Eventually Clemens settled his family in Switzerland, then hired Joseph Very, a courier who had served him on an earlier European trip, and proceeded to boat down the Rhône in a flat-bottom boat which Very had bought for five dollars.

The Clemenses spent the winter in Berlin. For a while Clemens was down with pneumonia, and Livy wasn't feeling well either. They were advised by doctors to move to a warmer climate, at least temporarily. Leaving the children behind, they proceeded to the south of France with Very. In the course of their journeying they came upon and rented the Villa Viviani near Settignano, Italy. They spent the summer of 1892 in Bad Nauheim, Germany, however.

Clemens's financial affairs were worsening, partly because of the *Library of American Literature*, which increasingly demanded large infusions of capital. Also, financially 1893 was a hard year for the United States as a whole. On August 29 of that year Clemens sailed for the United States. He lived in New York, where one evening he was introduced to Henry H. Rogers, "of the Standard Oil group of financiers," as Paine characterized him. It was an eventful moment for Clemens, for Rogers was not only an admirer of his work. He was to become Clemens's financial savior as well.

By early 1894 the affairs of Clemens's publishing house, Charles L. Webster & Co., were in a very bad way. Finally, on the afternoon of April 18, 1894, the firm executed assignment papers and went out of business through voluntary bankruptcy. Rogers, representing Clemens at meetings of the creditors, insisted that Livy was the chief creditor (she had lent the firm more than $60,000 of her own money) and that therefore Clemens's copyrights should belong to her. He added that the Hartford house was already hers. Aside from the claim, the firm's debts amounted to about $100,000. Thus ended Clemens's publishing venture after less than a decade, during which its most notable publication was the General Grant *Memoirs*.

In May of that year Clemens sailed for Europe, where he joined Livy. In the fall, under Rogers's guidance, the Paige typesetting machine was tested in Chicago. It proved finally and without question to be too complicated and fragile: a failure.

Early the following year Clemens arranged to make a lecture tour around the world. Paine has written, "He was nearly sixty years old, and time had not lessened his loathing for the platform. More than once, however, in earlier years, he had turned to it as a debt payer, and never yet had his burden been so great as now." Clemens embarked on his world tour in mid-July and sailed for Vancouver in the fourth week of August. He was accompanied by Livy and his daughter Clara. Jean and Susy, his other daughters, stayed behind with their aunt at Quarry Farm in Elmira.

It was in mid-August of 1896 when Clemens, alone in England (Livy and Clara were on their way to the United States), received one of the great blows of his life. He wrote in his autobiography, "I was standing in our dining room, thinking of nothing in particular, when a cablegram was put into my hand. It said, 'Susy was peacefully released today.'

"It is one of the mysteries of our nature that a man, all unprepared, can receive a thunder-stroke like that and live. There is but one reasonable explanation of it. The intellect is stunned by the shock and but gropingly gathers the meaning of the words. The power to realize their full import is mercifully wanting. The mind has a dumb sense of vast loss—that is all."

Susy had died of meningitis.

The Clemens family spent the fall and winter of 1897 in the Hotel Metropole in Vienna. Clemens gave the following speech in German at a gathering of journalists in that city and later translated it literally. He enjoyed the humor inherent in such translations, whether from the German or from the French.

HORRORS OF THE GERMAN LANGUAGE

It has me deeply touched, my gentlemen, here so hospitably received to be. From colleagues out of my own profession, in this from my own home so far distant land. My heart is full of gratitude, but my poverty of German words forces me to greater economy of expression. Excuse you, my gentlemen, that I read off, what I you say will.

[But he didn't read].

The German language speak I not good, but have numerous connoisseurs me assured that I her write like an angel. Maybe—maybe—I know not. Have till now no acquaintance with the angels had. That comes later—when it the dear God please—it has no hurry.

Since long, my gentlemen, have I the passionate longing nursed a speech on German to hold, but one has me not permitted. Men, who no feeling for the art had, laid me ever hindrance in the way and made naught my desire—sometimes by excuses, often by force. Always said these men to me, "Keep you still, your Highness! Silence! For God's sake seek another way and means yourself obnoxious to make."

In the present case, as usual it is me difficult become for me the permission to obtain. The committee sorrowed deeply but could me the permission not grant on account of a law which from the Concordia demands she shall the German language protect. Du liebe Zeit! How so had one to me this say could—might—dared—should?

I am indeed the truest friend of the German language, and not only now but from long since—yes, before twenty years already. And never have I the desire had the noble language to hurt. To the contrary, only wished she to improve, I would her only reform. It is the dream of my life been. I have already visits by the various German governments paid and for contracts prayed. I am now to Austria in the same task come. I would only some changes effect. I would only the language method, the luxurious, elaborate construction compress, the eternal parenthesis suppress, do away with, annihilate; the introduction of more than thirteen subjects in one sentence forbid; the verb so far to the front pull that one it without a telescope discover can.

With one word, my gentlemen, I would your beloved language simplify so that, my gentlemen, when you her for prayer need, One her yonder-up understands.

I beseech you, from me yourself counsel to let, execute these mentioned reforms. Then will you an elegant language possess, and afterward, when you something say will, will you at least yourself understand what you said had. But often nowadays, when you a mile-long sentence from you given and you yourself somewhat have rested, then must you have a touching inquisitiveness have yourself to determine what you actually spoken have. Before several days has the correspondent of a local paper a sentence constructed which hundred and twelve words contain, and therein were seven parentheses smuggled in, and the subject seven times changed. Think you only, my gentlemen, in the course of the voyage of a single sentence must the poor, persecuted, fatigued subject seven times change position!

Now, when we the mentioned reforms execute, will it no longer so bad be. Doch noch eins. I might gladly the separable verb also a little bit reform. I might none do let what Schiller did. He has the whole history of the Thirty Years' War between the two members of a separable verb in-pushed. That has even Germany itself aroused, and one has Schiller the permission refused the History of the Hundred Years' War to compose—God be it thanked! After all these reforms established be will, will the German language the noblest and the prettiest on the world be.

Since to you now, my gentlemen, the character of my mission known is, beseech I you so friendly to be and to me your valuable help grant. Mr. Pötzl has the public believed make would that I to Vienna come am in order the bridges to clog up and the traffic to hinder, while I observations gather and note. Allow you yourselves but not from him deceived. My frequent presence on the bridges has an entirely innocent ground. Yonder gives it the necessary space, yonder can one a noble long German sentence elaborate, the bridge-railing along, and his whole contents with one glance overlook. On the one end of the railing pasted I the first member of a separable verb and the final member cleave I to the other end, then spread the body of the sentence between it out. Usually are for my purposes the bridges of the city long enough, when I but Pötzl's writings study will I ride out and use the glorious endless imperial bridge.

But this is a calumny. Pötzl writes the prettiest German. Perhaps not so pliable as the mine, but in many details much better. Excuse you these flatteries. These are well deserved.

Now I my speech execute—no, I would say I bring her to the close. I am a foreigner, but here, under you, have I it entirely forgotten. And so again and yet again proffer I you my heartiest thanks.

October 1897

❦ 42 ❧

Clemens was finally out of debt the end of January 1898. There was universal praise for him. "Honest men must be pretty scarce," he said, "when they make so much fuss over even a defective specimen."

According to Paine, Clemens's apartment in the Hotel Metropole was "much more like an embassy than the home of a mere literary man. Celebrities in every walk of life, persons of social and official rank, writers for the press, assembled there on terms hardly possible in any other home in Vienna. Wherever Mark Twain appeared in public he was a central figure. Now and then he read or spoke to aid some benefit, and there were great gatherings attended by members of the royal family."

The following speech was made in Budapest at the Jubilee Celebration of the Emancipation of the Hungarian press. Paine has written, "The ministry and members of Parliament were present. The subject was the 'Ausgleich'—that is, the arrangement for the apportionment of the taxes between Hungary and Austria. Paragraph 14 of the Ausgleich fixes the proportion each country must pay to the support of the army. It is the paragraph which caused the trouble and prevented its renewal."

THE AUSGLEICH

N ow that we are all here together I think it will be a good idea to arrange the ausgleich. If you will act for Hungary I shall be quite willing to act for Austria, and this is the very time for it. There couldn't be a better, for we are all feeling friendly, fair-minded and hospitable now, and full of admiration for each other, full of confidence in each other, full of the spirit of welcome, full of the grace of forgiveness and the disposition to let bygones be bygones.

Let us not waste this golden, this beneficent, this providential opportunity. I am willing to make any concession you want, just so we get it settled. I am not only willing to let grain come in free, I am willing to pay the freight on it, and you may send delegates to the Reichsrath if you like. All I require is that they shall be quiet, peaceable people like your own deputies and not disturb our proceedings.

If you want the Gegenseitigengeldbeitragendenverhältnismässigkeiten rearranged and readjusted I am ready for that. I will let you off at twenty-eight per cent—twenty-seven—even twenty-five if you insist, for there is nothing illiberal about me when I am out on a diplomatic debauch.

Now, in return for these concessions I am willing to take anything in reason, and I think we may consider the business settled and the ausgleich ausgegloschen at last for ten solid years, and we will sign the papers in blank and do it here and now.

Well, I am unspeakably glad to have that ausgleich off my hands. It has kept me awake nights for anderthalbjahr.

But I never could settle it before, because always when I called at the Foreign Office in Vienna to talk about it there wasn't anybody at home, and that is not a place where you can go in and see for yourself whether it is a mistake or not, because the person who takes care of the front door there is of a size that discourages liberty of action and the free spirit of investigation. To think the ausgleich is abgemacht at last! It is a grand and beautiful consummation, and I am glad I came.

The way I feel now I do honestly believe I would rather be just my own humble self at this moment than paragraph 14.

March 1899

❦ 43 ❦

By the end of May 1899 the Clemenses were living in London. Early in June Clemens agreed to visit the Savage Club in London, which had elected him an honorary member, on condition that no speech would be expected from him. Paine has written, "The toastmaster, in proposing the health of their guest, said that as a Scotchman, and therefore as born expert, he thought Mark Twain had little or no claim to the title of humorist. Mr. Clemens had tried to be funny but had failed, and his true role in life was statistics; that he was a master of statistics, and loved them for their own sake, and it would be the easiest task he ever undertook if he would try to count all the real jokes he had ever made. While the toastmaster was speaking, the members saw Mr. Clemens's eyes begin to sparkle and his cheeks to flush. He jumped up and made a characteristic speech."

STATISTICS

Perhaps I am not a humorist. But I am a first-class fool, a simpleton. For up to this moment I have believed Chairman Mac-Alister to be a decent person whom I could allow to mix up with my friends and relatives.

The exhibition he has just made of himself reveals him to be a scoundrel and a knave of the deepest dye. I have been cruelly deceived, and it serves me right for trusting a Scotchman.

Yes, I do understand figures, and I can count. I have counted the words in MacAlister's drivel (I certainly cannot call it a speech), and there were exactly three thousand four hundred and thirty-nine. I also carefully counted the lies—there were exactly three thousand four hundred and thirty-nine. Therefore I leave MacAlister to his fate.

I was sorry to have my name mentioned as one of the great authors, because they have a sad habit of dying off. Chaucer is dead, Spenser is dead, so is Milton, so is Shakespeare, and I am not feeling very well myself.

June 1899

44

The Whitefriars Club, London, gave Clemens a dinner in June 1899. He had been an honorary member since 1874. Two hundred guests were present, including the American ambassador, Joseph H. Choate. Louis Frederic Austin of the *Illustrated London News* introduced Clemens, comparing him to Walter Scott, who like Clemens had paid off debts due to failures in business ventures, specifically publishing ones.

Sala was an English journalist. Depew—Chauncey M. Depew, an American attorney and senator-elect from New York at the time. Hayes—Isaac Israel Hayes, an American explorer. Nansen—Fridtjof Nansen, Norwegian explorer. Robert Buchanan was a British writer.

MASTERS OF ORATORY

Mr. chairman and brethren of the vow—in whatever the vow is. For although I have been a member of this club for five-and-twenty years I don't know any more about what that vow is than Mr. Austin seems to. But whatever the vow is, I don't care what it is. I have made a thousand vows.

There is no pleasure comparable to making a vow in the presence of one who appreciates that vow, in the presence of men who honor and appreciate you for making the vow, and men who admire you for making the vow. There is only one pleasure higher than that, and that is to get outside and break the vow.

A vow is always a pledge of some kind or other for the protection of your own morals and principles or somebody else's, and generally, by the irony of fate, it is for the protection of your own morals. Hence we have pledges that make us eschew tobacco or wine. And while you are taking the pledge there is a holy influence about that makes you feel you are reformed, and that you can never be so happy again in this world—until you get outside and take a drink.

I had forgotten that I was a member of this club. It is so long ago. But now I remember that I was here five-and-twenty years ago and that I was then at a dinner of the Whitefriars Club. And it was in those old days when you had just made two great finds. All London was talking about nothing else than that they had found Livingstone, and that the lost Sir Roger Tichborne had been found—and they were trying him for it. And at the dinner, Chairman . . . (I do not know who he was) failed to come to time. The gentleman who had been appointed to pay me the customary compliments and to introduce me forgot the compliments and did not know what they were.

And George Augustus Sala came in at the last moment just when I was about to go without compliments altogether. And that man was a gifted man. They just called on him instantaneously, while he was going to sit down, to introduce the stranger. And Sala made one of those marvelous speeches which he was capable of making.

I think no man talked so fast as Sala did. One did not need wine while he was making a speech. The rapidity of his utterance made a man drunk in a minute. An incomparable speech was that, an impromptu speech, and an impromptu speech is a seldom thing, and he did it so well.

He went into the whole history of the United States and made it entirely new to me. He filled it with episodes and incidents that Washington never heard of, and he did it so convincingly that although I knew none of it had happened, from that day to this I do not know any history but Sala's.

I do not know anything so sad as a dinner where you are going to get up and say something by and by and you do not know what it is. You sit and wonder and wonder what the gentleman is going to say who is going to introduce you. You know that if he says something severe, that if he will deride you or traduce you or do anything of that kind, he will furnish you with a text, because anybody can get up and talk against that. Anybody can get up and straighten out his character. But when a gentleman gets up and merely tells the truth about you, what can you do?

Mr. Austin has done well. He has supplied so many texts that I will have to drop out a lot of them, and that is about as difficult as when you do not have any text at all. Now, he made a beautiful and smooth speech without any difficulty at all, and I could have done that if I had gone on with the schooling with which I began.

I see here a gentleman on my left who was my master in the art of oratory more than twenty-five years ago. When I look upon the inspiring face of Mr. Depew it carries me a long way back. An old and valued friend of mine is he, and I saw his career as it came along, and it has reached pretty well up to now, when he, by another miscarriage of justice, is a United States Senator. But those were delightful days when I was taking lessons in oratory. My other master, the Ambassador, is not here yet. Under those two gentlemen I learned to make after-dinner speeches, and it was charming.

You know the New England dinner is the great occasion on the other side of the water. It is held every year to celebrate the landing of the Pilgrims. Those Pilgrims were a lot of people who were not needed in England, and you know they had great rivalry, and they were persuaded to go elsewhere, and they chartered a ship called *Mayflower* and set sail, and I have heard it said that they pumped the Atlantic Ocean through that ship sixteen times. They fell in over there with the Dutch from Rotterdam, Amsterdam and a lot of other places with profane names, and it is from that gang that Mr. Depew is descended.

On the other hand Mr. Choate is descended from those Puritans who landed on a bitter night in December. Every year those people used to meet at a great banquet in New York, and those masters of mine in oratory had to make speeches. It was Doctor Depew's business to get up there and apologize for the Dutch, and Mr. Choate had to get up later and explain the crimes of the Puritans, and grand, beautiful times we used to have.

It is curious that after long lapse of time I meet the Whitefriars again, some looking as young and fresh as in the old days, others showing a certain amount of wear and tear. And here, after all this time, I find one of the masters of oratory and the other named in the list. And here we three meet again as exiles on one pretext or another, and you will notice that while we are absent there is a pleasing tranquility in America, a building up of public confidence. We are doing the best we can for our country. I think we have spent our lives in serving our country, and we never serve it to greater advantage than when we get out of it.

But impromptu speaking—that is what I was trying to learn. That is a difficult thing. I used to do it in this way. I used to begin about a week ahead and write out my impromptu speech and get it by heart. Then I brought it to the New England dinner printed on a piece of paper in my pocket so that I could pass it to the reporters all cut and dried. And in order to do an impromptu speech as it should be done you have to indicate the places for pauses and hesitations. I put them all in it. And then you want the applause in the right places.

When I got to the place where it should come in, if it did not come in I did not care, but I had it marked in the paper. And these masters of mine used to wonder why it was my speech came out in the morning in the first person, while theirs went through the butchery of synopsis.

I do that kind of speech (I mean an offhand speech) and do it well—and make no mistake—in such a way as to deceive the audience completely and make that audience believe it is an impromptu speech. That is art.

I was frightened out of it at last by an experience of Doctor Hayes. He was a sort of Nansen of that day. He had been to the North Pole and it made him celebrated. He had even seen the polar bear climb the pole. He had made one of those magnificent voyages such as Nansen made. And in those days when a man did anything which greatly distinguished him for the moment he had to come on to the lecture platform and tell all about it.

Doctor Hayes was a great, magnificent creature like Nansen, superbly built. He was to appear in Boston. He wrote his lecture out and it was his purpose to read it from manuscript. But in an evil hour he concluded that it would be a good thing to preface it with something rather handsome, poetical and beautiful that he could get off by heart and deliver as if it were the thought of the moment. He had not had my experience and could not do that. He came on the platform, held his manuscript down and began with a beautiful piece of oratory. He spoke something like this.

"When a lonely human being, a pigmy in the midst of the architecture of nature, stands solitary on those icy waters and looks abroad to the horizon and sees mighty castles and temples of eternal ice raising up their pinnacles tipped by the pencil of the departing sun—"

Here a man came across the platform and touched him on the shoulder and said, "One minute."

And then to the audience, "Is Mrs. John Smith in the house? Her husband has slipped on the ice and broken his leg."

And you could see the Mrs. John Smiths get up everywhere and drift out of the house, and it made great gaps everywhere.

Then Doctor Hayes began again.

"When a lonely man, a pigmy in the architecture—"

The janitor came in again and shouted, "It is not Mrs. John Smith! It is Mrs. John Jones!"

Then all the Mrs. Joneses got up and left.

Once more the speaker started, and was in the midst of the sentence when he was interrupted again, and the result was that the lecture was not delivered. But the lecturer interviewed the janitor afterward in a private room, and of the fragments of the janitor they took "twelve basketsful."

Now, I don't want to sit down just in this way. I have been talking with so much levity that I have said no serious thing, and you are really no better or wiser, although Robert Buchanan has suggested that I am a person who deals in wisdom. I have said nothing which would make you better than when you came here. I should be sorry to sit down without having said one serious word which you can carry home and relate to your children and the old people who are not able to get away.

And this is just a little maxim which has saved me from many a difficulty and many a disaster, and in times of tribulation and uncertainty has come to my rescue, as it shall be yours if you observe it as I do day and night. I always use it in an emergency. And you can take it home as a legacy from me. And it is: "When in doubt, tell the truth."

June 1899

⟪ 45 ⟫

The following speech was given at a dinner in honor of Clemens and his wife, Olivia, by the New Vagabonds Club of London in June of 1899. According to Paine, the New Vagabonds Club was "made up of the leading younger literary men of the day." George Grossmith was an English singer and comedian.

ON BEING MORALLY PERFECT

It has always been difficult—leave that word difficult—not exceedingly difficult but just difficult, nothing more than that, not the slightest shade to add to that, just difficult—to respond properly, in the right phraseology, when compliments are paid to me. But it is more than difficult when the compliments are paid to a better than I, my wife.

And while I am not here to testify against myself (I can't be expected to do so, a prisoner in your own country is not admitted to do so) as to which member of the family wrote my books, I could say in general that really I wrote the books myself. My wife puts the facts in and they make it respectable. My modesty won't suffer while compliments are being paid to literature and through literature to my family. I can't get enough of them.

I am curiously situated tonight. It so rarely happens that I am introduced by a humorist. I am generally introduced by a person of grave walk and carriage. That makes the proper background of gravity for brightness. I am going to alter to suit, and haply I may say some humorous things.

When you start with a blaze of sunshine and upburst of humor, when you begin with that, the proper office of humor is to reflect, to put you into that pensive mood of deep thought, to make you think of your sins, if you wish half an hour to fly. Humor makes me reflect now tonight, it sets the thinking machinery in motion. Always when I am thinking there come suggestions of what I am and what we all are and what we are coming to. A sermon comes from my lips always when I listen to a humorous speech.

I seize the opportunity to throw away frivolities, to say something to plant the seed, and make all better than when I came. In Mr. Grossmith's remarks there was a subtle something suggesting my favorite theory of the difference between theoretical morals and practical morals. I try to instil practical morals in the place of theatrical—I mean theoretical—but as an addendum, an annex, something added to theoretical morals.

When your chairman said it was the first time he had ever taken the chair, he did not mean that he had not taken lots of other things. He attended my first lecture and took notes. This indicated the man's disposition. There was nothing else flying round, so he took notes. He would have taken anything he could get.

I can bring a moral to bear here which shows the difference between theoretical morals and practical morals. Theoretical morals are the sort you get on your mother's knee, in good books and from the pulpit. You gather them in your head and not in your heart. They are theory without practice. Without the assistance of practice to perfect them it is difficult to teach a child to "be honest, don't steal."

I will teach you how it should be done, lead you into temptation, teach you how to steal so that you may recognize when you have stolen and feel the proper pangs. It is no good going round and bragging you have never taken the chair.

As by the fires of experience, so by commission of crime you learn real morals. Commit all the crimes, familiarize yourself with all sins, take them in rotation (there are only two or three thousand of them), stick to it, commit two or three every day, and by and by you will be proof aginst them. When you are through you will be proof against all sins and morally perfect. You will be vaccinated against every possible commission of them. This is the only way.

I will read you a written statement upon the subject that I wrote three years ago to read to the Sabbath schools. [Here Mark Twain turned his pockets out but without success.] No! I have left it at home. Still, it was a mere statement of fact, illustrating the value of practical morals produced by the commission of crime.

It was in my boyhood—just a statement of fact, reading is only more formal, merely facts, merely pathetic facts, which I can state so as to be understood. It relates to the first time I ever stole a watermelon. That is, I think it was the first time. Anyway, it was right along there somewhere.

I stole it out of a farmer's wagon while he was waiting on another customer. "Stole" is a harsh term. I withdrew—I retired that watermelon. I carried it to a secluded corner of a lumber yard. I broke it open. It was green, the greenest watermelon raised in the valley that year.

The minute I saw it was green I was sorry and began to reflect. Reflection is the beginning of reform. If you don't reflect when you commit a crime then that crime is of no use. It might just as well have been committed by someone else. You must reflect or the value is lost. You are not vaccinated against committing it again.

I began to reflect.

I said to myself, "What ought a boy to do who has stolen a green watermelon? What would George Washington do, the father of his country, the only American who could not tell a lie? What would he do? There is only one right, high, noble thing for any boy to do who has stolen a watermelon of that class. He must make restitution. He must restore that stolen property to its rightful owner."

I said I would do it when I made that good resolution. I felt it to be a noble, uplifting obligation.

I rose up spiritually stronger and refreshed. I carried that watermelon back, what was left of it, and restored it to the farmer and made him give me a ripe one in its place.

Now you see that this constant impact of crime upon crime protects you against further commission of crime. It builds you up. A man can't become morally perfect by stealing one or a thousand green watermelons. But every little helps.

I was at a great school yesterday (St. Paul's), where for four hundred years they have been busy with brains, and building up England by producing Pepyses, Miltons and Marlboroughs. Six hundred boys left to nothing in the world but theoretical morality. I wanted to become the professor of practical morality. But the high master was away, so I suppose I shall have to go on making my living the same old way, by adding practical to theoretical morality.

What are the glory that was Greece, the grandeur that was Rome, compared to the glory and grandeur and majesty of a perfected morality such as you see before you?

The New Vagabonds are old vagabonds (undergoing the old sort of reform). You drank my health. I hope I have not been unuseful. Take this system of morality to your hearts. Take it home to your neighbors and your graves. And I hope that it will be a long time before you arrive there.

June 1899

<h1 style="text-align:center">✧ 46 ✧</h1>

The Clemenses sailed for New York early in October of 1900, stayed for a while in the Hotel Earlington and debated whether to move back into the Hartford house. After a solitary visit to the house Clemens wrote to a friend, "I realize that if we ever enter the house again to live, our hearts will break. I am not sure that we shall ever be strong enough to endure that strain." Susy had died in the house.

Clemens rented a large, handsomely furnished house at 14 West Tenth Street in New York. The following speech was given at the Galveston, Texas, Orphans Bazaar, a benefit for the survivors of a disastrous hurricane that struck Galveston. The bazaar was held at the Waldorf-Astoria hotel in New York.

PLAYING A PART

I expected that the Governor of Texas would occupy this place first and would speak to you, and in the course of his remarks would drop a text for me to talk from. But with the proverbial obstinacy that is proverbial with governors, they go back on their duties, and he has not come here, and has not furnished me with a text, and I am here without a text.

I have no text except what you furnish me with your handsome faces, and—but I won't continue that, for I could go on forever about attractive faces, beautiful dresses and other things. But, after all, compliments should be in order in a place like this.

I have been in New York two or three days and have been in a condition of strict diligence night and day, the object of this diligence being to regulate the moral and political situation on this planet—put it on a sound basis. And when you are regulating the conditions of a planet it requires a great deal of talk in a great many kinds of ways. And when you have talked a lot the emptier you get, and get also in a position of corking. When I am situated like that, with nothing to say, I feel as though I were a sort of fraud. I seem to be playing a part for want of something better, and this is not unfamiliar to me. I have often done this before.

When I was here about eight years ago I was coming up in a car of the elevated road. Very few people were in that car, and on one end of it there was no one, except on the opposite seat, where sat a man about fifty years old, with a most winning face and an elegant eye, a beautiful eye. And I took him from his dress to be a master mechanic, a man who had a vocation. He had with him a very fine little child of about four or five years. I was watching the affection which existed between those two. I judged he was the grandfather, perhaps. It was really a pretty child, and I was admiring her, and as soon as he saw I was admiring her he began to notice me.

I could see his admiration of me in his eye, and I did what everybody else would do—admired the child four times as much, knowing I would get four times as much of his admiration. Things went on very pleasantly. I was making my way into his heart.

By and by, when he almost reached the station where he was to get off, he got up, crossed over, and he said, "Now I am going to say something to you which I hope you will regard as a compliment."

And then he went on to say, "I have never seen Mark Twain, but I have seen a portrait of him, and any friend of mine will tell you that when I have once seen a portrait of a man I place it in my eye and store it away in my memory. And I can tell you now that you look enough like Mark Twain to be his brother. Now," he said. "I hope you take this as a compliment. Yes, you are a very good imitation. But when I come to look closer, you are probably not that man."

I said, "I will be frank with you. In my desire to look like that excellent character I have dressed for the character. I have been playing a part."

He said, "That is all right, that is all right. You look very well on the outside. But when it comes to the inside you are not in it with the original."

So when I come to a place like this with nothing valuable to say I always play a part.

But I will say before I sit down that when it comes to saying anything here I will express myself in this way. I am heartily in sympathy with you in your efforts to help those who were sufferers in this calamity, and in your desire to help those who were rendered homeless. And in saying this I wish to impress on you the fact that I am not playing a part.

October 1900

ᐒ 47 ᐕ

In August 1895, just before sailing for Australia, Clemens had issued the following statement.

"It has been reported that I sacrificed for the benefit of the creditors the property of the publishing firm whose financial backer I was, and that I am now lecturing for my own benefit.

"This an error. I intend the lectures, as well as the property, for the creditors. The law recognizes no mortgage on a man's brains, and a merchant who has given up all he has may take advantage of the laws of insolvency and may start free again for himself. But I am not a business man, and honor is a harder master than the law. It cannot compromise for less than one hundred cents on a dollar, and its debts are never outlawed.

"I had a two-thirds interest in the publishing firm whose capital I furnished. If the firm had prospered I would have expected to collect two-thirds of the profits. As it is, I expect to pay all the debts. My partner has no resources, and I do not look for assistance to my wife, whose contributions in cash from her own means have nearly equalled the claims of all the creditors combined. She has taken nothing. On the contrary, she has helped and intends to help me to satisfy the obligations due to the rest of the creditors.

"It is my intention to ask my creditors to accept that as a legal discharge and trust to my honor to pay the other fifty per cent as fast as I can earn it. From my reception thus far on my lecturing tour, I am confident that if I live I can pay off the last debt within four years.

"After which, at the age of sixty-four, I can make a fresh and unincumbered start in life. I am going to Australia, India and South Africa, and next year I hope to make a tour of the great cities of the United States."

On his return to the United States after an extended absence, Clemens was honored at a great dinner given by the Lotos Club in New York in November of 1900, at which he made the talk I have called "Home Conditions." The *New York Daily Tribune* ran the headline "Mark Twain at the Lotos" and reported, "The Lotos Club gave a dinner last night in honor of Mark Twain. The dinner was to begin at 6:30 o'clock. Mark Twain reached the clubhouse at 8 o'clock. Because of the anxiety of several members of

[177]

the club, arising from a rumor that the famous author had been run over by a Broadway cable car, a delegation from the club was sent about 7:15 o'clock to the Hotel Earlington, where Mark Twain is staying. The delegation inquired how seriously the author of 'Innocence [sic] Abroad' had been injured by the cable car, when Mark Twain himself appeared. On guessing the mission of his visitors the invited guest exclaimed, 'Why, this is too bad! I had forgotten all about it. Just wait fifteen minutes and I'll get right into my clothes.'

"When Mark Twain reached the clubhouse he was escorted to the table of honor, which had been placed in a large doorway opening from the front drawing room into the café. The doorway was heavily festooned with oak leaves, red from the autumn's frost. Both drawing room and café were filled with tables and crowded with guests and members of the club. At the dinner two hundred persons were seated."

The *New York Journal* headlined its story, "Mark Twain, Like Little Boy Blue, Fell Fast Asleep, And Lotos Club Didn't Know Where to Find Him."

Joseph Clifford Hendrix was an American banker; Thomas Bracket Reed was an American statesman; and Benjamin Barker Odell, Jr., was governor of New York at the time.

HOME CONDITIONS

I thank you all out of my heart for this fraternal welcome, and it seems almost too fine, almost too magnificent, for a humble Missourian such as I am, far from his native haunts on the banks of the Mississippi. Yet my modesty is in a degree fortified by observing that I am not the only Missourian who has been honored here tonight, for I see at this very table—here is a Missourian [indicating St. Clair McKelway], and there is a Missourian [indicating Chauncey Depew], and there is another Missourian—and Hendrix and Clemens.

And last but not least, the greatest Missourian of them all—here he sits—Tom Reed, who has always concealed his birth till now. And since I have been away I know what has been happening in his case. He has deserted politics and now is leading a creditable life. He has reformed, and God prosper him. And I judge, by a remark which he made upstairs awhile ago, that he had found a new business that is utterly suited to his make and constitution, and all he is doing now is that he is around raising the average of personal beauty.

But I am grateful to the president for the kind words which he has said of me. And it is not for me to say whether these praises were deserved or not. I prefer to accept them just as they stand, without concerning myself with the statistics upon which they have been built, but only with that large matter, that essential matter, the good-fellowship, the kindliness, the magnanimity and generosity that prompted their utterance.

Well, many things have happened since I sat here before. And now that I think of it, the president's reference to the debts which were left by the bankrupt firm of Charles L. Webster & Co. gives me an opportunity to say a word which I very much wish to say— not for myself but for ninety-five men and women whom I shall always hold in high esteem and in pleasant remembrance: the creditors of that firm. They treated me well. They treated me handsomely. There were ninety-six of them, and by not a finger's weight did ninety-five of them add to the burden of that time for me. Ninety-five out of the ninety-six. They didn't indicate by any word or sign that they were anxious about their money. They treated me well, and I shall not forget it. I could not forget it if I wanted to.

Many of them said, "Don't you worry, don't you hurry." That's what they said.

Why, if I could have that kind of creditors always, and that experience, I would recognize it as a personal loss to be out of debt.

I owe those ninety-five creditors a debt of homage, and I pay it now in such measure as one may pay so fine a debt in mere words. Yes, they said that very thing. I was not personally acquainted with ten of them, and yet they said, "Don't you worry, and don't you hurry." I know that phrase by heart, and if all the other music should perish out of the world it would still sing to me. I appreciate that. I am glad to say this word. People say so much about me, and they forget those creditors. They were handsomer than I was—or Tom Reed.

You have been doing many things in this time that I have been absent. You have done lots of things, some that are well worth remembering, too. Now, we have fought a righteous war since I have gone, and that is rare in history. A righteous war is so rare that it is almost unknown in history. But by the grace of that war we set Cuba free and we joined her to those three or four nations that exist on this earth. And we started out to set those poor Filipinos free too, and why, why, why that most righteous purpose of ours has apparently miscarried I suppose I never shall know.

But we have made a most creditable record in China in these days. Our sound and level-headed administration has made a most creditable record over there. And there are some of the Powers that cannot say that by any means. The Yellow Terror is threatening this world today. It is looming vast and ominous on that distant horizon. I do not know what is going to be the result of that Yellow Terror, but our government has had no hand in evoking it, and let's be happy in that and proud of it.

We have nursed free silver. We watched by its cradle. We have done the best we could to raise that child. But those pestiferous Republicans have—well, they keep giving it the measles every chance they get, and we never shall raise that child. Well, that's no matter, there's plenty of other things to do, and we must think of something else. We have tried a President four years, criticized him and found fault with him the whole time, and turned around a day or two ago with votes enough to spare to elect another.

O consistency! Consistency! Thy name—I don't know what thy name is—Thompson will do—any name will do—but you see there is the fact, there is the consistency.

Then we have tried for governor an illustrious Rough Rider. And we liked him so much in that great office that now we have made him Vice President—not in order that that office shall give him distinction but that he may confer distinction upon that office. And it's needed, too, it's needed. And now, for a while anyway, we shall not be stammering and embarrassed when a stranger asks us, "What is the name of the Vice President?" This one is known. This one is pretty well known, pretty widely known, and in some quarters favorably.

I am not accustomed to dealing in these fulsome compliments, and I am probably overdoing it a little. But—well, my old affectionate admiration for Governor Roosevelt has probably betrayed me into the complimentary excess. But I know him, and you know him. And if you give him rope enough—I mean if—oh yes, he will justify that compliment. Leave it just as it is.

And now we have put in his place Mr. Odell, another Rough Rider, I suppose. All the fat things go to that profession now. Why, I could have been a Rough Rider myself if I had known that this political Klondike was going to open up. And I would have been a Rough Rider if I could have gone to war on an automobile—but not on a horse! No, I know the horse too well. I have known the horse in war and in peace, and there is no place where a horse is comfortable. The horse has too many caprices, and he is too much given to initiative. He invents too many new ideas. No, I don't want anything to do with a horse.

And then we have taken Chauncey Depew out of a useful and active life and made him a Senator—embalmed him, corked him up. And I am not grieving. That man has said many a true thing about me in his time, and I always said something would happen to him. Look at that [pointing to Depew] gilded mummy! He has made my life a sorrow to me at many a banquet on both sides of the ocean, and now he has got it. Perish the hand that pulls that cork!

All these things have happened, all these things have come to pass, while I have been away. And it just shows how little a Mugwump can be missed in a cold, unfeeling world even when he is the last one that is left—a GRAND OLD PARTY all by himself.

And there is another thing that has happened, perhaps the most imposing event of them all. The institution called the Daughters of the Crown—the Daughters of the Royal Crown—has established itself and gone into business. Now, there's an American idea for you. There's an idea born of God knows what kind of specialized insanity, but not softening of the brain—you cannot soften a thing that doesn't exist—the Daughters of the Royal Crown! Nobody eligible but American descendants of Charles II. Dear me, how the fancy product of that old harem still holds out!

Well, I am truly glad to foregather with you again and partake of the bread and salt of this hospitable house once more. Seven years ago when I was your guest here, when I was old and despondent, you gave me the grip and the word that lift a man up and make him glad to be alive. And now I come back from my exile young again, fresh and alive, and ready to begin life once more. And your welcome puts the finishing touch upon my restored youth and makes it real to me, and not a gracious dream that must vanish with the morning. I thank you.

November 1900

48

The following talk was given at a reception for Clemens by the Society of American Authors in New York later the same month, November 1900. So many members surrounded him that Clemens asked, "Is this genuine popularity or is it all a part of a prearranged program?"
Judge Ransom: Rastus S. Ransom.

MY REAL SELF

It seems a most difficult thing for any man to say anything about me that is not complimentary. I don't know what the charm is about me which makes it impossible for a person to say a harsh thing about me and say it heartily, as if he was glad to say it. If this thing keeps on it will make me believe that I am what these kind chairmen say of me.

In introducing me, Judge Ransom spoke of my modesty as if he was envious of me. I would like to have one man come out flat-footed and say something harsh and disparaging of me, even if it were true. I thought at one time, as the learned Judge was speaking, that I had found that man, but he wound up like all the others by saying complimentary things.

I am constructed like everybody else and enjoy a compliment as well as any other fool but I do like to have the other side presented. And there is another side. I have a wicked side. Estimable friends who know all about it would tell you and take a certain delight in telling you things that I have done, and things further that I have not repented. The real life that I live and the real life that I suppose all of you live is a life of interior sin. That is what makes life valuable and pleasant. To lead a life of undiscovered sin! That is true joy.

Judge Ransom seems to have all the virtues that he ascribes to me. But oh my! if you could throw an X-ray through him. We are a pair. I have made a life study of trying to appear to be what he seems to think I am. Everybody believes that I am a monument of all the virtues, but it is nothing of the sort. I am living two lives and it keeps me pretty busy.

Some day there will be a chairman who will forget some of these merits of mine and then he will make a speech. I have more personal vanity than modesty, and twice as much veracity as the two put together. When that fearless and forgetful chairman is found there will be another story told.

At the Press Club recently I thought that I had found him. He started in in the way that I knew I should be painted with all sincerity, and was leading to things that would not be to my credit. But when he said that he never read a book of mine I knew at once that he was a liar, because he never could have had all the wit and intelligence with which he was blessed unless he had read my works as a basis.

I like compliments. I like to go home and tell them all over again to the members of my family. They don't believe them, but I like to tell them in the home circle all the same. I like to dream of them if I can.

I thank everybody for their compliments but I don't think that I am praised any more than I am entitled to be.

November 1900

❦ 49 ❦

This address was given at a dinner of the Nineteenth Century Club in New York, also held in November of 1900. Winchester and Trent were professors of English literature at Wesleyan University and Columbia University respectively. Eliot was Charles William Eliot.

DISAPPEARANCE OF LITERATURE

It wasn't necessary for your chairman to apologize for me in Germany. It wasn't necessary at all. Instead of that he ought to have impressed upon those poor benighted Teutons the service I rendered them. Their language had needed untangling for a good many years. Nobody else seemed to want to take the job, and so I took it. And I flatter myself that I made a pretty good job of it.

The Germans have an inhuman way of cutting up their verbs. Now a verb has a hard time enough of it in this world when it's all together. It's downright inhuman to split it up. But that's just what those Germans do. They take part of a verb and put it down here, like a stake, and they take the other part of it and put it away over yonder like another stake, and between these two limits they just shovel in German. I maintain that there is no necessity for apologizing for a man who helped in a small way to stop such mutilation.

We have heard a discussion tonight on the disappearance of literature. That's no new thing. That's what certain kinds of literature have been doing for several years. The fact is, my friends, that the fashion in literature changes, and the literary tailors have to change their cuts or go out of business. Professor Winchester here, if I remember fairly correctly what he said, remarked that few if any of the novels produced today would live as long as the novels of Walter Scott. That may be his notion. Maybe he is right. But so far as I am concerned I don't care if they don't.

Professor Winchester also said something about there being no modern epics like *Paradise Lost*. I guess he's right. He talked as if he was pretty familiar with that piece of literary work, and nobody would suppose that he never had read it. I don't believe any of you have ever read *Paradise Lost*, and you don't want to. That's something that you just want to take on trust. It's a classic, just as Professor Winchester says, and it meets his definition of a classic— something that everybody wants to have read and nobody wants to read.

Professor Trent also had a good deal to say about the disappearance of literature. He said that Scott would outlive all his critics. I guess that's true. The fact of the business is, you've got to be one of two ages to appreciate Scott. When you're eighteen you can read *Ivanhoe*. And you want to wait until you are ninety to read some of the rest. It takes a pretty well-regulated, abstemious critic to live ninety years.

But as much as these two gentlemen have talked about the disappearance of literature, they didn't say anything about my books. Maybe they think they've disappeared. If they do, that just shows their ignorance on the general subject of literature. I am not as young as I was several years ago, and maybe I'm not so fashionable, but I'd be willing to take my chances with Mr. Scott tomorrow morning in selling a piece of literature to the Century Publishing Company. And I haven't got much of a pull here, either. I often think that the highest compliment ever paid to my poor efforts was paid by Darwin through President Eliot of Harvard College. At least Eliot said it was a compliment, and I always take the opinion of great men like college presidents on all such subjects as that.

I went out to Cambridge one day a few years ago and called on President Eliot. In the course of the conversation he said that he had just returned from England and that he was very much touched by what he considered the high compliment Darwin was paying to my books. And he went on to tell me something like this.

"Do you know that there is one room in Darwin's house, his bedroom, where the housemaid is never allowed to touch two things? One is a plant he is growing and studying while it grows" (it was one of those insect-devouring plants which consumed bugs and beetles and things for the particular delectation of Mr. Darwin) "and the other some books that lie on the night table at the head of his bed. They are your books, Mr. Clemens, and Mr. Darwin reads them every night to lull him to sleep."

My friends, I thoroughly appreciated that compliment and considered it the highest one that was ever paid to me. To be the means of soothing to sleep a brain teeming with bugs and squirming things like Darwin's was something that I had never hoped for. And now that he is dead I never hope to be able to do it again.

November 1900

〜 **50** 〜

This talk was given at the Berkeley Lyceum of the Public Education Association in New York, also held in November of 1900. Clemens's anti-imperialism was well known. He was referring to the Boxer Rebellion of 1900. The Boxer—a member of the Chinese secret society of the time.

FEEDING A DOG ON ITS OWN TAIL

I don't suppose that I am called here as an expert on education, for that would show a lack of foresight on your part and a deliberate intention to remind me of my shortcomings.

As I sat here looking around for an idea it struck me that I was called for two reasons. One was to do good to me, a poor unfortunate traveler on the world's wide ocean, by giving me a knowledge of the nature and scope of your society and letting me know that others beside myself have been of some use in the world. The other reason that I can see is that you have called me to show by way of contrast what education can accomplish if administered in the right sort of doses.

Your worthy president said that the school pictures, which have received the admiration of the world at the Paris Exposition, have been sent to Russia. And this was a compliment from that government, which is very surprising to me.

Why, it is only an hour since I read a cablegram in the newspapers beginning "Russia Proposes to Retrench." I was not expecting such a thunderbolt, and I thought what a happy thing it will be for Russians when the retrenchment will bring home the thirty thousand Russian troops now in Manchuria, to live in peaceful pursuits. I thought this was what Germany should do also without delay, and that France and all the other nations in China should follow suit.

Why should not China be free from the foreigners, who are only making trouble on her soil? If they would only all go home, what a pleasant place China would be for the Chinese! We do not allow Chinamen to come here, and I say in all seriousness that it would be a graceful thing to let China decide who shall go there.

China never wanted foreigners any more than foreigners wanted Chinamen, and on this question I am with the Boxers every time. The Boxer is a patriot. He loves his country better than he does the countries of other people. I wish him success. The Boxer believes in driving us out of his country. I am a Boxer too, for I believe in driving him out of our country.

When I read the Russian despatch further my dream of world peace vanished. It said that the vast expense of maintaining the army had made it necessary to retrench, and so the government had decided that to support the army it would be necessary to withdraw the appropriation from the public schools. This is a monstrous idea to us. We believe that out of the public school grows the greatness of a nation.

It is curious to reflect how history repeats itself the world over. Why, I remember the same thing was done when I was a boy on the Mississippi River. There was a proposition in a township there to discontinue public schools because they were too expensive. An old farmer spoke up and said if they stopped the schools they would not save anything, because every time a school was closed a jail had to be built.

It's like feeding a dog on his own tail. He'll never get fat. I believe it is better to support schools than jails.

The work of your association is better and shows more wisdom than the Czar of Russia and all his people. This is not much of a compliment but it's the best I've got in stock.

November 1900

❧ **51** ❧

The following address was given at an annual dinner of the St. Nicholas Society in New York. It was a lavish affair, held in Delmonico's, a famous restaurant of the time, in December of 1900. Some three hundred people were present, many of them of Dutch ancestry. Donald Sage Mackay, a minister, said in response to the toast "St. Nicholas," "Mark Twain is as true a preacher of true righteousness as any bishop, priest, or minister of any church today, because he moves men to forget their faults by cheerful well-doing instead of making them sour and morbid by everlastingly bending their attention to the seamy and sober side of life." Bishop Potter—Henry Codman Potter, Episcopal clergyman.

NEW YORK

These are indeed prosperous days for me. Night before last, in a speech, the Bishop of the Diocese of New York complimented me for my contribution to theology, and tonight the Reverend Doctor Mackay has elected me to the ministry. I thanked Bishop Potter then for his compliment and I thank Doctor Mackay now for that promotion. I think that both have discerned in me what I long ago discerned but what I was afraid the world would never learn to recognize.

In this absence of nine years I find a great improvement in the city of New York. I am glad to speak on that as a toast—"The City of New York." Some say it has improved because I have been away. Others, and I agree with them, say it has improved because I have come back. We must judge of a city, as of a man, by its external appearances and by its inward character. In externals the foreigner coming to these shores is more impressed at first by our skyscrapers. They are new to him. He has not done anything of the sort since he built the tower of Babel. The foreigner is shocked by them.

In the daylight they are ugly. They are—well, too chimneyfied and too snaggy, like a mouth that needs attention from a dentist, like a cemetery that is all monuments and no gravestones. But at night, seen from the river where they are columns towering against the sky, all sparkling with light, they are fairylike. They are beauty more satisfactory to the soul and more enchanting than anything that man has dreamed of since the Arabian nights. We can't always have the beautiful aspect of things. Let us make the most of our sights that are beautiful and let the others go. When your foreigner makes disagreeable comments on New York by daylight, float him down the river at night.

What has made these skyscrapers possible is the elevator. The cigar box which the European calls a "lift" needs but to be compared with our elevators to be appreciated. The lift stops to reflect between floors. That is all right in a hearse but not in elevators. The American elevator acts like the man's patent purge—it worked. As the inventor said, "This purge doesn't waste any time fooling around. It attends strictly to business."

That New Yorkers have the cleanest, quickest and most admirable system of street railways in the world has been forced upon you by the abnormal appreciation you have of your hackman. We ought always to be grateful to him for that service. Nobody else would have brought such a system into existence for us. We ought to build him a monument. We owe him one as much as we owe one to anybody. Let it be a tall one. Nothing permanent, of course. Build it of plaster, say. Then gaze at it and realize how grateful we are for the time being. And then pull it down and throw it on the ash heap. That's the way to honor your public heroes.

As to our streets, I find them cleaner than they used to be. I miss those dear old landmarks, the symmetrical mountain ranges of dust and dirt that used to be piled up along the streets for the wind and rain to tear down at their pleasure. Yes, New York is cleaner than Bombay. I realize that I have been in Bombay, that I now am in New York, that it is not my duty to flatter Bombay but rather to flatter New York.

Compared with the wretched attempts of London to light that city, New York may fairly be said to be a well-lighted city. Why, London's attempt at good lighting is almost as bad as London's attempt at rapid transit. There is just one good system of rapid transit in London—the "Tube," and that, of course, had been put in by Americans. Perhaps after a while those Americans will come back and give New York also a good underground system. Perhaps they have already begun. I have been so busy since I came back that I haven't had time as yet to go down cellar.

But it is by the laws of the city, it is by the manners of the city, it is by the ideals of the city, it is by the customs of the city and by the municipal government which all these elements correct, support and foster, by which the foreigner judges the city. It is by these that he realizes that New York may indeed hold her head high among the cities of the world. It is by these standards that he knows whether to class the city higher or lower than the other municipalities of the world.

Gentlemen, you have the best municipal government in the world, the purest and the most fragrant. The very angels envy you, and wish they could establish a government like it in heaven. You got it by a noble fidelity to civic duty. You got it by stern and ever-watchful exertion of the great powers with which you are charged, by the rights which were handed down to you by your forefathers, by your manly refusal to let base men invade the high places of your government, and by instant retaliation when any public officer has insulted you in the city's name by swerving in the slightest from the upright and full performance of his duty. It is you who have made this city the envy of the cities of the world. God will bless you for it—God will bless you for it. Why, when you approach the final resting place the angels of heaven will gather at the gates and cry out,

"Here they come! Show them to the archangel's box and turn the limelight on them!"

December 1900

52

The talk was given at a dinner of the City Club in New York in January 1901. The bishop referred to is, again, Henry Codman Potter. Bryan— William Jennings Bryan, American politician and presidential candidate. According to Paine, "Bishop Potter told how an alleged representative of Tammany Hall asked him in effect if he would cease his warfare upon the police department if a certain captain and inspector were dismissed. He replied that he would never be satisfied until the 'man at the top' and the 'system' which permitted evils in the police department were crushed."

THE ANTI-DOUGHNUT PARTY

The Bishop has just spoken of a condition of things which none of us can deny, and which ought not to exist. That is, the lust of gain, a lust which does not stop short of the penitentiary or the jail to accomplish its ends. But we may be sure of one thing, and that is that this sort of thing is not universal. If it were, this country would not be. You may put this down as a fact: that out of every fifty men, forty-nine are clean.

Then why is it, you may ask, that the forty-nine don't have things the way they want them? I'll tell you why it is. A good deal has been said here tonight about what is to be accomplished by organization. That's just the thing. It's because the fiftieth fellow and his pals are organized and the other forty-nine are not that the dirty one rubs it into the clean fellows every time.

You may say organize, organize, organize. But there may be so much organization that it will interfere with the work to be done. The Bishop here had an experience of that sort and told all about it downtown the other night. He was painting a barn (it was his own barn) and yet he was informed that his work must stop. He was a non-union painter and couldn't continue at that sort of job.

Now, all these conditions of which you complain should be remedied and I am here to tell you just how to do it. I've been a statesman without salary for many years and I have accomplished great and widespread good. I don't know that it has benefited anybody very much even if it was good. But I do know that it hasn't harmed me very much and it hasn't made me any richer.

We hold the balance of power. Put up your best men for office and we shall support the better one. With the election of the best man for mayor would follow the selection of the best man for police commissioner and chief of police.

My first lesson in the craft of statesmanship was taken at an early age. Fifty-one years ago I was fourteen years old, and we had a society in the town I lived in, patterned after the Freemasons or the Ancient Order of United Farmers or some such thing—just what it was patterned after doesn't matter. It had an inside guard and an outside guard and a past-grand warden and a lot of such things so as to give dignity to the organization and offices to the members.

Generally speaking it was a pretty good sort of organization, and some of the very best boys in the village, including—but I mustn't get personal on an occasion like this. And the society would have got along pretty well had it not been for the fact that there were a certain number of the members who could be bought. They got to be an infernal nuisance. Every time we had an election the candidates had to go around and see the purchasable members. The price per vote was paid in doughnuts and it depended somewhat on the appetites of the individuals as to the price of the votes.

This thing ran along until some of us, the really very best boys in the organization, decided that these corrupt practices must stop. And for the purpose of stopping them we organized a third party. We had a name but we were never known by that name. Those who didn't like us called us the Anti-Doughnut party. But we didn't mind that.

We said, "Call us what you please. The name doesn't matter. We are organized for a principle."

By and by the election came around and we made a big mistake. We were triumphantly beaten. That taught us a lesson. Then and there we decided never again to nominate anybody for anything. We decided simply to force the other two parties in the society to nominate their very best men. Although we were organized for a principle we didn't care much about that. Principles aren't of much account anyway, except at election time. After that you hang them up to let them season.

The next time we had an election we told both the other parties that we'd beat any candidates put up by any one of them of whom we didn't approve. In that election we did business. We got the man we wanted. I suppose they called us the Anti-Doughnut party because they couldn't buy us with their doughnuts. They didn't have enough of them. Most reformers arrive at their price sooner or later, and I suppose we would have had our price. But our opponents weren't offering anything but doughnuts, and those we spurned.

Now it seems to me that an Anti-Doughnut party is just what is wanted in the present emergency. I would have the Anti-Doughnuts felt in every city and hamlet and school district in this State and in the United States. I was an Anti-Doughnut in my boyhood and I'm an Anti-Doughnut still. The modern designation is Mugwump. There used to be quite a number of us Mugwumps but I think I'm the only one left. I had a vote this fall and I began to make some inquiries as to what I had better do with it.

I don't know anything about finance and I never did but I know some pretty shrewd financiers and they told me that Mr. Bryan wasn't safe on any financial question. I said to myself then that it wouldn't do for me to vote for Bryan, and I rather thought—I know now—that McKinley wasn't just right on this Philippine question. And so I just didn't vote for anybody.

I've got that vote yet and I've kept it clean, ready to deposit at some other election. It wasn't cast for any wildcat financial theories and it wasn't cast to support the man who sends our boys as volunteers out into the Philippines to get shot down under a polluted flag.

January 1901

53

That same month, January of 1901, Clemens was invited to speak at the annual meeting of the Hebrew Technical School for Girls, held in Temple Emanu-El, New York. He was introduced by the school's president, Nathaniel Meyer, who said, "In one of Mr. Clemens's works he expressed his opinion of men, saying he had no choice between Hebrew and Gentile, black men or white. To him all men were alike. But I never could find that he expressed his opinion of women. Perhaps that opinion was so exalted that he could not express it. We shall now be called to hear what he thinks of women."

WOMEN'S RIGHTS

It is a small help that I can afford but it is just such help that one can give as coming from the heart through the mouth. The report of Mr. Meyer was admirable and I was as interested in it as you have been. Why, I'm twice as old as he and I've had so much experience that I would say to him when he makes his appeal for help, "Don't make it for today or tomorrow, but collect the money on the spot." We are all creatures of sudden impulse. We must be worked up by steam, as it were. Get them to write their wills now or it may be too late by and by.

Fifteen or twenty years ago I had an experience I shall never forget. I got into a church which was crowded by a sweltering and panting multitude. The city missionary of our town (Hartford) made a telling appeal for help. He told of personal experiences among the poor in cellars and top lofts requiring instances of devotion and help.

The poor are always good to the poor. When a person with his millions gives a hundred thousand dollars it makes a great noise in the world. But he does not miss it. It's the widow's mite that makes no noise but does the best work.

I remember on that occasion in the Hartford church the collection was being taken up. The appeal had so stirred me that I could hardly wait for the hat or plate to come my way. I had four hundred dollars in my pocket and I was anxious to drop it in the plate and wanted to borrow more. But the plate was so long in coming my way that the fever heat of beneficence was going down lower and lower, going down at the rate of a hundred dollars a minute.

The plate was passed too late. When it finally came to me my enthusiasm had gone down so much that I kept my four hundred dollars—and stole a dime from the plate. So you see time sometimes leads to crime.

Oh, many a time have I thought of that and regretted it, and I adjure you all to give while the fever is on you.

Referring to woman's sphere in life, I'll say that woman is always right. For twenty-five years I've been a woman's rights man. I have always believed, long before my mother died, that, with her gray hairs and admirable intellect, perhaps she knew as much as I did. Perhaps she knew as much about voting as I.

I should like to see the time come when women shall help to make the laws. I should like to see that whiplash, the ballot, in the hands of women. As for this city's government, I don't want to say much except that it is a shame, a shame. But if I should live twenty-five years longer, and there is no reason why I shouldn't, I think I'll see women handle the ballot. If women had the ballot today, the state of things in this town would not exist.

If all the women in this town had a vote today they would elect a mayor at the next election. And they would rise in their might and change the awful state of things now existing here.

January 1901

54

Clemens was the chairman at the celebration of Abraham Lincoln's ninety-second birthday anniversary, held in Carnegie Hall, New York City, to raise funds for the Lincoln Memorial University. Many prominent people attended, including Andrew Carnegie, J. P. Morgan, Whitelaw Reid and generals representing both the Union and the Confederate armies. As chairman, Clemens introduced the principal speaker, Henry Watterson, editor of the *Louisville Courier-Journal*. According to Paine, "Colonel Watterson's forbears had intermarried with the Lamptons, Mark Twain's maternal ancestors."

LINCOLN'S BIRTHDAY

The remainder of my duties as presiding chairman here this evening are but two, only two. One of them is easy and the other difficult. That is to say I must introduce the orator and then keep still and give him a chance.

The name of Henry Watterson carries with it its own explanation. It is like an electric light on top of Madison Square Garden. You touch the button and the light flashes up out of the darkness. You mention the name of Henry Watterson and your minds are at once illuminated with the splendid radiance of his fame and achievements. A journalist, a soldier, an orator, a statesman, a rebel. Yes, he was a rebel. And, better still, now he is a reconstructed rebel.

It is a curious circumstance that without collusion of any kind but merely in obedience to a strange and pleasant and dramatic freak of destiny he and I, kinsmen by blood (for we are that—and one-time rebels—for we were that) were chosen out of a million surviving quondam rebels to come here and bare our heads in reverence and love of that noble soul whom forty years ago we tried with all our hearts and all our strength to defeat and dispossess—Abraham Lincoln!

Is the Rebellion ended and forgotten? Are the Blue and the Gray one today? By authority of this sign we may answer yes. There was a Rebellion. That incident is closed.

I was born and reared in a slave state. My father was a slave owner. And in the Civil War I was a second lieutenant in the Confederate service. For a while. This second cousin of mine, Colonel Watterson, the orator of this present occasion, was born and reared in a slave state, was a colonel in the Confederate service, and rendered me such assistance as he could in my self-appointed task of annihilating the Federal armies and breaking up the Union.

I laid my plans with wisdom and foresight, and if Colonel Watterson had obeyed my orders I should have succeeded in my giant undertaking. It was my intention to drive General Grant into the Pacific—if I could get transportation—and I told Colonel Watterson to surround the Eastern armies and wait till I came.

But he was insubordinate and stood upon a punctilio of military etiquette. He refused to take orders from a second lieutenant. And the Union was saved.

This is the first time this secret has been revealed. Until now no one outside the family has known the facts. But there they stand. Watterson saved the Union. Yet to this day that man gets no pension.

Those were great days, splendid days. What an uprising it was! For the hearts of the whole nation, North and South, were in the war. We of the South were not ashamed, for like the men of the North we were fighting for flags we loved. And when men fight for these things and under these convictions, with nothing sordid to tarnish their cause, that cause is holy, the blood spilled for it is sacred, the life that is laid down for it is consecrated.

Today we no longer regret the result. Today we are glad that it came out as it did. But we are not ashamed that we did our endeavor. We did our bravest best against despairing odds for the cause which was precious to us and which our conscience approved. And we are proud, and you are proud, the kindred blood in your veins answers when I say it, you are proud of the record we made in those mighty collisions in the fields.

What an uprising it was! We did not have to supplicate for soldiers on either side. "We are coming, Father Abraham, three hundred thousand strong!" That was the music North and South. The very choicest young blood and brawn and brain rose up from Maine to the Gulf and flocked to the standards, just as men always do when in their eyes their cause is great and fine and their hearts are in it. Just as men flocked to the Crusades, sacrificing all they possessed to the cause, and entering cheerfully upon hardships which we cannot even imagine in this age, and upon toilsome and wasting journeys which in our time would be the equivalent of circumnavigating the globe five times over.

North and South we put our hearts into that colossal struggle. And out of it came the blessed fulfilment of the prophecy of the immortal Gettysburg speech which said, "We here highly resolve that these dead shall not have died in vain; that this nation, under God, shall have a new birth of freedom; and that a government of the people, by the people, for the people, shall not perish from the earth."

We are here to honor the birthday of the greatest citizen, and the noblest and the best after Washington, that this land or any other has yet produced. The old wounds are healed. You and we are brothers again. You testify by honoring two of us, once soldiers of the Lost Cause and foes of your great and good leader, with the privilege of assisting here. And we testify it by laying our honest homage at the feet of Abraham Lincoln and in forgetting that you of the North and we of the South were ever enemies, and remembering only that we are now indistinguishably fused together and namable by one common great name—Americans.

February 1901

~ 55 ~

In November of 1901, Clemens was invited to address the one hundred and forty-fifth annual dinner of the St. Andrew's Society of the State of New York, held in Delmonico's banquet hall in New York City, Andrew Carnegie presiding. Next day the *New York Times* headlines read: "Sons of Scotland/Feast and Make Merry/Haggis, Whisky, and the Pibroch/Features of the Occasion/A Token for Mr. Carnegie/He tells the St. Andrew's Society King/Edward Is America's Friend—Mark/Twain Discusses Scotch Humor."

"President Carnegie occupied the centre of the guests' table, behind the great fleece-covered snuffbox of the society," the *Times* reported. Some of the most prominent guests were named. "Little local color was lent to the scene by the appearance of many of the Scots in their national costume," the story continued. "Besides ex-Pipe Major James MacDonald of the Black Watch, attired in his full regimentals, only one member of the society wore kilt and tartan. He was George Austin Morrison, Jr., the Secretary of the society, who wore the plaid of the Clan Morrison. The pipe playing of Major MacDonald aroused much enthusiasm, especially when the shrill notes of the 'Cock o' the North' were heard. His piping of 'Carnegie of Skibo,' which he composed especially for the occasion, also was enthusiastically received. Major MacDonald had to divide favor with a band, stationed in the gallery, which played 'Annie Laurie' and 'Robin Adair,' and then 'Little Annie Rooney' and the 'Bowery,' the members joining lustily in the chorus of the last two.

"The menu consisted of all the good things of the season, but prominent among them was the national dish of the Scots—haggis, flanked by the national beverage—Scotch whisky. The haggis was borne into the dining hall upon the shoulders of a dozen waiters and the procession was headed around the tables by the Pipe Major tootling merrily on his pibroch 'The Bannocks of Barley.' The company received the procession standing and cheering loudly. The same ceremony was not observed when the whisky was borne in."

HUMOR

The President of St. Andrew's, the Lord Rector of Dublin—. No, Glasgow, isn't it? No. Well, he is higher up than I thought he was. Told me that Scotch humor is non-existent. How is he a Lord Rector, anyway? What does he know about ecclesiastics? I suppose he don't care so long as the salary is satisfactory.

I have never examined the subject of humor until now. I am surprised to find how much ground it covers. I have got its divisions and frontiers down on a piece of paper. I find it defined as a production of the brain, as the power of the brain to produce something humorous, and the capacity of perceiving humor.

The third subdivision is possessed by all English-speaking people, even the Scotch. Even the Lord Rector is humorous. He has offered of his own motion to send me a fine lot of whisky. That is certainly humor.

Goldsmith said that he had found some of the Scotch possessed wit, which is next door to humor. He didn't overurge the compliment. Josh Billings defined the difference between humor and wit as that between the lightning bug and the lightning. There is a conscious and unconscious humor. That whisky offer of the Lord Rector's was one of unconscious humor. A peculiarity of that sort is a man is apt to forget it.

I have here a few anecdotes to illustrate these definitions. I hope you will recognize them. I like anecdotes which have had the benefit of experience and travel, those which have stood the test of time, those which have laid claim to immortality. Here is one passed around a year ago, and twelve years old in its Scotch form.

A man receives a telegram telling him that his mother-in-law is dead and asking, "Shall we embalm, bury or cremate her?"

He wires back, "If these fail, try dissection."

Now, the unconscious humor of this was that he thought they'd try all of the three means suggested, anyway.

An old Scotch woman wrote to a friend, "First the child died, then the callant." For the benefit of those not Scotchmen here, I will say that a callant is a kind of shepherd dog. That is, this is the definition of the Lord Rector, who spends six months in his native land every year to preserve his knowledge of its tongue.

Another instance of unconscious humor was of the Sunday school boy who defined a lie as "An abomination before the Lord and an ever present help in time of trouble." That may have been unconscious humor but it looked more like hard, cold experience and knowledge of facts.

Then you have the story of the two fashionable ladies talking before a sturdy old Irish washerwoman. One said to the other, "Where did you spend the summer?"

"Oh, at Long Branch," was the reply. "But the Irish there. Oh, the Irish! Where were you?" she asked her companion in turn.

"At Saratoga. But the Irish there. Oh, the Irish!"

Then spoke up the old Irish woman and asked, "Why didn't you go to Hades? You wouldn't have found any Irish there."

Let me tell you now of a case of conscious humor. It was of William Cary, late of the *Century*, who died a few weeks ago, a man of the finest spirit and thought. One day a distinguished American called at the *Century* office. There was a new boy on duty as sentry. He gruffly gave the gentleman a seat and bade him wait. A short time after, Mr. Cary came along and said, "Why, what are you doing here?" After explanations Mr. Cary brought out three pictures, one of Washington, one of Lincoln and one of Grant.

"Now, young man," he said to the boy, "didn't you know that gentleman? Now, look at these pictures carefully, and if any of these gentlemen call show them right in."

I am grateful for this double recognition. I find that, like St. Andrew, my birthday comes on the 30th of November. In fact, I was sixty-six years old about thirty-four minutes ago.

It was cold weather when I was born. What a chance there was of my catching cold! My friends never explained their carelessness, except on the plea of custom. But what does a child of that age care for custom?

November 1901

ॐ 56 ॐ

The twentieth anniversary dinner of the Society of Medical Jurisprudence was held in New York in March of 1902, and Clemens was the guest speaker. Judge Morgan Joseph O'Brien was an American jurist.

PROGRESS IN MEDICINE

It is a pleasure to watch a company of gentlemen in that condition which is peculiar to gentlemen who have had their dinners. That is a time when the real nature of man comes out. As a rule we go about with masks, we go about looking honest and we are able to conceal ourselves all through the day. But when the time comes that man has had his dinner, then the true man comes to the surface.

I could see it here this evening. I noticed the burst of applause when Judge O'Brien got up to speak, and I knew that he was either an exceedingly able man or else that a lot of you practice in his court. You have been giving yourselves away all evening. One speaker got up here and urged you to be honest, and there was no response.

Now, I want you to remember that medicine has made all its progress during the past fifty years. One member of this society sent me a typewritten judicial decision of the year 1809 in a medical case, with the suggestion that this was the kind of medicine to have, and that the science of medicine had not progressed, but gone back. This decision went on and described a sort of medicine I used to take myself fifty years ago and which was in use also in the time of the Pharaohs. And all the knowledge up to fifty years ago you got from five thousand years before that.

I now hold in my hand Jaynes's *Medical Dictionary*, published in 1745. In that book there is a suggestion as to what medicine was like a long time ago. How many operations that are in use now were known fifty years ago? They were not operations, they were executions. I read in this book the case of a man who "died from a severe headache." Why "severe?" The man was dead. Didn't that cover the ground?

This book goes on to say, "A certain merchant about fifty years of age, of a melancholy habit, and deeply involved in affairs of the world, was, during the dog days" (with a capital D) "seized with a violent pain of his head, which some time after kept him in bed. I being called" (remember this man was a regular) "ordered vennisection in the arms, bleeding. I also ordered the applications of leeches to the vessels of his nostrils. I also ordered the application of leeches to his forehead and temples, and also behind his ears."

Now you see, he has got him fringed all over with leeches. But that was not enough, for he goes on to say: "I likewise ordered the application of cup glasses, with scarification on his back." Now he has township maps carved all over him, and all this is for a headache. But notwithstanding these precautions the man dies, or rather, perhaps, I might have said, because of these precautions the man dies. Now this physician goes on to say, "If any surgeon skilled in arterial anatomy had been present I should also have ordered an operation."

He was not satisfied with what he had done, with the precautions he had already taken, but he wanted apparently to put a pump into that man and pump out what was left.

Now all that has passed away, and modern medicine and surgery have come in. Medicine was like astronomy, which did not move for centuries. When a comet appeared in the heavens it was a sign that a Prince was going to die. It was also a sign of earthquakes and of pestilence and other dreadful things. But they began to drop one thing after another. They finally got down to earthquakes and the death of a Prince as the result of the appearance of a comet, until in 1818 a writer in *The Gentlemen's Magazine* found at least one thing that a comet was sent for, because it was of record that when the comet appeared in 1818 all the flies in London went blind and died. Now they had got down to flies.

In 1829 a clergyman found still one other thing that a comet was sent for, because while it was in the heavens all the cats in Westphalia got sick. But in 1868 that whole scheme was swept away and the comet was recognized to be only a pleasant summer visitor. And as for the cats and flies, they never were so healthy as they were then. From that time dates the great step forward that your profession has taken.

March 1902

ᘓ 57 ᘔ

August 1902 was a fateful month for the Clemenses, for it marked the beginning of Livy's final and fatal illness, which lasted twenty-two months and which kept her and Clemens almost entirely apart even though they lived in close proximity. Her health, never strong, had seemed to Clemens fragile earlier in the year. Some years later he wrote of her in his auto-biography, "Under a grave and gentle exterior burned inextinguishable fires of sympathy, energy, devotion, enthusiasm and absolutely limitless affection. She was *always* frail in body and she lived upon her spirit, whose hopefulness and courage were indestructible."

In November of that year Colonel George Harvey, president of Harper & Brothers, publishers, gave a dinner in honor of Clemens's sixty-seventh birthday, which was held at the Metropolitan Club in New York. Clemens was the ninth speaker. The previous speakers had teased him by pre-tending to discuss his shortcomings. Howells—William Dean Howells. John Hay—American diplomat and author. Reverend Twichell—Joseph Twichell, Clemens's close friend and fellow resident of Hartford. Wayne MacVeagh—American politician and public servant. Charles A. Dana— American journalist. Bangs—John Kendrick Bangs, American writer and humorist. St. Clair McKelway—American journalist. Rogers—Henry H. Rogers, American financier and friend of Clemens. Van Dyke—Henry Van Dyke, American clergyman, author and professor of English liter-ature.

I HAVE TRIED TO DO GOOD

I think I ought to be allowed to talk as long as I want to, for the reason that I have cancelled all my winter's engagements of every kind, for good and sufficient reasons, and am making no new en-gagements for this winter, and, therefore, this is the only chance I shall have to disembowel my skull for a year—close the mouth in that portrait for a year.

I want to offer thanks and homage to the chairman for this innovation which he has introduced here, which is an improvement, as I consider it, on the old-fashioned style of conducting occasions like this. That was bad—that was a bad, bad, bad arrangement. Under that old custom the chairman got up and made a speech, he introduced the prisoner at the bar and covered him all over with compliments, nothing but compliments, not a thing but compliments, never a slur, and sat down and left that man to get up and talk without a text.

You cannot talk on compliments. That is not a text. No modest person, and I was born one, can talk on compliments. A man gets up and is filled to the eyes with happy emotions but his tongue is tied. He has nothing to say. He is in the condition of Doctor Rice's friend who came home drunk and explained it to his wife, and his wife said to him, "John, when you have drunk all the whisky you want, you ought to ask for sarsaparilla."

He said, "Yes, but when I have drunk all the whisky I want I can't say sarsaparilla."

And so I think it is much better to leave a man unmolested until the testimony and pleadings are all in. Otherwise he is dumb, he is at the sarsaparilla stage.

Before I get to the higgledy-piggledy point, as Mr. Howells suggested I do, I want to thank you, gentlemen, for this very high honor you are doing me. And I am quite competent to estimate it at its value.

I see around me captains of all the illustrious industries, most distinguished men. There are more than fifty here, and I believe I know thirty-nine of them well. I could probably borrow money from—from the others, anyway. It is a proud thing to me, indeed, to see such a distinguished company gather here on such an occasion as this, when there is no foreign prince to be fêted, when you have come here not to do honor to hereditary privilege and ancient lineage but to do reverence to mere moral excellence and elemental veracity—and, dear me, how old it seems to make me.

I look around me and I see three or four persons I have known so many, many years. I have known Mr. Secretary Hay—John Hay, as the nation and the rest of his friends love to call him—I have known John Hay and Tom Reed and the Reverend Twichell close upon

thirty-six years. Close upon thirty-six years I have known those venerable men. I have known Mr. Howells nearly thirty-four years, and
I knew Chauncey Depew before he could walk straight and before
he learned to tell the truth. Twenty-seven years ago I heard him
make the most noble and eloquent and beautiful speech that has
ever fallen from even his capable lips.

Tom Reed said that my principal defect was inaccuracy of statement. Well, suppose that that is true. What's the use of telling the
truth all the time? I never tell the truth about Tom Reed. But that is
his defect, truth. He speaks the truth always. Tom Reed has a good
heart and he has a good intellect but he hasn't any judgment.

Why, when Tom Reed was invited to lecture to the Ladies' Society for the Procreation or Procrastination, or something, of morals,
I don't know what it was—advancement, I suppose, of pure morals—he had the immortal indiscretion to begin by saying that some
of us can't be optimists, but by judiciously utilizing the opportunities that Providence puts in our way we can all be bigamists.
You perceive his limitations. Anything he has in mind he states, if
he thinks it is true. Well, that was true, but that was no place to say
it. So they fired him out.

A lot of accounts have been settled here tonight for me. I have
held grudges against some of these people but they have all been
wiped out by the very handsome compliments that have been paid
me. Even Wayne MacVeagh—I have had a grudge against him
many years. The first time I saw Wayne MacVeagh was at a private
dinner party at Charles A. Dana's. And when I got there he was
clattering along, and I tried to get a word in here and there. But you
know what Wayne MacVeagh is when he is started. And I could not
get in five words to his one—or one word to his five. I struggled
along and struggled along and—well, I wanted to tell and I was
trying to tell a dream I had had the night before, and it was a remarkable dream, a dream worth people's while to listen to, a dream
recounting Sam Jones the revivalist's reception in heaven.

I was on a train and was approaching the celestial way station—I
had a through ticket—and I noticed a man sitting alongside of me
asleep, and he had his ticket in his hat. He was the remains of the
Archbishop of Canterbury. I recognized him by his photograph. I
had nothing against him, so I took his ticket and let him have mine.

He didn't object. He wasn't in a condition to object. And presently when the train stopped at the heavenly station—well, I got off, and he went on by request.

But there they all were, the angels, you know, millions of them, every one with a torch. They had arranged for a torch light procession. They were expecting the Archbishop. And when I got off they started to raise a shout. But it didn't materialize. I don't know whether they were disappointed. I suppose they had a lot of superstitious ideas about the Archbishop and what he should look like, and I didn't fill the bill, and I was trying to explain to Saint Peter, and was doing it in the German tongue, because I didn't want to be too explicit.

Well, I found it was no use. I couldn't get along. For Wayne MacVeagh was occupying the whole place.

And I said to Mr. Dana, "What is the matter with that man? Who is that man with the long tongue? What's the trouble with him, that long, lank cadaver, old oil derrick out of a job. Who is that?"

"Well now," Mr. Dana said, "you don't want to meddle with him. You had better keep quiet. Just keep quiet, because that's a bad man. Talk! He was born to talk. Don't let him get out with you. He'll skin you."

I said, "I have been skinned, skinned and skinned for years. There is nothing left."

He said, "Oh, you'll find there is. That man is the very seed and inspiration of that proverb which says, 'No matter how close you skin an onion, a clever man can always peel it again.'"

I reflected and I quieted down. That would never occur to Tom Reed. He's got no discretion.

Well, MacVeagh is just the same man. He hasn't changed a bit in all those years. He has been peeling Mr. Mitchell lately. That's the kind of man he is.

Mr. Howells—that poem of his is admirable. That's the way to treat a person. Howells has a peculiar gift for seeing the merits of people and he has always exhibited them in my favor. Howells has never written anything about me that I couldn't read six or seven times a day. He is always just and always fair. He has written more appreciatively of me than anyone in this world, and published it in the *North American Review*.

He did me the justice to say that my intentions (he italicized that) that my intentions were always good, that I wounded people's conventions rather than their convictions. Now, I wouldn't want anything handsomer than that said of me. I would rather wait, with anything harsh I might have to say, till the convictions become conventions.

Bangs has traced me all the way down. He can't find that honest man. But I will look for him in the looking glass when I get home. It was intimated by the Colonel that it is New England that makes New York and builds up this country and makes it great, overlooking the fact that there's a lot of people here who came from elsewhere, like John Hay from away out West, and Howells from Ohio, and St. Clair McKelway and me from Missouri, and we are doing what we can to build up New York a little—elevate it.

Why, when I was living in that village of Hannibal, Missouri on the banks of the Mississippi, and Hay up in the town of Warsaw, also on the banks of the Mississippi River—it is an emotional bit of the Mississippi, and when it is low water you have to climb up to it on a ladder, and when it floods you have to hunt for it with a deep-sea lead, but it is a great and beautiful country. In that old time it was a paradise for simplicity. It was a simple, simple life, cheap but comfortable, and full of sweetness, and there was nothing of this rage of modern civilization there at all. It was a delectable land.

I went out there last June and I met in that town of Hannibal a schoolmate of mine, John Briggs, whom I had not seen for more than fifty years. I tell you, that was a meeting! That pal whom I had known as a little boy long ago, and knew now as a stately man three or four inches over six feet and browned by exposure to many climes, he was back there to see that old place again. We spent a whole afternoon going about here and there and yonder and hunting up the scenes and talking of the crimes which we had committed so long ago.

It was a heartbreaking delight, full of pathos, laughter and tears all mixed together. And we called the roll of boys and girls that we picnicked and sweethearted with so many years ago, and there were hardly half a dozen of them left. The rest were in their graves. And we went up there on the summit of that hill, a treasured place in my memory, the summit of Holiday's Hill, and looked out again over that magnificent panorama of the Mississippi River sweeping along league after league, a level green paradise on one side, and retreating capes and promontories as far as you could see on the other, fading away in the soft, rich lights of the remote distance.

I recognized then that I was seeing now the most enchanting river view the planet could furnish. I never knew it when I was a boy. It took an educated eye that had traveled over the globe to know and appreciate it.

And John said, "Can you point out the place where Bear Creek used to be before the railroad came?"

I said, "Yes, it ran along yonder."

"And can you point out the swimming hole?"

"Yes, out there."

And he said, "Can you point out the place where we stole the skiff?"

Well, I didn't know which one he meant. Such a wilderness of events had intervened since that day more than fifty years ago, it took me more than five minutes to call back that little incident. And then I did call it back. It was a white skiff, and we painted it red to allay suspicion. And the saddest, saddest man came along, a stranger he was, and he looked that red skiff over so pathetically. And he said, "Well, if it weren't for the complexion I'd know whose skiff that was."

He said it in that pleading way, you know, that appeals for sympathy for him but we weren't in any condition to offer suggestions.

I can see him yet as he turned away with that same sad look on his face and vanished out of history forever. I wonder what became of that man. I know what became of the skiff. Well, it was a beautiful life, a lovely life. There was no crime. Merely little things like pillaging orchards and watermelon patches and breaking the Sabbath. We didn't break the Sabbath often enough to signify. Once a week, perhaps.

But we were good boys, good Presbyterian boys, all Presbyterian boys, and loyal and all that. Anyway, we were good Presbyterian boys when the weather was doubtful. When it was fair we did wander a little from the fold.

Look at John Hay and me. There we were in obscurity. And look where we are now. Consider the ladder which he has climbed, the illustrious vocations he has served. And vocations is the right word. He has in all those vocations acquitted himself with high credit and honor to his country and to the mother that bore him. Scholar, soldier, diplomat, poet, historian. Now, see where we are. He is Secretary of State and I am a gentleman. It could not happen in any other country.

Our institutions give men the positions that of right belong to them through merit. All you men have won your places not by heredities and not by family influence or extraneous help but only by the natural gifts God gave you at your birth, made effective by your own energies. This is the country to live in.

Now, there is one invisible guest here. A part of me is present. The larger part, the better part, is yonder at her home. That is my wife, and she has a good many personal friends here. And I think it won't distress any one of them to know that although she is going to be confined to that bed for many months to come from that nervous prostration there is not any danger and she is coming along very well. And I think it quite appropriate that I should speak of her.

I knew her for the first time just in the same year that I first knew John Hay and Tom Reed and Mr. Twichell, thirty-six years ago, and she has been the best friend I have ever had, and that is saying a good deal. She has reared me, she and Twichell together, and what I am I owe to them.

Twichell—why, it is such a pleasure to look upon Twichell's face! For five-and-twenty years I was under the Rev. Mr. Twichell's tuition, I was in his pastorate, occupying a pew in his church, and held him in due reverence. That man is full of all the graces that go to make a person companionable and beloved. And wherever Twichell goes to start a church the people flock there to buy the land. They find real estate goes up all around the spot. And the envious and the thoughtful always try to get Twichell to move to their neighborhood and start a church. And wherever you see him go you can go and buy land there with confidence, feeling sure that there will be a double price for you before very long. I am not saying this to flatter Mr. Twichell. It is the fact. Many and many a time I have attended the annual sale in his church and bought up all the pews on a margin. And it would have been better for me spiritually and financially if I had stayed under his wing.

I have tried to do good in this world, and it is marvelous in how many different ways I have done good, and it is comfortable to reflect—now, there's Mr. Rogers. Just out of the affection I bear that man many a time I have given him points in finance that he had never thought of, and if he could lay aside envy, prejudice and superstition, and utilize those ideas in his business it would make a difference in his bank account.

Well, I like the poetry. I like all the speeches and the poetry too. I liked Doctor Van Dyke's poem. I wish I could return thanks in proper measure to you, gentlemen, who have spoken and violated your feelings to pay me compliments. Some were merited and some you overlooked, it is true. And Colonel Harvey did slander every one of you and put things into my mouth that I never said, never thought of at all.

And now, my wife and I out of our single heart return you our deepest and most grateful thanks, and—yesterday was her birthday.

November 1902

58

A doctor in attendance on Livy thought she had a nervous breakdown and prescribed absolute rest, seclusion and careful nursing. Another doctor said she was suffering from "nervous prostration" and ordered her to be isolated from most members of her family, including Clemens. Howells thought she was suffering from heart disease. In later times there was speculation that she had had an attack of asthma, with a consequent strain on her heart, and that her illnesses were at least to some extent psychosomatic in origin.

Early in April 1903 Clemens wrote to a friend from Riverdale, New York, that his daughter Clara was spelling the trained nurse in the afternoons and that he himself was allowed to see Livy only twenty minutes twice a day and to write her only two letters a day provided they excluded any news—almost any news might upset her and cause a relapse. Several days earlier her physicians and a nerve specialist from New York had ordered her to spend the next winter in Italy, so Clara was now writing to a friend in Florence in the hope of finding a suitable villa near that city.

The Clemens family sailed for Genoa on October 24, 1903, and settled down in the Villa Reale di Quarto in the hills west of Florence. Livy died there the evening of June 5, 1904. Two hours later Clemens was writing an account of her death.

"She has been dead two hours. It is impossible. The words have no meaning. But they are true; I know it, without realizing it. She was my life, and she is gone; she was my riches, and I am a pauper. . . . How grateful I was that she had been spared the struggle she had so dreaded. And that I, too, had so dreaded for her. Five times in the last four months she spent an hour and more fighting violently for breath, and she lived in the awful fear of death by strangulation. Mercifully she was granted the gentlest and swiftest of deaths—by heart-failure—and she never knew, she never knew! She was the most beautiful spirit, and the highest and the noblest I have known. And now she is dead."

Livy was fifty-eight and a half at her death. She had been married thirty-four years. Clemens, ten years older, had six more years to live. Clemens and his entourage returned to the United States in July. By November he was preparing to establish himself in a house at the corner of Fifth Avenue and Ninth Street in New York.

At the close of November 1905 Clemens turned seventy. His birthday occasioned a great banquet in Delmonico's famous red room in New York, complete with music provided by a forty-piece orchestra from the Metropolitan Opera House. As a souvenir of the occasion, each guest was presented with a foot-high plaster bust of the author. The menu included Baltimore terrapin, saddle of lamb, fillet of kingfish, quail, redhead duck, champagne, sauterne and brandy. The host was Colonel George Harvey, editor of *Harper's Weekly* and of the *North American Review*.

The joke at the beginning of the speech refers to a twenty-eight-line "sonnet" which William Dean Howells, the evening's toastmaster, read. "I jolly the whole earth,/But most I love to jolly my own kind,/Joke of a people great, gay, bold, and free,/I type their master-mood. Mark Twain made me." Howells concluded with, "Now, ladies and gentlemen and Colonel Harvey, I will try not to be greedy on your behalf in wishing the health of our honored and, in view of his great age, our revered guest. I will not say, 'Oh King, live forever!' but 'Oh King, live as long as you like!'" Rising amid applause and the waving of napkins, the audience drank to Mark Twain.

"An insurance moral" and "associating with insurance presidents" refer to insurance company scandals of the time, resulting from speculative use of insurance company funds. "Leopold, the pirate King of Belgium"—Clemens savaged him in his *King Leopold's Soliloquy* (1905) for his severe exploitation of Congo native labor.

HOW TO REACH SEVENTY

Well, if I made that joke it is the best one I ever made. And it is in the prettiest language, too. I never can get quite to that height. But I appreciate that joke and I shall remember it. And I shall use it when occasion requires.

I have had a great many birthdays in my time. I remember the first one very well and I always think of it with indignation. Everything was so crude, unaesthetic, primeval. Nothing like this at all. No proper appreciative preparation made. Nothing really ready. Now, for a person born with high and delicate instincts—nothing ready at all. I hadn't any hair. I hadn't any teeth. I hadn't any clothes. I had to go to my first banquet just like that.

Well, everybody came swarming in. It was the merest little bit of a village. Hardly that. Just a little hamlet in the backwoods of Missouri, where nothing ever happened. And the people were all interested and they all came. They looked me over to see if there was anything fresh in my line.

Why, nothing ever happened in that village. I was the only thing that had really happened there for months and months and months. And although I say it myself that shouldn't, I came the nearest to being a real event that had happened in that village in more than two years.

Well, those people came, they came with that curiosity which is so provincial, with that frankness which also is so provincial, and they examined me all around and gave their opinion. Nobody asked them. And I shouldn't have minded if anybody had paid me a compliment but nobody did. Their opinions were all just green with prejudice. And I feel those opinions to this day. Well, I stood that as long as—well, you know I was born courteous, and I stood it to the limit. I stood it an hour and then the worm turned. I knew very well the strength of my position. I knew that I was the only spotlessly pure and innocent person in that whole town. And I came out and said so. And they could not say a word. It was so true. They blushed. They were embarrassed. Well, that was the first after-dinner speech I ever made. I think it was after dinner.

It's a long stretch between that first birthday speech and this one. That was my cradle song and this is my swan song, I suppose. I am used to swan songs. I have sung them several times. This is my seventieth birthday, and I wonder if you all rise to the size of that proposition, realizing all the significance of that phrase, seventieth birthday.

The seventieth birthday! It is the time of life when you arrive at a new and awful dignity. When you may throw aside the decent reserves which have oppressed you for a generation and stand unafraid and unabashed upon your seven-terraced summit and look down and teach, unrebuked. You can tell the world how you got there. It is what they all do. You shall never get tired of telling by what delicate arts and deep moralities you climbed up to that great place. You will explain the process and dwell on the particulars with senile rapture. I have been anxious to explain my own system this long time. And now at last I have the right.

I have achieved my seventy years in the usual way: by sticking strictly to a scheme of life which would kill anybody else. It sounds like an exaggeration but that is really the common rule for attaining to old age. When we examine the program of any of these garrulous old people we always find that the habits which have preserved them would have decayed us, that the way of life which enabled them to live upon the property of their heirs so long, as Mr. Choate says, would have put us out of commission ahead of time. I will offer here as a sound maxim this: that we can't reach old age by another man's road.

I will now teach, offering my way of life to whomsoever desires to commit suicide by the scheme which has enabled me to beat the doctor and the hangman for seventy years. Some of the details may sound untrue but they are not. I am not here to deceive. I am here to teach.

We have no permanent habits until we are forty. Then they begin to harden. Presently they petrify. Then business begins. Since forty I have been regular about going to bed and getting up. And that is one of the main things. I have made it a rule to go to bed when there wasn't anybody left to sit up with. And I have made it a rule to get up when I had to. This has resulted in an unswerving regularity of irregularity. It has saved me sound. But it would injure another person.

In the matter of diet, which is another main thing, I have been persistently strict in sticking to the things which didn't agree with me until one or the other of us got the best of it. Until lately I got the best of it myself. But last spring I stopped frolicking with mince pie after midnight. Up to then I had always believed it wasn't loaded.

For thirty years I have taken coffee and bread at eight in the morning, and no bite nor sup until seven-thirty in the evening. Eleven hours. That is all right for me, and is wholesome, because I have never had a headache in my life. But headachy people would not reach seventy comfortably by that road and they would be foolish to try it.

And I wish to urge upon you this, which I think is wisdom, that if you find you can't make seventy by any but an uncomfortable road, don't you go. When they take off the Pullman and retire you to the rancid smoker, put on your things, count your checks and get out at the first way station where there's a cemetery.

I have made it a rule never to smoke more than one cigar at a time. I have no other restriction as regards smoking. I do not know just when I began to smoke, I only know that it was in my father's lifetime and that I was discreet. He passed from this life early in 1847 when I was a shade past eleven. Ever since then I have smoked publicly. As an example to others, and not that I care for moderation myself, it has always been my rule never to smoke when asleep and never to refrain when awake. It is a good rule. I mean for me. But some of you know quite well that it wouldn't answer for everybody that's trying to get to be seventy.

I smoke in bed until I have to go to sleep. I wake up in the night, sometimes once, sometimes twice, sometimes three times, and I never waste any of these opportunities to smoke. This habit is so old and dear and precious to me that I would feel as you, sir, would feel if you should lose the only moral you've got—meaning the chairman—if you've got one. I am making no charges. I will grant here that I have stopped smoking now and then for a few months at a time but it was not on principle, it was only to show off. It was to pulverize those critics who said I was a slave to my habits and couldn't break my bonds.

Today it is all of sixty years since I began to smoke the limit. I have never bought cigars with life belts around them. I early found that those were too expensive for me. I have always bought cheap cigars—reasonably cheap, at any rate. Sixty years ago they cost me four dollars a barrel. But my taste has improved latterly and I pay seven now. Six or seven. Seven, I think. Yes, it's seven. But that includes the barrel. I often have smoking parties at my house. But the people that come have always just taken the pledge. I wonder why that is.

As for drinking, I have no rule about that. When the others drink I like to help. Otherwise I remain dry by habit and preference. This dryness does not hurt me but it could easily hurt you. Because you are different. You let it alone.

Since I was seven years old I have seldom taken a dose of medicine and have still seldomer needed one. But up to seven I lived exclusively on allopathic medicines. Not that I needed them, for I don't think I did. It was for economy. My father took a drug store for a debt, and it made cod-liver oil cheaper than the other breakfast foods. We had nine barrels of it and it lasted me seven years. Then I was weaned. The rest of the family had to get along with rhubarb and ipecac and such things. Because I was the pet.

I was the first Standard Oil Trust. I had it all. By the time the drug store was exhausted my health was established, and there has never been much the matter with me since. But you know very well it would be foolish for the average child to start for seventy on that basis. It happened to be just the thing for me but that was merely an accident. It couldn't happen again in a century.

I have never taken any exercise except sleeping and resting, and I never intend to take any. Exercise is loathsome. And it cannot be any benefit when you are tired. And I was always tired. But let another person try my way and see where he will come out.

I desire now to repeat and emphasize that maxim. We can't reach old age by another man's road. My habits protect my life but they would assassinate you.

I have lived a severely moral life. But it would be a mistake for other people to try that or for me to recommend it. Very few would succeed. You have to have a perfectly colossal stock of morals. And you can't get them on a margin. You have to have the whole thing and put them in your box. Morals are an acquirement like music, like a foreign language, like piety, poker, paralysis. No man is born with them. I wasn't myself, I started poor. I hadn't a single moral. There is hardly a man in this house that is poorer than I was then.

Yes, I started like that, the world before me, not a moral in the slot. Not even an insurance moral. I can remember the first one I ever got. I can remember the landscape, the weather, the—I can remember how everything looked. It was an old moral, an old second-hand moral, all out of repair, and didn't fit, anyway. But if you are careful with a thing like that and keep it in a dry place and save it for processions and Chautauquas and World's Fairs and so on, and disinfect it now and then, and give it a fresh coat of whitewash once in a while, you will be surprised to see how well she will last and how long she will keep sweet, or at least inoffensive.

When I got that mouldy old moral she had stopped growing because she hadn't any exercise. But I worked her hard, I worked her Sundays and all. Under this cultivation she waxed in might and stature beyond belief and served me well and was my pride and joy for sixty-three years. Then she got to associating with insurance presidents and lost flesh and character and was a sorrow to look at and no longer competent for business. She was a great loss to me. Yet not all loss. I sold her—ah, pathetic skeleton as she was—I sold her to Leopold, the pirate King of Belgium. He sold her to our Metropolitan Museum, and it was very glad to get her, for without a rag on she stands 57 feet long and 16 feet high and they think she's a brontosaur. Well, she looks it. They believe it will take nineteen geological periods to breed her match.

Morals are of inestimable value, for every man is born crammed with sin microbes, and the only thing that can extirpate these sin microbes is morals. Now you take a sterilized Christian. I mean, you take *the* sterilized Christian, for there's only one. Dear sir, I wish you wouldn't look at me like that.

Threescore years and ten! It is the Scriptural statute of limitations. After that you owe no active duties. For you the strenuous life is over. You are a time-expired man, to use Kipling's military phrase. You have served your term, well or less well, and you are mustered out. You are become an honorary member of the republic. You are emancipated. Compulsions are not for you, nor any bugle call but "lights out." You pay the time-worn duty bills if you choose, or decline if you prefer, and without prejudice, for they are not legally collectable.

The previous-engagement plea, which in forty years has cost you so many twinges, you can lay aside forever. On this side of the grave you will never need it again. If you shrink at thought of night and winter and the late home-coming from the banquet and the lights and the laughter through the deserted streets—a desolation which would not remind you now, as for a generation it did, that your friends are sleeping and you must creep in a-tiptoe and not disturb them, but would only remind you that you need not tiptoe, you can never disturb them more—if you shrink at thought of these things you need only reply, "Your invitation honors me and pleases me because you still keep me in your remembrance. But I am seventy.

Seventy, and would nestle in the chimney-corner and smoke my pipe and read my book and take my rest, wishing you well in all affection, and that when you in your turn shall arrive at pier No. 70 you may step aboard your waiting ship with a reconciled spirit and lay your course toward the sinking sun with a contented heart."

December 1905

59

Clemens also spoke in December of 1905 at a benefit for Russian Jews who suffered at the hands of the revolution of 1905. Earlier in the evening Sarah Bernhardt, the famous French actress, presented a one-act play, *L'Escarpolette.*

LOST OPPORTUNITY

It seems a sort of cruelty to inflict upon an audience like this our rude English tongue after we have heard that divine speech flowing in that lucid Gallic tongue. It has always been a marvel to me, that French language. It has always been a puzzle to me.

How beautiful that language is. How expressive it seems to be. How full of grace it is. And when it comes from lips like those, how eloquent and how liquid it is. And I am always deceived. I always think I am going to understand it.

It is such a delight to me to meet Madame Bernhardt and laugh hand to hand and heart to heart with her. I have seen her play, as we all have, and that is divine. But I have always wanted to know Madame Bernhardt herself, her fiery self. I have wanted to know that beautiful character. Why, she is the youngest person I ever saw, except myself. For I always feel young when I come in the presence of young people.

I have a pleasant recollection of an incident so many years ago, when Madame Bernhardt came to Hartford, where I lived, and she was going to play and the tickets were three dollars, and there were two lovely women, a widow and her daughter, neighbors of ours, highly cultivated ladies they were. Their tastes were fine and elevated, but they were very poor, and they said, "Well, we must not spend six dollars on a pleasure of the mind, a pleasure of the intellect. We must spend it, if it must go at all, to furnish to somebody bread to eat."

And so they sorrowed over the fact that they had to give up that great pleasure of seeing Madame Bernhardt. But there were two neighbors equally highly cultivated and who could not afford bread, and those good-hearted Joneses sent that six dollars, deprived themselves of it, and sent it to those poor Smiths to buy bread with. And those Smiths took it and bought tickets with it to see Madame Bernhardt. Oh yes, some people have taste and intelligence also.

Now, I was going to make a speech. I supposed I was, but I am not. It is late, late. And so I am going to tell a story. And there is this advantage about a story, anyway, that whatever moral or valuable thing you put into a speech, why, it gets diffused among those involuted sentences and possibly your audience goes away without finding out what that valuable thing was that you were trying to confer upon it. But, dear me, you put the same jewel into a story and it becomes the keystone of that story, and you are bound to get it—it flashes, it flames, it is the jewel in the toad's head. You don't overlook that.

Now, if I am going to talk on such a subject as, for instance, the lost opportunity—oh, the lost opportunity. Anybody in this house who has reached the turn of life—sixty or seventy or even fifty, or along there—when he goes back along his history, there he finds it mile-stoned all the way with the lost opportunity. And you know how pathetic that is. You younger ones cannot know the full pathos that lies in those words—the lost opportunity. But anybody who is old, who has really lived and felt this life, he knows the pathos of the lost opportunity.

Now, I will tell you a story whose moral is that, whose lesson is that, whose lament is that. I was in a village which is a suburb of New Bedford several years ago. Well, New Bedford is a suburb of Fair Haven, or perhaps it is the other way. In any case it took both of those towns to make a great center of the great whaling industry of the first half of the nineteenth century. And I was up there at Fair Haven some years ago with a friend of mine. There was a dedication of a great town hall, a public building, and we were there in the afternoon. This great building was filled, like this great theater, with rejoicing villagers, and my friend and I started down the center aisle.

He saw a man standing in that aisle, and he said, "Now, look at that bronzed veteran, at that mahogany-faced man. Now, tell me, do you see anything about that man's face that is emotional? Do you see anything about it that suggests that inside that man anywhere there are fires that can be started? Would you ever imagine that that is a human volcano?"

"Why, no," I said, "I would not. He looks like a wooden Indian in front of a cigar store."

"Very well," said my friend, "I will show you that there is emotion even in that unpromising place. I will just go to that man and I will just mention in the most casual way an incident in his life. That man is getting along toward ninety years old. He is past eighty. I will mention an incident of fifty or sixty years ago. Now, just watch the effect, and it will be so casual that if you don't watch you won't know when I do say that thing. But you just watch the effect."

He went on down there and accosted this antiquity and made a remark or two. I could not catch up. They were so casual I could not recognize which one it was that touched that bottom, for in an instant that old man was literally in eruption and was filling the whole place with profanity of the most exquisite kind. You never heard such accomplished profanity. I never heard it also delivered with such eloquence.

I never enjoyed profanity as I enjoyed it then—more than if I had been uttering it myself. There is nothing like listening to an artist— all his passions passing away in lava, smoke, thunder, lightning and earthquake.

Then this friend said to me, "Now I will tell you about that. About sixty years ago that man was a young fellow of twenty-three and had just come home from a three years' whaling voyage. He came into that village of his happy and proud because now, instead of being chief mate, he was going to be master of a whale ship, and he was proud and happy about it.

"Then he found that there had been a kind of a cold frost come upon that town and the whole region roundabout, for while he had been away the Father Mathew temperance excitement had come upon the whole region. Therefore everybody had taken the pledge.

There wasn't anybody for miles and miles around that had not taken the pledge.

"So you can see what a solitude it was to this young man, who was fond of his grog. And he was just an outcast, because when they found he would not join Father Mathew's Society they ostracized him, and he went about that town three weeks, day and night, in utter loneliness—the only human being in the whole place who ever took grog, and he had to take it privately.

"If you don't know what it is to be ostracized, to be shunned by your fellow man, may you never know it. Then he recognized that there was something more valuable in this life than grog, and that is the fellowship of your fellow man. And at last he gave it up, and at nine o'clock one night he went down to the Father Mathew Temperance Society and with a broken heart he said, 'Put my name down for membership in this society.'

"And then he went away crying, and at earliest dawn the next morning they came for him and routed him out, and they said that new ship of his was ready to sail on a three years' voyage. In a minute he was on board that ship and gone. And he said—well, he was not out of sight of that town till he began to repent. But he had made up his mind that he would not take a drink, and so that whole voyage of three years was a three years' agony to that man because he saw all the time the mistake he had made.

"He felt it all through. He had constant reminders of it, because the crew would pass him with their grog, come out on the deck and take it, and there was the torturous smell of it. He went through the whole three years of suffering, and at last coming into port it was snowy, it was cold, he was stamping through the snow two feet deep on the deck and longing to get home, and there was his crew torturing him to the last minute with hot grog.

"But at last he had his reward. He really did get to shore at last, and jumped and ran and bought a jug and rushed to the society's office and said to the secretary,

"'Take my name off your membership books, and do it right away! I have got a three years' thirst on.'

"And the secretary said, 'It is not necessary. You were blackballed.'"

December 1905

🞿 60 🞿

Also in December of 1905 Clemens addressed the Society of Illustrators at a dinner given at the Aldine Association Club in New York. Paine has written, "Just before Mr. Clemens made his speech, a young woman attired as Joan of Arc, with a page bearing her flag of battle, courtesied reverently and tendered Mr. Clemens a laurel wreath on a satin pillow. He tried to speak, but his voice failed from excess of emotion. 'I thank you!' he finally exclaimed, and, pulling himself together, he began his speech." Daniel Carter Beard was an American illustrator, and Sir Purdon Clarke was an English architect and authority on art.

JACK VAN NOSTRAND

Now there is an illustration [pointing to the retreating Joan of Arc]. That is exactly what I wanted, precisely what I wanted, when I was describing to myself Joan of Arc after studying her history and her character for twelve years diligently. That was the product—not the conventional Joan of Arc. Wherever you find the conventional Joan of Arc in history she is an offense to anybody who knows the story of that wonderful girl.

Why, she was—she was almost supreme in several details. She had a marvelous intellect. She had a great heart, had a noble spirit, was absolutely pure in her character, her feeling, her language, her words, her everything—she was only eighteen years old. Now put that heart into such a breast—eighteen years old—and give it that masterly intellect which showed in the face, and furnish it with that almost god-like spirit, and what are you going to have? The conventional Joan of Arc? Not by any means. That is impossible. I cannot comprehend any such thing as that.

You must have a creature like that young and fair and beautiful girl we just saw. And her spirit must look out of the eyes. The figure should be—the figure should be in harmony with all that, but oh, what we get in the conventional picture, and it is always the conventional picture!

I hope you will allow me to say that your guild, when you take the conventional, you have got it at secondhand. Certainly if you had studied and studied, then you might have something else as a result, but when you have the common convention you stick to that.

You cannot prevail upon the artist to do it. He always gives you a Joan of Arc, that lovely creature that started a great career at thirteen but whose greatness arrived when she was eighteen. And merely because she was a girl he cannot see the divinity in her and so he paints a peasant, a coarse and lubberly figure, the figure of a cotton bale, and he clothes that in the coarsest raiment of the peasant region—just like a fishwoman, her hair cropped short like a Russian peasant, and that face of hers, which should be beautiful and which should radiate all the glories which are in the spirit and in her heart—that expression in that face is always just the fixed expression of a ham.

But now Mr. Beard has intimated a moment ago, and so has Sir Purdon Clarke also, that the artist, the illustrator, does not often get the idea of the man whose book he is illustrating. Here is a very remarkable instance of the other thing in Mr. Beard, who illustrated a book of mine. You may never have heard of it. I will tell you about it now—*A Yankee in King Arthur's Court.*

Now, Beard got everything that I put into that book and a little more besides. Those pictures of Beard's in that book—oh, from the first page to the last—are one vast sardonic laugh at the trivialities, the servilities, of our poor human race, and also at the professions and the insolence of priestcraft and kingcraft—those creatures that make slaves of themselves and have not the manliness to shake it off. Beard put it all in that book. I meant it to be there. I put a lot of it there and Beard put the rest.

That publisher of mine in Hartford had an eye for the pennies, and he saved them. He did not waste any on the illustrations. He had a very good artist, Williams, who had never taken a lesson in drawing. Everything he did was original. The publisher hired the cheapest wood engraver he could find, and in my early books you can see a trace of that. You can see that if Williams had had a chance he would have made some very good pictures. He had a good heart and good intentions. I had a character in the first book he illustrated, *The Innocents Abroad.* That was a boy seventeen or eighteen years old, Jack Van Nostrand, a New York boy who to my mind was a very remarkable creature. He and I tried to get Williams to understand that boy and make a picture of Jack that would be worthy of Jack.

Jack was a most singular combination. He was born and reared in New York here. He was as delicate in his feelings, as clean and pure and refined in his feelings, as any lovely girl that ever was. But whenever he expressed a feeling he did it in Bowery slang, and it was a most curious combination, that delicacy of his and that apparent coarseness. There was no coarseness inside of Jack at all, and Jack in the course of seventeen or eighteen years had acquired a capital of ignorance that was marvelous—ignorance of various things, not of all things. For instance, he did not know anything about the Bible. He had never been in Sunday school. Jack got more out of the Holy Land than anybody else, because the others knew what they were expecting, but it was a land of surprises to him.

I said in the book that we found him watching a turtle on a log, stoning that turtle, and he was stoning that turtle because he had read that "The song of the turtle was heard in the land," and this turtle wouldn't sing. It sounded absurd but it was charged on Jack as a fact, and as he went along through that country he had a proper foil in an old rebel colonel who was superintendent and head engineer in a large Sunday school in Wheeling, West Virginia. That man was full of enthusiasm wherever he went and would stand and deliver himself of speeches, and Jack would listen to those speeches of the colonel and wonder.

Jack had made a trip as a child almost across this continent in the first overland stage coach. That man's name who ran that line of stages . . . well, I declare that name is gone. Well, names will go. . . .

Holloday—ah, that's the name—Ben Holloday, your uncle [turning to Andrew Carnegie]. That was the fellow —Ben Holloday—and Jack was full of admiration at the prodigious speed that that line of stages made. And it was good speed, one hundred and twenty-five miles a day, going day and night, and it was the event of Jack's life, and there at the Fords of the Jordan the colonel was inspired to a speech (he was always making a speech), so he called us up to him.

He called up five sinners and three saints.

It has been only lately that Mr. Carnegie beatified me.

And he said, "Here are the Fords of the Jordan, a monumental place. At this very point, when Moses brought the children of Israel through—he brought the children of Israel from Egypt through the desert you see there—he guided them through that desert patiently, patiently during forty years, and brought them to this spot safe and sound. There you see—there is the scene of what Moses did."

And Jack said, "Moses who?"

"Oh," he says, "Jack, you ought not to ask that! Moses the great law-giver! Moses the great patriot! Moses the great warrior! Moses the great guide, who, as I tell you, brought these people through these three hundred miles of sand in forty years and landed them safe and sound."

Jack said, "There's nothin' in that three hundred miles in forty years. Ben Holloday would have snaked 'em through in thirty-six hours."

Well, I was speaking of Jack's innocence, and it was beautiful. Jack was not ignorant on all subjects. That boy was a deep student in the history of Anglo-Saxon liberty, and he was a patriot all the way through to the marrow. There was a subject that interested him all the time. Other subjects were of no concern to Jack, but that quaint, inscrutable innocence of his I could not get Williams to put into the picture.

Yes, Williams wanted to do it.

He said, "I will make him as innocent as a virgin."

He thought a moment and then said, "I will make him as innocent as an unborn virgin," which covered the ground.

I was reminded of Jack because I came across a letter today which is over thirty years old that Jack wrote. Jack was doomed to consumption. He was very long and slim, poor creature, and in a year or two after he got back from that excursion to the Holy Land he went on a ride on horseback through Colorado, and he did not last but a year or two.

He wrote this letter not to me but to a friend of mine, and he said: "I have ridden horseback"—this was three years after—"I have ridden horseback four hundred miles through a desert country where you never see anything but cattle now and then, and now and then a cattle station—ten miles apart, twenty miles apart. Now you tell Clemens that in all that stretch of four hundred miles I have seen only two books—the Bible and *Innocents Abroad*. Tell Clemens the Bible was in a very good condition."

I say that he had studied, and he had, the real Saxon liberty, the acquirement of our liberty, and Jack used to repeat some verses (I don't know where they came from but I thought of them today when I saw that letter). And that boy could have been talking of himself in those quoted lines from that unknown poet:

> *For he had sat at Sidney's feet*
> *And walked with him in plain apart,*
> *And through the centuries heard the beat*
> *Of Freedom's march through Cromwell's heart.*

And he was that kind of a boy.

He should have lived, and yet he should not have lived, because he died at that early age—he couldn't have been more than twenty. He had seen all there was to see in the world that was worth the trouble of living in it. He had seen all of this world that is valuable. He had seen all of this world that was illusion. And illusion is the only valuable thing in it.

He had arrived at that point where presently the illusions would cease and he would have entered upon the realities of life, and God help the man that has arrived at that point.

December 1905

~ 61 ~

In January of 1906, Clemens was invited to address a meeting, held in Carnegie Hall, New York, to raise funds for Tuskegee Institute. Joseph H. Choate, the speaker preceding Clemens, in Paine's words "made fun of him because he made play his work, and because when he worked hardest he did so lying in bed." Charles Henry Parkhurst was a Congregational pastor active in municipal reform. The Washington referred to was Booker T. Washington, the American educator prominent in the establishment of Tuskegee.

PRIVATE AND PUBLIC MORALS

I came here in the responsible capacity of policeman to watch Mr. Choate. This is an occasion of grave and serious importance and it seems necessary for me to be present, so that if he tried to work off any statement that required correction, reduction, refutation or exposure there would be a tried friend of the public to protect the house. He has not made one statement whose veracity fails to tally exactly with my own standard. I have never seen a person improve so.

This makes me thankful and proud of a country that can produce such men—two such men. And all in the same country. We can't be with you always, we are passing away, and then—well, everything will have to stop, I reckon. It is a sad thought. But in spirit I shall still be with you. Choate too—if he can.

Every born American among the eighty millions, let his creed or destitution of creed be what it may, is indisputably a Christian to this degree—that his moral constitution is Christian. There are two kinds of Christian morals, one private and the other public. These two are so distinct, so unrelated, that they are no more akin to each other than are archangels and politicians.

During three hundred and sixty-three days in the year the American citizen is true to his Christian private morals and keeps undefiled the nation's character at its best and highest. Then in the other two days of the year he leaves his Christian private morals at home and carries his Christian public morals to the tax office and the polls and does the best he can to damage and undo his whole year's faithful and righteous work. Without a blush he will vote for an unclean boss if that boss is his party's Moses, without compunction he will vote against the best man in the whole land if he is on the other ticket. Every year in a number of cities and States he helps put corrupt men in office, whereas if he would but throw away his Christian public morals and carry his Christian private morals to the polls he could promptly purify the public service and make the possession of office a high and honorable distinction.

Once a year he lays aside his Christian private morals and hires a ferry boat and piles up his bonds in a warehouse in New Jersey for three days and gets out his Christian public morals and goes to the tax office and holds up his hand and swears he wishes he may never-never if he's got a cent in the world, so help him. The next day the list appears in the papers—a column and a quarter of names in fine print, and every man in the list a billionaire and member of a couple of churches.

I know all those people. I have friendly, social and criminal relations with the whole lot of them. They never miss a sermon when they are so's to be around, and they never miss swearing-off day, whether they are so's to be around or not.

I used to be an honest man. I am crumbling. No—I have crumbled. When they assessed me at $75,000 a fortnight ago I went out and tried to borrow the money and couldn't. Then when I found they were letting a whole crop of millionaires live in New York at a third of the price they were charging me I was hurt, I was indignant, and said, "This is the last feather. I am not going to run this town all by myself."

In that moment—in that memorable moment—I began to crumble. In fifteen minutes the disintegration was complete. In fifteen minutes I had become just a mere moral sand pile. And I lifted up my hand along with those seasoned and experienced deacons and swore off every rag of personal property I've got in the world, clear down the cork leg, glass eye and what is left of my wig.

Those tax officers were moved. They were profoundly moved. They had long been accustomed to seeing hardened old grafters act like that, and they could endure the spectacle, but they were expecting better things of me, a chartered, professional moralist, and they were saddened. I fell visibly in their respect and esteem and I should have fallen in my own except that I had already struck bottom and there wasn't any place to fall to.

At Tuskegee they will jump to misleading conclusions from insufficient evidence, along with Doctor Parkhurst, and they will deceive the student with the superstition that no gentleman ever swears. Look at those good millionaires. Aren't they gentlemen? Well, they swear. Only once in a year, maybe, but there's enough bulk to it to make up for the lost time. And do they lose anything by it? No, they don't. They save enough in three minutes to support the family seven years. When they swear, do we shudder? No—unless they say "damn!" Then we do. It shrivels us all up. Yet we ought not to feel so about it, because we all swear—everybody. Including the ladies. Including Doctor Parkhurst, that strong and brave and excellent citizen, but superficially educated.

For it is not the word that is the sin, it is the spirit back of the word. When an irritated lady says "oh!" the spirit back of it is "damn!" and that is the way it is going to be recorded against her. It always makes me so sorry when I hear a lady swear like that. But if she says "damn," and says it in an amiable, nice way, it isn't going to be recorded at all.

The idea that no gentleman ever swears is all wrong. He can swear and still be a gentleman if he does it in a nice and benevolent and affectionate way. The historian, John Fiske, whom I knew well and loved, was a spotless and most noble and upright Christian gentleman, and yet he swore once. Not exactly that, maybe. Still, he— but I will tell you about it.

One day when he was deeply immersed in his work his wife came in, much moved and profoundly distressed, and said, "I am sorry to disturb you, John, but I must, for this is a serious matter and needs to be attended to at once."

Then, lamenting, she brought a grave accusation against their little son.

She said, "He has been saying his Aunt Mary is a fool and his Aunt Martha is a damned fool."

Mr. Fiske reflected upon the matter a minute, then said, "Oh, well, it's about the distinction I should make between them myself."

Mr. Washington, I beg you to convey these teachings to your great and prosperous and most beneficent educational institution, and add them to the prodigal mental and moral riches wherewith you equip your fortunate protégés for the struggle of life.

January 1906

‏ 62 ‏

In February of 1906, the Manhattan Dickens Fellowship gave a dinner in celebration of the ninety-fourth anniversary of the birth of Charles Dickens. Clemens was not averse to recycling the story of the poet who blew his brains out.

LYING

I always had taken an interest in young people who wanted to become poets. I remember I was particularly interested in one budding poet when I was a reporter. His name was Butter. One day he came to me and said disconsolately that he was going to commit suicide. He was tired of life, not being able to express his thoughts in poetic form. Butter asked me what I thought of the idea.

I said that it was a good idea.

"You can do me a friendly turn. You go off in a private place and do it there, and I'll get it all. You do it, and I'll do as much for you some time."

At first he determined to drown himself. Drowning is so nice and clean and writes up so well in a newspaper. But things ne'er do go smoothly in weddings, suicides or courtships. Only there at the edge of the water, where Butter was to end himself, lay a life preserver, a big round canvas one which would float after the scrap iron was soaked out of it.

Butter wouldn't kill himself with the life preserver in sight, and so I had an idea. I took it to a pawnshop and sold it for a revolver. The pawnbroker didn't think much of the exchange but when I explained the situation he acquiesced.

We went up on top of a high building, and this is what happened to the poet. He put the revolver to his forehead and blew a tunnel straight through his head. The tunnel was about the size of your finger. You could look right through it. The job was complete. There was nothing in it.

Well, after that that man never could write prose. But he could write poetry. He could write it after he had blown his brains out. There is lots of that talent all over the country. But the trouble is they don't develop it.

I am suffering now from the fact that I, who have told the truth a good many times in my life, have lately received more letters than anybody else urging me to lead a righteous life. I have more friends who want to see me develop on a high level than anybody else.

Young John D. Rockefeller, two weeks ago, taught his Bible class all about veracity, and why it was better that everybody should always keep a plentiful supply on hand. Some of the letters I have received suggest that I ought to attend his class and learn too. Why, I know Mr. Rockefeller and he is a good fellow. He is competent in many ways to teach a Bible class. But when it comes to veracity he is only thirty-five years old. I'm seventy years old. I have been familiar with veracity twice as long as he.

And the story about George Washington and his little hatchet has also been suggested to me in these letters—in a fugitive way, as if I needed some of George Washington and his hatchet in my constitution. Why, dear me, they overlook the real point in that story. The point is not the one that is usually suggested, and you can readily see that.

The point is not that George said to his father, "Yes, father, I cut down the cherry tree. I can't tell a lie," but that the little boy (only seven years old) should have his sagacity developed under such circumstances. He was a boy wise beyond his years. His conduct then was a prophecy of later years. Yes, I think he was the most remarkable man the country ever produced—up to my time, anyway.

Now then, little George realized that circumstantial evidence was against him. He knew that his father would know from the size of the chips that no full-grown hatchet cut that tree down and that no man would have haggled it so. He knew that his father would send around the plantation and inquire for a small boy with a hatchet, and he had the wisdom to come out and confess it.

Now, the idea that his father was overjoyed when he told little

George that he would rather have him cut down a thousand cherry trees than tell a lie is all nonsense. What did he really mean? Why, that he was absolutely astonished that he had a son who had the chance to tell a lie and didn't.

I admire old George—if that was his name—for his discernment. He knew when he said that his son couldn't tell a lie that he was stretching it a good deal. He wouldn't have to go to John D. Rockefeller's Bible class to find that out. The way the old George Washington story goes down it doesn't do anybody any good. It only discourages people who can tell a lie.

February 1906

⋙ **63** ⋙

Both the exact date and the occasion of the following talk are unknown. "The Reverend Doctor Van Dyke" was the distinguished author and Princeton professor Henry Van Dyke. Simon Hanks may have been a fictional creation; he is not identified in any sources.

THE GENTLEMAN

I am here ostensibly to introduce to you the lecturer of the occasion, the Reverend Doctor Van Dyke of Princeton University. Not to tell you who he is—you know that already. Not to praise his delicious books—they praise themselves better than any words of mine could do it for them.

Then is there any real use or advantage in my being here at all? Yes. I am here to talk and put in the time while Doctor Van Dyke reflects upon what he is going to say and whether he had better say it or not.

Chance has furnished me a text, a text which offers me an opportunity to teach, an opportunity to be instructive. And if I have a passion for anything it is for teaching. It is noble to teach oneself. It is still nobler to teach others, and less trouble.

My text is a telegram from the *Daily Review*, an Illinois newspaper, which says, "In what book of yours will we find a definition of a gentleman?"

This question has been asked me a number of times by mail in the past month or two and I have not replied. But if it is now going to be taken up by telegraph it is time for me to say something, and I think that this is the right time and place for it.

The source of these inquiries was an Associated Press telegram of a month or so ago which said, in substance, that a citizen of Joplin,

Missouri, who had just died had left ten thousand dollars to be devoted to the dissemination among young men of Mark Twain's idea of the true gentleman. This was a puzzle to me, for I had never in my life uttered in print a definition of that word, a word which once had a concrete meaning but has no clear and definite meaning now either in America or elsewhere.

In England long ago and in America in early times the term was compact and definite and was restricted to a certain grade of birth, and it had nothing to do with character. A gentleman could commit all the crimes and bestialities known to the Newgate Calendar and be shunned and despised by everybody great and small, and no one could dispute it. But in our day how would you define that loose and shackly and shadowy and colorless word? In case you had thirty-five years to do it in. None but a very self-complacent and elaborately incompetent person would ever try to define it. And then the result wouldn't be worth the violent mental strain it had cost.

The weeks drifted along and I remained puzzled. But at last when this telegram came I suddenly remembered. Remembered that I had once defined the word? Not at all. What I remembered was this. In the first fortnight of March, four years ago, a New York lady defined the word in a published interview. The main feature of her definition was that no man is a gentleman who hasn't had a college education.

Oh dear me—Adam, for instance! And Arkwright—and Watt—and Stephenson—and Whitney—and Franklin—and Fulton—and Morse—and Elias Howe—and Edison—and Graham Bell—and Lincoln—and Washington—and—and me.

What a project! To select and set apart a majestic and monumental class for the people's reverence and homage, then degrade it, belittle it, make it trivial, make it comical, make it grotesque, by leaving out of it the makers of history, the uplifters of man, the creators and preservers of civilizations. The idea of leaving *us* out!

It was my privilege to laugh if I did it privately. Very well, I did it privately. Considering the fact that the person who proposes to define that word must be equipped with almost limitless knowledge and daring and placid self-confidence, it seemed to me that the late Simon Hanks of Cape Cod had surely changed his sex and was come again.

The poet says:

> *The Lord knows all things, great and small;*
> *With doubt He's never vexed;*
> *Ah yes, the good Lord knows it all—*
> *But Simon Hanks comes next.*

The matter seemed settled. But the New York papers have long known that no large question is ever really settled until I have been consulted. It is the way they feel about it. And they show it by always sending to me when they get uneasy. So the interviewers came up to Riverdale to get the verdict.

I was in bed, trying to amuse the bronchitis, therefore I got myself excused. I said not a word upon the subject to anyone. Yet there was a long and fictitious interview pretending to come from me in one of the papers the next morning, the only instance in which a paper on either side of the Atlantic had treated me uncourteously and unfairly for many years. I was made to speak in the first person and to furnish my idea of what a gentleman is.

You will perceive that there is a sort of grotesque and degraded humor about that situation. All definers of the modern gentleman are agreed that among his qualities must be honesty, courtesy and truthfulness. Very well, here is a journalist who sends to me a forger to represent him, then prints the forger's product and filches money with it from his deceived readers. Yet if I should assert that he is not a gentleman his friends could quite properly require me to prove it, and I couldn't do it, for I don't know what a gentleman is—a gentleman on the indefinite modern plan. It's the fourth dimension to me, with the unsquared circle and the nebular theory added.

There is also another humorous detail or two about the situation. The forged interview deceived and beguiled that trusting and well-meaning citizen of Joplin before he died, and pillaged his heirs after he was in his grave. They can't get the bequeathed money, for it has to go to the dissemination of my definition of what a gentleman is. The proposed class in gentlemanliness can't get it, for my definition doesn't exist and has never existed. The money is tied up for good and all. I believe it is the most dismally and pathetically and sardonically humorous incident I have ever come across.

Now then, can't we define the American gentleman at all? As a whole, no. We can define the best part of him, the valuable part. It is as far as we can get. The rest of him is hazy, diffused, uncertain. It is this, that and the other thing. It is everything and nothing, according to Tom, Dick and Harry's undigested notion. And when you've got the jumble all jumbled together to suit you, if it still seems to lack something whitewash it with a college education and call game.

What shall we say is the best part, the accepted part, the essential part of the American gentleman? Let us say it is courtesy and a blemishless character. What is courtesy? Consideration for others. Is there a good deal of it in the American character? So far as I have observed, no. Is it an American characteristic? So far as I have observed, the most striking, the most prominent, the most American of all American characteristics is the poverty of it in the American character. Even the foreigner loses his kindly politeness as soon as we get him Americanized.

When we have been abroad among either the naked savages or the clothed civilized for even so brief a time as a year the first thing we notice when we get back home is the wanton and unprovoked discourtesies that assail us at every turn. They begin at the customs pier and they follow us everywhere. Such of you as have been abroad will feel with remembered pangs and cheek burnings that I am speaking the truth.

The rest of you will confess it some day when you come home from abroad. You will step into the trolley with your heart so full of thankfulness to be at home again that you can't speak. You are so glad, so happy, so grateful that the tears blur everything, and you say to yourself, "Oh, *am* I really and truly at home once more?"

Then the conductor bawls out, "Come, step lively, will you!" and you realize that you are.

You realize that in no country on the planet, savage òr civilized, but your own could you hear your unoffending old father and mother and your gentle young sister assailed with that brutal insult. Also that no people on the planet but ours is meek enough to stand it.

We allow our commonest rights to be trampled underfoot every day and everywhere. Among us citizenship is an unknown virtue.

We have never claimed to be the Uncourteous Nation, the Unpolite Nation, I don't know where, there being no competition. Is it because we are also the Too-Modest Nation? Probably. Is that why we still keep that old, quiet, courtly uninsolent, uncharacteristic E PLURIBUS UNUM for our national motto instead of replacing it with an up-to-date one full of national character—"Come, *step* lively!"

I am working hard, day and night without salary or hope of applause, upon my high and self-appointed task of reforming our national manners. And I ask for your help. Am I polite, do you ask? Well . . . no. I'm an American myself. Why don't I begin by reforming my own manners? I have already explained that in the beginning. I said, it is noble to teach oneself, but still nobler to teach others—and less trouble.

Having now finished this extraneous and unofficial lecture, I invite the real lecturer to approach and deliver to you his message. But I do it courteously. You will never hear me say to Reverend Doctor Van Dyke, whom I and the nation revere, "Come, *step* lively!"

about February 1906

~ 64 ~

In March of 1906 Clemens was a guest at a reception in his honor at Barnard College in New York. The student who introduced him said it gave her and her fellow students great pleasure to have him there "because we all love you." Onteora is a summer resort in the Catskills where he once stayed.

MEMORIES

If anyone here loves me she has my sincere thanks. Nay, if anyone here is so good as to love me—why, I'll be a brother to her. She shall have my sincere, warm, unsullied affection.

When I was coming up in the car with the very kind young lady who was delegated to show me the way, she asked me what I was going to talk about. And I said I wasn't sure. I said I had some illustrations and I was going to bring them in. I said I was certain to give those illustrations but that I hadn't the faintest notion what they were going to illustrate.

Now, I've been thinking it over in this forest glade [indicating the woods of Arcady on the scene setting], and I've decided to work them in with something about morals and the caprices of memory. That seems to me to be a pretty good subject. You see, everybody has a memory and it's pretty sure to have caprices. And, of course, everybody has morals.

It's my opinion that every one I know has morals, though I wouldn't like to ask. I know I have. But I'd rather teach them than practice them any day. "Give them to others"—that's my motto. Then you never have any use for them when you're left without.

Now, speaking of the caprices of memory in general and of mine in particular, it's strange to think of all the tricks this little mental process plays on us. Here we're endowed with a faculty of mind that ought to be more supremely serviceable to us than them all. And what happens? This memory of ours stores up a perfect record of the most useless facts and anecdotes and experiences. And all the things that we ought to know, that we need to know, that we'd profit by knowing, it casts aside with the careless indifference of a girl refusing her true lover. It's terrible to think of this phenomenon. I tremble in all my members when I consider all the really valuable things that I've forgotten in seventy years—when I meditate upon the caprices of my memory.

There's a bird out in California that is one perfect symbol of the human memory. I've forgotten the bird's name (just because it would be valuable for me to know it—to recall it to your own minds, perhaps). But this fool of a creature goes around collecting the most ridiculous things you can imagine and storing them up. He never selects a thing that could ever prove of the slightest help to him, but he goes about gathering iron forks and spoons and tin cans and broken mouse traps—all sorts of rubbish that is difficult for him to carry and yet be any use when he gets it. Why, that bird will go by a gold watch to bring back one of those patent cake pans.

Now, my mind is just like that, and my mind isn't very different from yours, and so our minds are just like that bird. We pass by what would be of inestimable value to us, and pack our memories with the most trivial odds and ends that never by any chance, under any circumstances whatsoever, could be of the slightest use to anyone. Now, things that I have remembered are constantly popping into my head. And I am repeatedly startled by the vividness with which they recur to me after the lapse of years and their utter uselessness in being remembered at all.

I was thinking over some on my way up here. They were the illustrations I spoke about to the young lady on the way up. And I've come to the conclusion, curious though it is, that I can use every one of these freaks of memory to teach you all a lesson. I'm convinced that each one has its moral. And I think it's my duty to hand the moral on to you.

Now, I recall that when I was a boy I was a good boy—I was a very good boy. Why, I was the best boy in my school. I was the best boy in that little Mississippi town where I lived. The population was only about twenty million. You may not believe it, but I was the best boy in that State—and in the United States, for that matter.

But I don't know why I never heard anyone say that but myself. I always recognized it. But even those nearest and dearest to me couldn't seem to see it. My mother, especially, seemed to think there was something wrong with that estimate. And she never got over that prejudice.

Now, when my mother got to be eighty-five years old her memory failed her. She forgot little threads that hold life's patches of meaning together. She was living out West then, and I went to visit her. I hadn't seen my mother in a year or so. And when I got there she knew my face, knew I was married, knew I had a family and that I was living with them. But she couldn't, for the life of her, tell my name or who I was. So I told her I was her boy.

"But you don't live with me," she said.

"No," said I, "I'm living in Hartford."

"What are you doing there?"

"Going to school."

"Large school?"

"Very large."

"All boys?"

"All boys."

"And how do you stand?" said my mother.

"I'm the best boy in that school," I answered.

"Well," said my mother, with a return of her old fire, "I'd like to know what the other boys are like."

Now, one point in this story is the fact that my mother's mind went back to my school days, and remembered my little youthful self-prejudice when she'd forgotten everything else about me.

The other point is the moral. There's one there that you will find if you search for it.

Now, here's something else I remember. It's about the first time I ever stole a watermelon. "Stole" is a strong word. Stole? Stole? No, I don't mean that. It was the first time I ever withdrew a watermelon. It was the first time I ever extracted a watermelon. That is exactly the word I want—"extracted." It is definite. It is precise. It perfectly conveys my idea. Its use in dentistry connotes the delicate shade of meaning I am looking for. You know we never extract our own teeth.

And it was not my watermelon that I extracted. I extracted that watermelon from a farmer's wagon while he was inside negotiating with another customer. I carried that watermelon to one of the secluded recesses of the lumberyard and there I broke it open. It was a green watermelon.

Well, do you know when I saw that I began to feel sorry—sorry—sorry. It seemed to me that I had done wrong. I reflected deeply. I reflected that I was young. I think I was just eleven. But I knew that though immature I did not lack moral advancement. I knew what a boy ought to do who had extracted a watermelon—like that. I considered George Washington and what action he would have taken under similar circumstances. Then I knew there was just one thing to make me feel right inside, and that was: restitution.

So I said to myself, "I will do that. I will take that green watermelon back where I got it from."

And the minute I had said it I felt that great moral uplift that comes to you when you've made a noble resolution.

So I gathered up the biggest fragments and I carried them back to the farmer's wagon and I restored the watermelon—what was left of it. And I made him give me a good one in place of it, too. And I told him he ought to be ashamed of himself going around working off his worthless old green watermelons on trusting purchasers who had to rely on him. How could they tell from the outside whether the melons were good or not? That was his business. And if he didn't reform, I told him I'd see that he didn't get any more of my trade—nor anybody else's I knew, if I could help it.

You know that man was as contrite as a revivalist's last convert. He said he was all broken up to think I'd gotten a green watermelon. He promised me he would never carry another green watermelon if he starved for it. And he drove off—a better man.

Now, do you see what I did for that man? He was on a downward path and I rescued him. But all I got out of it was a watermelon.

Yet I'd rather have that memory, just that memory of the good I did for that depraved farmer, than all the material gain you can think of. Look at the lesson he got. I never got anything like that from it. But I ought to be satisfied. I was only eleven years old but I secured everlasting benefit to other people.

The moral in this is perfectly clear, and I think there's one in the next memory I'm going to tell you about.

To go back to my childhood, there's another little incident that comes to me. It's about one of the times I went fishing. You see, in our house there was a sort of family prejudice against going fishing if you hadn't permission. But it would frequently be bad judgment to ask. So I went fishing secretly, as it were—way up the Mississippi. It was an exquisitely happy trip, I recall, with a very pleasant sensation.

Well, while I was away there was a tragedy in our town. A stranger stopping over on his way East from California was stabbed to death in an unseemly brawl. Now, my father was justice of the peace, and because he was justice of the peace he was coroner, and since he was coroner he was also constable, and being constable he was sheriff, and out of consideration for his holding the office of sheriff he was likewise county clerk and a dozen other officials I don't think of just this minute.

I thought he had power of life or death, only he didn't use it over other boys. He was sort of an austere man. Somehow I didn't like being round him when I'd done anything he disapproved of. So that's the reason I wasn't often around.

Well, when this gentleman got knifed they communicated with the proper authority, the coroner, and they laid the corpse out in the coroner's office, our front sitting room, in preparation for the inquest the next morning. About 9 or 10 o'clock I got back from fishing. It was a little too late for me to be received by my folks, so I took my shoes off and slipped noiselessly up the back way to the sitting room. I was very tired and I didn't wish to disturb my people. So I groped my way to the sofa and lay down.

Now, I didn't know anything of what had happened during my absence. But I was sort of nervous on my own account, afraid of being caught, and rather dubious about the morning affair. And I had been lying there a few moments when my eyes gradually got used to the darkness and I became aware of something on the other side of the room. It was something foreign to the apartment. It had an uncanny appearance. And I sat up looking very hard, and wondering what in heaven this long, formless, vicious-looking thing might be.

First I thought I'd go and see. Then I thought, "Never mind that."

Mind you, I had no cowardly sensations whatever but it didn't seem exactly prudent to investigate. But I somehow couldn't keep my eyes off the thing. And the more I looked at it the more disagreeably it grew on me. But I was resolved to play the man. So I decided to turn over and count a hundred and let the patch of moonlight creep up and show me what the dickens it was.

Well, I turned over and tried to count but I couldn't keep my mind on it. I kept thinking of that gruesome mass. I was losing count all the time and going back and beginning over again. Oh no, I wasn't frightened, just annoyed. But by the time I'd gotten to the century mark I turned cautiously over and opened my eyes with great fortitude.

The moonlight revealed to me a marble-white human hand. Well, maybe I wasn't embarrassed! But then that changed to a creepy feeling again and I thought I'd try the counting again. I don't know how many hours or weeks it was that I lay there counting hard. But the moonlight crept up that white arm and it showed me a lead face and a terrible wound over the heart.

I could scarcely say that I was terror-stricken or anything like that. But somehow his eyes interested me so that I went right out of the window. I didn't need the sash. But it seemed easier to take it than leave it behind.

Now, let that teach you a lesson—I don't know just what it is. But at seventy years old I find that memory of peculiar value to me. I have been unconsciously guided by it all these years. Things that seemed pigeon-holed and remote are a perpetual influence. Yes, you're taught in so many ways. And you're so felicitously taught when you don't know it.

Here's something else that taught me a good deal. When I was seventeen I was very bashful, and a sixteen-year-old girl came to stay a week with us. She was a peach and I was seized with a happiness not of this world.

One evening my mother suggested that to entertain her I take her to the theater. I didn't really like to, because I was seventeen and sensitive about appearing in the streets with a girl. I couldn't see my way to enjoying my delight in public. But we went.

I didn't feel very happy. I couldn't seem to keep my mind on the play. I became conscious after a while that that was due less to my lovely company than my boots. They were sweet to look upon, as smooth as skin, but fitted ten times as close. I got oblivious to the play and the girl and the other people and everything but my boots until I hitched one partly off. The sensation was sensuously perfect. I couldn't help it. I had to get the other off, partly. Then I was obliged to get them off altogether, except that I kept my feet in the legs so they couldn't get away.

From that time I enjoyed the play. But the first thing I knew the curtain came down, like that, without my notice, and I hadn't any boots on. What's more, they wouldn't go on. I tugged strenuously. And the people in our row got up and fussed and said things until the peach and I simply had to move on.

We moved—the girl on one arm and the boots under the other. We walked home that way, sixteen blocks, with a retinue a mile long. Every time we passed a lamp post death gripped me at the throat. But we got home—and I had on white socks. If I live to be nine hundred and ninety-nine years old I don't suppose I could ever forget that walk. I remember it about as keenly as the chagrin I suffered on another occasion.

At one time in our domestic history we had a colored butler who had a failing. He could never remember to ask people who came to the door to state their business. So I used to suffer a good many calls unnecessarily. One morning when I was especially busy he brought me a card engraved with a name I did not know.

So I said, "What does he wish to see me for?" and Sylvester said, "Ah couldn't ask him, sah. He wuz a genlmun."

"Return instantly," I thundered, "and inquire his mission. Ask him what's his game."

Well, Sylvester returned with the announcement that he had lightning rods to sell.

"Indeed," said I, "things are coming to a fine pass when lightning rod agents send up engraved cards."

"He has pictures," added Sylvester.

"Pictures, indeed! He may be peddling etchings. Has he a Russia leather case?"

But Sylvester was too frightened to remember.

I said, "I am going down to make it hot for that upstart!"

I went down the stairs, working up my temper all the way. When I got to the parlor I was in a fine frenzy concealed beneath a veneer of frigid courtesy. And when I looked in the door, sure enough he had a Russia leather case in his hand. But I didn't happen to notice that it was our Russia leather case.

And if you'd believe me, that man was sitting with a whole gallery of etchings spread out before him. But I didn't happen to notice that they were our etchings, spread out by some member of my family for some unguessed purpose.

Very curtly I asked the gentleman his business. With a surprised, timid manner he faltered that he had met my wife and daughter at Onteora, and they had asked him to call. Fine lie, I thought, and I froze him.

He seemed to be kind of nonplussed, and sat there fingering the etchings in the case until I told him he needn't bother, because we had those. That pleased him so much that he leaned over, in an embarrassed way, to pick up another from the floor. But I stopped him.

I said, "We've got that, too."

He seemed pitifully amazed, but I was congratulating myself on my great success.

Finally the gentleman asked where Mr. Winton lived. He'd met him in the mountains too. So I said I'd show him gladly. And I did on the spot. And when he was gone I felt queer, because there were all his etchings spread out on the floor.

Well, my wife came in and asked me who had been in. I showed her the card and told her all exultantly. To my dismay she nearly fainted. She told me he had been a most kind friend to them in the country, and had forgotten to tell me that he was expected our way. And she pushed me out of the door and commanded me to get over to the Wintons in a hurry and get him back.

I came into the drawing room, where Mrs. Winton was sitting up very stiff in a chair, beating me at my own game. Well, I began to put another light on things. Before many seconds Mrs. Winton saw it was time to change her temperature. In five minutes I had asked the man to luncheon, and she to dinner, and so on.

We made that fellow change his trip and stay a week and we gave him the time of his life. Why, I don't believe we let him get sober the whole time.

I trust that you will carry away some good thought from these lessons I have given you, and that the memory of them will inspire you to higher things and elevate you to plans far above the old— and—and—

And I tell you one thing, young ladies: I've had a better time with you today than with that peach fifty-three years ago.

March 1906

⚬ 65 ⚬

The same month as his appearance at Barnard, March 1906, Clemens attended a dinner of the Freundschaft Society in New York. Edward Marshall Grout was an American attorney and a New York City official. Charles Putzel was a tax commissioner and the society's former president. David Leventritt was an American attorney and a justice of the New York Supreme Court. When the toastmaster introduced Clemens he referred to the maxim in *Pudd'nhead Wilson*, "When in doubt, tell the truth."

NEW YORK MORALS

That maxim I did invent but never expected it to be applied to me. I did say, "When you are in doubt." But when I am in doubt myself I use more sagacity.

Mr. Grout suggested that if I have anything to say against Mr. Putzel or any criticism of his career or his character I am the last person to come out on account of that maxim and tell the truth. That is altogether a mistake. I do think it is right for other people to be virtuous so that they can be happy hereafter. But if I knew every impropriety that even Mr. Putzel has committed in his life I would not mention one of them. My judgment has been maturing for seventy years and I have got to that point where I know better than that.

Mr. Putzel stands related to me in a very tender way (through the tax office), and it does not behoove me to say anything which could by any possibility militate against that condition of things. Now, that word—taxes, taxes, taxes! I have heard it tonight. I have heard it all night. I wish somebody would change that subject. That is a very sore subject to me.

I was so relieved when Judge Leventritt did find something that was not taxable—when he said that the commissioner could not tax your patience. And that comforted me. We've got so much taxation. I don't know of a single foreign product that enters this country untaxed except the answer to prayer.

On an occasion like this the proprieties require that you merely pay compliments to the guest of the occasion. And I am merely here to pay compliments to the guest of the occasion, not to criticize him in any way, and I can say only complimentary things to him.

When I went down to the tax office some time ago, for the first time in New York, I saw Mr. Putzel sitting in the "Seat of Perjury." I recognized him right away. I warmed to him on the spot. I didn't know that I had ever seen him before, but just as soon as I saw him I recognized him. I had met him twenty-five years before and at that time had achieved a knowledge of his abilities and something more than that.

I thought, "Now, this is the man whom I saw twenty-five years ago."

On that occasion I not only went free at his hands but carried off something more than that. I hoped it would happen again.

It was twenty-five years ago when I saw a young clerk in Putnam's book store. I went in there and asked for George Haven Putnam and handed him my card, and then the young man said Mr. Putnam was busy and I couldn't see him. Well, I had merely called in a social way and so it didn't matter.

I was going out when I saw a great big, fat, interesting-looking book lying there, and I took it up. It was an account of the invasion of England in the fourteenth century by the Preaching Friar, and it interested me.

I asked him the price of it, and he said four dollars.

"Well," I said, "what discount do you allow to publishers?"

He said "Forty per cent off."

I said, "All right, I am a publisher."

He put down the figure, forty per cent off, on a card.

Then I said, "What discount do you allow to authors?"

He said, "Forty per cent off."

"Well," I said, "set me down as an author."

"Now," said I, "what discount do you allow to the clergy?"

He said, "Forty per cent off."

I said to him that I was only on the road, and that I was studying for the ministry. I asked him wouldn't he knock off twenty per cent for that. He set down the figure and he never smiled once.

I was working off these humorous brilliancies on him and getting no return, not a scintillation in his eye, not a spark of recognition of what I was doing there. I was almost in despair.

I thought I might try him once more, so I said, "Now, I am also a member of the human race. Will you let me have the ten per cent off for that?"

He set it down and never smiled.

Well, I gave it up. I said, "There is my card with my address on it. But I have not any money with me. Will you please send the bill to Hartford?"

I took up the book and was going away.

He said, "Wait a minute. There is forty cents coming to you."

When I met him in the tax office I thought maybe I could make something again. But I could not. But I had not any idea I could when I came, and as it turned out I did get off entirely free.

I put up my hand and made a statement. It gave me a good deal of pain to do that. I was not used to it. I was born and reared in the higher circles of Missouri, and there we don't do such things— didn't in my time. But we have got that little matter settled, got a sort of tax levied on me.

Then he touched me. Yes, he touched me this time. Because he cried—cried! He was moved to tears to see that I, a virtuous person only a year before, after immersion for one year—during one year in the New York morals—had no more conscience than a millionaire.

March 1906

~ 66 ~

Clemens gave still another address in March of 1906, this time at a public meeting of the New York State Association for Promoting the Interests of the Blind, held at the Waldorf-Astoria hotel in New York. Laurence Hutton was an American editor and author. Helen Keller and Anna M. Sullivan, her gifted and devoted teacher, of course need no introduction.

THE SOCK

If you detect any awkwardness in my movements and infelicities in my conduct I will offer the explanation that I never presided at a meeting of any kind before in my life, and that I do find it out of my line. I supposed I could do anything anybody else could. But I recognize that experience helps, and I do feel the lack of that experience. I don't feel as graceful and easy as I ought to be in order to impress an audience. I shall not pretend that I know how to umpire a meeting like this, and I shall just take the humble place of the Essex band.

There was a great gathering in a small New England town about twenty-five years ago. I remember that circumstance because there was something that happened at that time. It was a great occasion. They gathered in the militia and orators and everybody from all the towns around. It was an extraordinary occasion.

The little local paper threw itself into ecstasies of admiration and tried to do itself proud from beginning to end. It praised the orators, the militia and all the bands that came from everywhere, and all this in honest country newspaper detail. But the writer ran out of adjectives toward the end. Having exhausted his whole magazine of praise and glorification, he found he still had one band left over. He had to say something about it, and he said, "The Essex band done the best it could." I am an Essex band on this occasion, and I am going to get through as well as inexperience and good intentions will enable me.

I have got all the documents here necessary to instruct you in the objects and intentions of this meeting and also of the association which has called the meeting. But they are too voluminous. I could not pack those statistics into my head and I had to give it up. I shall have to just reduce all that mass of statistics to a few salient facts. There are too many statistics and figures for me. I never could do anything with figures, never had any talent for mathematics, never accomplished anything in my efforts at that rugged study, and today the only mathematics I know is multiplication, and the minute I get away up in that, as soon as I reach nine times seven—

[Mark Twain lapsed into deep thought for a moment. He was trying to figure out nine times seven but it was a hopeless task, and he turned to St. Clair McKelway, who sat near him. McKelway whispered the answer and the speaker resumed.]

I've got it now. It's eighty-four. Well, I can get that far all right with a little hesitation. After that I am uncertain and I can't manage a statistic.

This association for the—

[Mark Twain was in another dilemma. Again he was obliged to turn to McKelway.]

Oh yes, for promoting the interests of the blind. It's a long name. If I could I would write it out for you and let you take it home and study it. But I don't know how to spell it. And Mr. Carnegie is down in Virginia somewhere. Well, anyway the object of that association which has been recently organized—five months ago, in fact—is in the hands of very, very energetic, intelligent and capable people, and they will push it to success very surely, and all the more surely if you will give them a little of your assistance out of your pockets.

The intention, the purpose, is to search out all the blind and find work for them to do so that they may earn their own bread. Now it is dismal enough to be blind. It is a dreary, dreary life at best but it can be largely ameliorated by finding something for these poor blind people to do with their hands. The time passes so heavily that it is never day or night with them, it is always night, and when they have to sit with folded hands and with nothing to do to amuse or entertain or employ their minds it is drearier and drearier.

And then the knowledge they have that they must subsist on charity, and so often reluctant charity. It would renew their lives if they could have something to do with their hands and pass their time and at the same time earn their bread and know the sweetness of the bread which is the result of the labor of one's own hands. They need that cheer and pleasure. It is the only way you can turn their night into day, to give them happy hearts, the only thing you can put in the place of the blessed sun. That you can do in the way I speak of.

Blind people generally who have seen the light know what it is to miss the light. Those who have gone blind since they were twenty years old—their lives are unendingly dreary. But they can be taught to use their hands and to employ themselves at a great many industries. That association from which this draws its birth in Cambridge, Massachusetts has taught its blind to make many things. They make them better than most people, and more honest than people who have the use of their eyes. The goods they make are readily salable. People like them. And so they are supporting themselves, and it is a matter of cheer, cheer. They pass their time now not so irksomely as they formerly did.

What this association needs and wants is $15,000. The figures are set down, and what the money is for, and there is no graft in it or I would not be here. And they hope to beguile that out of your pockets, and you will find affixed to the program an opportunity, that little blank which you will fill out and promise so much money now or tomorrow or some time. Then there is another opportunity which is still better, and that is that you shall subscribe an annual sum.

I have invented a good many useful things in my time but never anything better than that of getting money out of people who don't want to part with it. It is always for good objects, of course. This is the plan. When you call upon a person to contribute to a great and good object, and you think he should furnish about $1000, he disappoints you as like as not. Much the best way to work him to supply that thousand dollars is to split it into parts and contribute, say a hundred dollars a year, or fifty, or whatever the sum may be. Let him contribute ten or twenty a year. He doesn't feel that, but he does feel it when you call upon him to contribute a large amount. When you get used to it you would rather contribute than borrow money.

I tried it in Helen Keller's case. Mr. Hutton wrote me in 1896 or 1897 when I was in London and said, "The gentleman who has been so liberal in taking care of Helen Keller has died without making provision for her in his will, and now they don't know what to do."

They were proposing to raise a fund, and he thought $50,000 enough to furnish an income of $2400 or $2500 a year for the support of that wonderful girl and her wonderful teacher, Miss Sullivan, now Mrs. Macy.

I wrote to Mr. Hutton and said: "Go on, get up your fund. It will be slow, but if you want quick work I propose this system," the system I speak of, of asking people to contribute such and such a sum from year to year and drop out whenever they please, and he would find there wouldn't be any difficulty, people wouldn't feel the burden of it.

And he wrote back saying he had raised the $2400 a year indefinitely by that system in a single afternoon.

We would like to do something just like that tonight. We will take as many checks as you care to give. You can leave your donations in the big room outside.

I knew once what it was to be blind. I shall never forget that experience. I have been as blind as anybody ever was for three or four hours, and the sufferings that I endured and the mishaps and the accidents that are burning in my memory make my sympathy rise when I feel for the blind and always shall feel.

I once went to Heidelberg on an excursion. I took a clergyman along with me, the Rev. Joseph Twichell of Hartford, who is still among the living despite that fact. I always travel with clergymen when I can. It is better for them, it is better for me. And any preacher who goes out with me in stormy weather and without a lightning rod is a good one. The Reverend Twichell is one of those people filled with patience and endurance, two good ingredients for a man travelling with me, so we got along very well together. In that old town they have not altered a house nor built one in 1500 years. We went to the inn and they placed Twichell and me in a most colossal bedroom, the largest I ever saw or heard of. It was as big as this room.

I didn't take much notice of the place. I didn't really get my bearings. I noticed Twichell got a German bed about two feet wide, the kind in which you've got to lie on your edge, because there isn't room to lie on your back, and he was way down south in that big room, and I was way up north at the other end of it, with a regular Sahara in between.

We went to bed. Twichell went to sleep. But then he had his conscience loaded and it was easy for him to get to sleep. I couldn't get to sleep. It was one of those torturing kinds of lovely summer nights when you hear various kinds of noises now and then. A mouse away off in the southwest. You throw things at the mouse. That encourages the mouse. But I couldn't stand it, and about two o'clock I got up and thought I would give it up and go out in the square where there was one of those tinkling fountains, and sit on its brink and dream, full of romance.

I got out of bed, and I ought to have lit a candle, but I didn't think of it until it was too late. It was the darkest place that ever was. There has never been darkness any thicker than that. It just lay in cakes.

I thought that before dressing I would accumulate my clothes. I pawed around in the dark and found everything packed together on the floor except one sock. I couldn't get on the track of that sock. It might have occurred to me that maybe it was in the wash. But I didn't think of that. I went excursioning on my hands and knees. Presently I thought, "I am never going to find it. I'll go back to bed again." That is what I tried to do during the next three hours. I had lost the bearings of that bed. I was going in the wrong direction all the time. By and by I came in collision with a chair and that encouraged me.

It seemed to me, as far as I could recollect, there was only a chair here and there and yonder, five or six of them scattered over this territory, and I thought maybe after I found that chair I might find the next one. Well, I did. And I found another and another and another. I kept going around on my hands and knees, having those sudden collisions, and finally when I banged into another chair I almost lost my temper. And I raised up, garbed as I was, not for public exhibition, right in front of a mirror fifteen or sixteen feet high.

I hadn't noticed the mirror. Didn't know it was there. And when I saw myself in the mirror I was frightened out of my wits. I don't allow any ghosts to bite me. And I took up a chair and smashed at it. A million pieces. Then I reflected. That's the way I always do. And it's unprofitable unless a man has had much experience that way and has clear judgment. And I had judgment. And I would have had to pay for that mirror if I hadn't recollected to say it was Twichell who broke it.

Then I got down on my hands and knees and went on another exploring expedition. As far as I could remember there were six chairs in that Oklahoma and one table, a great big heavy table, not a good table to hit with your head when rushing madly along. In the course of time I collided with thirty-five chairs and tables enough to stock that dining room out there. It was a hospital for decayed furniture, and it was in a worse condition when I got through with it.

I went on and on and at last got to a place where I could feel my way up. And there was a shelf. I knew that wasn't in the middle of the room. Up to that time I was afraid I had gotten out of the city. I was very careful and pawed along that shelf. And there was a pitcher of water about a foot high, and it was at the head of Twichell's bed but I didn't know it. I felt that pitcher going and I grabbed at it but it didn't help any and came right down in Twichell's face and nearly drowned him. But it woke him up.

I was grateful to have company on any terms. He lit a match and there I was, way down south when I ought to have been back up yonder. My bed was out of sight it was so far away. You needed a telescope to find it. Twichell comforted me and I scrubbed him off and we got sociable.

But that night wasn't wasted. I had my pedometer on my leg. Twichell and I were in a pedometer match. Twichell had longer legs than I. The only way I could keep up was to wear my pedometer to bed. I always walk in my sleep, and on this occasion I gained sixteen miles on him.

After all, I never found that sock, I never have seen it from that day to this. But that adventure taught me what it is to be blind. That was one of the most serious occasions of my whole life, yet I never can speak of it without somebody thinking it isn't serious. You try it and see how serious it is to be as the blind are. And as I was that night.

March 1906

67

In April of 1906 Clemens attended a benefit meeting in Carnegie Hall, New York, which was held to raise funds for the Robert Fulton Monument Association. Clemens, when offered a fee of $1000 to address the association, had refused it, saying, "I shall be glad to do it but I must stipulate that you keep the $1000 and add it to the memorial fund as my contribution to erect a monument in New York to the memory of the man who applied steam to navigation." General Frederick D. Grant, Ulysses Grant's son, presided at the meeting.

A WANDERING ADDRESS

I wish to deliver a historical address. I've been studying the history of—er—a—let me see—a [Then he stopped in confusion and walked over to Gen. Fred D. Grant, who sat at the head of the platform. He leaned over in a whisper and then returned to the front of the stage and continued.]

Oh yes! I've been studying Robert Fulton. I've been studying a biographical sketch of Robert Fulton, the inventor of—er—a—let's see—oh yes, the inventor of the electric telegraph and the Morse sewing machine. Also, I understand he invented the air—diria—pshaw! I have it at last—the dirigible balloon. Yes, the dirigible—but it is a difficult word, and I don't see why anybody should marry a couple of words like that when they don't want to be married at all and are likely to quarrel with each other all the time. I should put that couple of words under the ban of the United States Supreme Court, under its decision of a few days ago, and take 'em out and drown 'em.

I used to know Fulton. It used to do me good to see him dashing through the town on a wild broncho. And Fulton was born in—er—a—well, it doesn't make much difference where he was born, does it? I remember a man who came to interview me once, to get a sketch of my life. I consulted with a friend, a practical man, before he came, to know how I should treat him.

"Whenever you give the interviewer a fact," he said, "give him another fact that will contradict it. Then he'll go away with a jumble that he can't use at all. Be gentle, be sweet, smile like an idiot—just be natural."

That's what my friend told me to do and I did it.

"Where were you born?" asked the interviewer.

"Well—er—a," I began, "I was born in Alabama, or Alaska, or the Sandwich Islands. I don't know where, but right around there somewhere. And you had better put it down before you forget it."

"But you weren't born in all those places," he said.

"Well, I've offered you three places. Take your choice. They're all at the same price."

"How old are you?" he asked.

"I shall be nineteen in June," I said.

"Why, there's such a discrepancy between your age and your looks," he said.

"Oh, that's nothing," I said, "I was born discrepantly."

Then we got to talking about my brother Samuel and he told me my explanations were confusing.

"I suppose he is dead," I said. "Some said that he was dead and some said that he wasn't."

"Did you bury him without knowing whether he was dead or not?" asked the reporter.

"There was a mystery," said I. "We were twins, and one day when we were two weeks old—that is, he was one week old and I was one week old—we got mixed up in the bathtub, and one of us drowned. We never could tell which. One of us had a strawberry birthmark on the back of his hand. There it is on my hand. This is the one that was drowned. There's no doubt about it."

"Where's the mystery?" he said.

"Why, don't you see how stupid it was to bury the wrong twin?" I answered.

I didn't explain it any more because he said the explanation confused him. To me it is perfectly plain.

But to get back to Fulton. I'm going along like an old man I used to know who used to start to tell a story about his grandfather. He had an awfully retentive memory and he never finished the story, because he switched off into something else. He used to tell about how his grandfather one day went into a pasture, where there was a ram. The old man dropped a silver dime in the grass and stooped over to pick it up. The ram was observing him and took the old man's action as an invitation.

Just as he was going to finish about the ram this friend of mine would recall that his grandfather had a niece who had a glass eye. She used to loan that glass eye to another lady friend, who used it when she received company. The eye didn't fit the friend's face, and it was loose. And whenever she winked it would turn over.

Then he got on the subject of accidents, and he would tell a story about how he believed accidents never happened.

"There was an Irishman coming down a ladder with a hod of bricks," he said, "and a Dutchman was standing on the ground below. The Irishman fell on the Dutchman and killed him. Accident? Never! If the Dutchman hadn't been there the Irishman would have been killed. Why didn't the Irishman fall on a dog which was next to the Dutchman? Because the dog would have seen him coming."

Then he'd get off from the Dutchman to an uncle named Reginald Wilson. Reginald went into a carpet factory one day and got twisted into the machinery's belt. He went excursioning around the factory until he was properly distributed and was woven into sixty-nine yards of the best three-ply carpet. His wife bought the carpet, and then she erected a monument to his memory. It read:

Sacred to the memory
of
sixty-nine yards of the best three-ply carpet
containing the mortal remainders of

REGINALD WILSON

Go thou and do likewise

And so on he would ramble about telling the story of his grandfather until we never were told whether he found the ten-cent piece or whether something else happened.

April 1906

✧ **68** ✧

In September of 1906 Clemens spoke at a dinner of the Associated Press, held at the Waldorf-Astoria hotel in New York. The illiterate letter turned out to be a literary production, and Clemens urged its author, Grace Donworth, to write a book of such letters, which she did, calling it *The Letters of Jennie Allen to Her Friend, Miss Musgrove.*

SIMPLIFIED SPELLING

I am here to make an appeal to the nations in behalf of the simplified spelling. I have come here because they cannot all be reached except through you. There are only two forces that can carry light to all the corners of the globe—only two—the sun in the heavens and the Associated Press down here.

I may seem to be flattering the sun but I do not mean it so. I am meaning only to be just and fair all around. You speak with a million voices. No one can reach so many races, so many hearts and intellects, as you—except Rudyard Kipling, and he cannot do it without your help. If the Associated Press will adopt and use our simplified forms and thus spread them to the ends of the earth, covering the whole spacious planet with them as with a garden of flowers, our difficulties are at an end.

Every day of the three hundred and sixty-five the only pages of the world's countless newspapers that are read by all the human beings and angels and devils that can read are these pages that are built out of Associated Press despatches. And so I beg you, I beseech you—oh, I implore you to spell them in our simplified forms. Do this daily, constantly, persistently, for three months—only three months—it is all I ask. The infallible result?—victory, victory all down the line. For by that time all eyes here and above and below will have become adjusted to the change and in love with it, and the present clumsy and ragged forms will be grotesque to the eye and revolting to the soul. And we shall be rid of phthisis and phthisic and pneumonia and pneumatics and diphtheria and pterodactyl, and all those other insane words which no man addicted to the simple Christian life can try to spell and not lose some of the bloom of his piety in the demoralizing attempt.

Do not doubt it. We are chameleons, and our partialities and prejudices change places with an easy and blessed facility, and we are soon wonted to the change and happy in it. We do not regret our old, yellow fangs and snags and tushes after we have worn nice, fresh, uniform store teeth a while.

Do I seem to be seeking the good of the world? That is the idea. It is my public attitude. Privately I am merely seeking my own profit. We all do it but it is sound and it is virtuous, for no public interest is anything other or nobler than a massed accumulation of private interests. In 1883, when the simplified-spelling movement first tried to make a noise, I was indifferent to it. More: I even irreverently scoffed at it. What I needed was an object lesson, you see. It is the only way to teach some people.

Very well, I got it. At that time I was scrambling along, earning the family's bread on magazine work at seven cents a word, compound words at single rates, just as it is in the dark present. I was the property of a magazine, a seven-cent slave under a boiler-iron contract.

One day there came a note from the editor requiring me to write ten pages on this revolting text: "Considerations concerning the alleged subterranean holophotal extemporaneousness of the conchyliaceous superimbrication of the Ornithorhyncus, as foreshadowed by the unintelligibility of its plesiosaurian anisodactylous aspects."

Ten pages of that. Each and every word a seventeen-jointed vestibuled railroad train. Seven cents a word. I saw starvation staring the family in the face. I went to the editor, and I took a stenographer along so as to have the interview down in black and white, for no magazine editor can ever remember any part of a business talk except the part that's got graft in it for him and the magazine.

I said, "Read that text, Jackson, and let it go on the record. Read it out loud."

He read it: "Considerations concerning the alleged subterranean holophotal extemporaneousness of the conchyliaceous superimbrication of the Ornithorhyncus, as foreshadowed by the unintelligibility of its plesiosaurian anisodactylous aspects."

I said, "You want ten pages of those rumbling, great, long, summer thunderpeals, and you expect to get them at seven cents a peal?"

He said, "A word's a word, and seven cents is the contract. What are you going to do about it?"

I said, "Jackson, this is cold-blooded oppression. What's an average English word?"

He said, "Six letters."

I said, "Nothing of the kind. That's French, and includes the spaces between the words. An average English word is four letters and a half. By hard, honest labor I've dug all the large words out of my vocabulary and shaved it down till the average is three letters and a half. I can put one thousand and two hundred words on your page, and there's not another man alive that can come within two hundred of it. My page is worth eighty-four dollars to me. It takes exactly as long to fill your magazine page with long words as it does with short ones—four hours. Now, then, look at the criminal injustice of this requirement of yours. I am careful, I am economical of my time and labor. For the family's sake I've got to be so. So I never write 'metropolis' for seven cents, because I can get the same money for 'city.' I never write 'policeman,' because I can get the same price for 'cop.' And so on and so on. I never write 'valetudinarian' at all, for not even hunger and wretchedness can humble me to the point where I will do a word like that for seven cents. I wouldn't do it for fifteen. Examine your obscene text, please. Count the words."

He counted and said it was twenty-four. I asked him to count the letters. He made it two hundred and three.

I said, "Now, I hope you see the whole size of your crime. With my vocabulary I would make sixty words out of those two hundred and five letters, and get four dollars and twenty cents for it. Whereas for your inhuman twenty-four I would get only one dollar and sixty-eight cents. Ten pages of these skyscrapers of yours would pay me only about three hundred dollars. In my simplified vocabulary the same space and the same labor would would pay me eight hundred and forty dollars. I do not wish to work upon this scandalous job by the piece. I want to be hired by the year."

He coldly refused.

I said, "Then for the sake of the family, if you have no feeling for me, you ought at least to allow me overtime on that word extemporaneousness."

Again he coldly refused.

I seldom say a harsh word to anyone but I was not master of myself then and I spoke right out and called him an anisodactylous plesiosaurian conchyliaceous Ornithorhyncus, and rotten to the heart with holophotal subterranean extemporaneousness. God forgive me for that wanton crime. He lived only two hours.

From that day to this I have been a devoted and hard-working member of the heaven-born institution, the International Association for the Prevention of Cruelty to Authors, and now I am laboring with Carnegie's Simplified Committee, and with my heart in the work.

Now then, let us look at this mighty question reasonably, rationally, sanely—yes, and calmly, not excitedly. What is the real function, the essential function, the supreme function, of language? Isn't it merely to convey ideas and emotions? Certainly. Then if we can do it with words of fonetic brevity and compactness, why keep the present cumbersome forms? But can we? Yes. I hold in my hand the proof of it.

Here is a letter written by a woman, right out of her heart of hearts. I think she never saw a spelling book in her life. The spelling is her own. There isn't a wasted letter in it anywhere. It reduces the fonetics to the last gasp, it squeezes the surplusage out of every word, there's no spelling that can begin with it on this planet outside of the White House. And as for the punctuation, there isn't any. It is all one sentence, eagerly and breathlessly uttered, without break or pause in it anywhere. The letter is absolutely genuine—I have the proofs of that in my possession. I can't stop to spell the words for you but you can take the letter presently and comfort your eyes with it. I will read the letter.

"Miss____dear freind I took some Close into the armerry and

give them to you to Send too the suffrers out to California and i
Hate to truble you but i got to have one of them Back it was a black
oll wolle Shevyott With a jacket to Mach trimed Kind of Fancy no
38 Burst measure and passy menterry acrost the front And the color
i woodent Trubble you but it belonged to my brothers wife and she
is Mad about it i thoght she was willin but she want she says she
want done with it and she was going to Wear it a Spell longer
she ant so free harted as what i am and she Has got more to do with
Than i have having a Husband to Work and slave For her i gess you
remember Me I am shot and stout and light complected i torked
with you quite a spell about the suffrars and said it was orful about
that erth quake I shoodent wondar if they had another one rite off
seeine general Condision of the country is Kind of Explossive i hate
to take that Black dress away from the suffrars but i will hunt round
And see if i can get another One if i can i will call to the armerry for
it if you will jest lay it asside so no more at present from your True
freind
i liked your
appearance very Much"

Now you see what simplified spelling can do. It can convey any
fact you need to convey, and it can pour out emotions like a sewer. I
beg you, I beseech you, to adopt our spelling and print all your
despatches in it.

Now I wish to say just one entirely serious word. I have reached a
time of life, seventy years and a half, where none of the concerns of
this world have much interest for me personally. I think I can speak
dispassionately upon this matter because in the little while that I
have got to remain here I can get along very well with these old-
fashioned forms, and I don't propose to make any trouble about it at
all. I shall soon be where they won't care how I spell so long as I
keep the Sabbath.

There are eighty-two millions of us people that use this orthography, and it ought to be simplified in our behalf, but it is kept in its
present condition to satisfy one million people who like to have their
literature in the old form. That looks to me to be rather selfish, and
we keep the forms as they are while we have got one million people
coming in here from foreign countries every year and they have got
to struggle with this orthography of ours, and it keeps them back

and damages their citizenship for years until they learn to spell the language, if they ever do learn. This is merely sentimental argument.

People say it is the spelling of Chaucer and Spenser and Shakespeare and a lot of other people who do not know how to spell anyway, and it has been transmitted to us and we preserved it and wish to preserve it because of its ancient and hallowed associations.

Now, I don't see that there is any real argument about that. If that argument is good, then it would be a good argument not to banish the flies and the cockroaches from hospitals because they have been there so long that the patients have got used to them and they feel a tenderness for them on account of the associations. Why, it is like preserving a cancer in a family because it is a family cancer, and we are bound to it by the test of affection and reverence and old, mouldy antiquity. I think that this declaration to improve this orthography of ours is our family cancer, and I wish we could reconcile ourselves to have it cut out and let the family cancer go.

Now, you see before you the wreck and ruin of what was once a young person like yourselves. I am exhausted by the heat of the day. I must take what is left of this wreck and run out of your presence and carry it away to my home and spread it out there and sleep the sleep of the righteous. There is nothing much left of me but my age and my righteousness, but I leave with you my love and my blessing, and may you always keep your youth.

September 1906

✑ 69 ✑

That same month, September 1906, Clemens spoke at the American concert debut of his daughter Clara in Norfolk, Connecticut.

STAGE FRIGHT

My heart goes out in sumpathy to anyone who is making his first appearance before an audience of human beings. By a direct process of memory I go back forty years, less one month—for I'm older than I look.

I recall the occasion of my first appearance. San Francisco knew me then only as a reporter, and I was to make my bow to San Francisco as a lecturer. I knew that nothing short of compulsion would get me to the theater. So I bound myself by a hard-and-fast contract so that I could not escape. I got to the theater forty-five minutes before the hour set for the lecture. My knees were shaking so that I didn't know whether I could stand up.

If there is an awful, horrible malady in the world it is stage fright—and seasickness. They are a pair. I had stage fright then for the first and last time. I was only seasick once, too. It was on a little ship on which there were two hundred other passengers. I—was—sick. I was so sick that there wasn't any left for those other two hundred passengers.

It was dark and lonely behind the scenes in that theater, and I peeked through the little peek holes they have in theater curtains and looked into the big auditorium. That was dark and empty too. By and by it lighted up and the audience began to arrive.

I had got a number of friends of mine, stalwart men, to sprinkle themselves through the audience armed with big clubs. Every time I said anything they could possibly guess I intended to be funny they were to pound those clubs on the floor. Then there was a kind lady in a box up there, also a good friend of mine, the wife of the Governor. She was to watch me intently, and whenever I glanced toward her she was going to deliver a gubernatorial laugh that would lead the whole audience into applause.

At last I began. I had the manuscript tucked under a United States flag in front of me where I could get at it in case of need. But I managed to get started without it. I walked up and down—I was young in those days and needed the exercise—and talked and talked.

Right in the middle of the speech I had placed a gem. I had put in a moving, pathetic part which was to get at the hearts and souls of my hearers. When I delivered it they did just what I hoped and expected. They sat silent and awed. I had touched them. Then I happened to glance up at the box where the Governor's wife was— you know what happened.

Well, after the first agonizing five minutes my stage fright left me, never to return. I know if I was going to be hanged I could get up and make a good showing, and I intend to. But I shall never forget my feelings before the agony left me, and I got up here to thank you for her for helping my daughter, by your kindness, to live through her first appearance. And I want to thank you for your appreciation of her singing, which is, by the way, hereditary.

September 1906

✑ 70 ✑

In December of 1906 Clemens was in Washington, D.C., to attend a hearing of the Congressional Committee on Patents, which was considering a proposed new copyright bill. Earlier in the day Clemens had sent Speaker Cannon of the House the following letter.

"Dear Uncle Joseph,

"Please get me the thanks of Congress, not next week but right away. It is very necessary. Do accomplish this for your affectionate old friend right away—by persuasion if you can, by violence if you must, for it is imperatively necessary that I get on the floor of the House for two or three hours and talk to the members, man by man, in behalf of support, encouragement and protection of one of the nation's most valuable assets and industries—its literature. I have arguments with me—also a barrel with liquid in it.

"Give me a chance. Get me the thanks of Congress. Don't wait for others—there isn't time. Furnish them to me yourself and let Congress ratify later. I have stayed away and let Congress alone for seventy-one years and am entitled to the thanks. Congress knows this perfectly well, and I have long felt hurt that this quite proper and earned expression of gratitude has been merely felt by the House and never publicly uttered.

"Send me an order on the sergeant-at-arms quick. When shall I come?

"With love and a benediction, Mark Twain."

Clemens wasn't the only author present at the hearing. Edward Everett Hale, William Dean Howells, Thomas Nelson Page and others were also there. And Frank Millet spoke on behalf of painters, and John Philip Sousa for musicians. The proposed feature, which Clemens liked, of extending copyright for the author's life plus fifty years didn't become law until the Copyright Act of 1906 was revised seventy years later.

COPYRIGHT

I have read this bill. At least I have read such portions as I could understand. Nobody but a practiced legislator can read the bill and thoroughly understand it, and I am not a practiced legislator.

I am interested particularly and especially in the part of the bill which concerns my trade. I like that extension of copyright life to the author's life and fifty years afterward. I think that would satisfy any reasonable author, because it would take care of his children. Let the grandchildren take care of themselves. That would take care of my daughters, and after that I am not particular. I shall then have long been out of this struggle, independent of it, indifferent to it.

It isn't objectionable to me that all the trades and professions in the United States are protected by the bill. I like that. They are all important and worthy, and if we can take care of them under the copyright law I should like to see it done. I should like to see oyster culture added, and anything else.

I am aware that copyright must have a limit, because that is required by the Constitution of the United States, which sets aside the earlier Constitution, which we call the decalogue. The decalogue says you shall not take away from any man his profit. I don't like to be obliged to use the harsh term. What the decalogue really says is, "Thou shalt not steal," but I am trying to use more polite language. The laws of England and America do take it away, do select but one class, the people who create the literature of the land. They always talk handsomely about the literature of the land, always what a fine, great, monumental thing a great literature is. And in the midst of their enthusiasm they turn around and do what they can to discourage it.

I know we must have a limit. But forty-two years is too much of a limit. I am quite unable to guess why there should be a limit at all to the possession of the product of a man's labor. There is no limit to real estate. Doctor Hale has suggested that a man might just as well, after discovering a coal mine and working it forty-two years, have the Government step in and take it away.

What is the excuse? It is that the author who produced that book has had the profit of it long enough, and therefore the Government takes a profit which does not belong to it and generously gives it to the 88,000,000 of people. But it doesn't do anything of the kind. It merely takes the author's property, takes his children's bread, and gives the publisher double profit. He goes on publishing the book and as many of his confederates as choose to go into the conspiracy do so. And they rear families in affluence. And they continue the enjoyment of those ill-gotten gains generation after generation forever, for they never die.

In a few weeks or months or years I shall be out of it, I hope under a monument. I hope I shall not be entirely forgotten, and I shall subscribe to the monument myself. But I shall not be caring what happens if there are fifty years left of my copyright. My copyright produces annually a good deal more than I can use. But my children can use it. I can get along. I know a lot of trades. But that goes to my daughters, who can't get along as well as I can because I have carefully raised them as young ladies, who don't know anything and can't do anything. I hope Congress will extend to them the charity which they have failed to get from me.

Why, if a man who is not even mad but only strenuous, strenuous about race suicide, should come to me and try to get me to use my large political and ecclesiastical influence to get a bill passed by this Congress limiting families to twenty-two children by one mother, I should try to calm him down. I should reason with him.

I should say to him, "Leave it alone. Leave it alone and it will take care of itself. Only one couple a year in the United States can reach that limit. If they have reached that limit let them go right on. Let them have all the liberty they want. In restricting that family to twenty-two children you are merely conferring discomfort and unhappiness on one family per year in a nation of 88,000,000, which is not worthwhile."

It is the very same with copyright. One author per year produces a book which can outlive the forty-two-year limit. That's all. This nation can't produce two authors a year that can do it. The thing is demonstrably impossible. All that the limited copyright can do is to take the bread out of the mouths of the children of that one author per year.

I made an estimate some years ago, when I appeared before a committee of the House of Lords, that we had published in this country since the Declaration of Independence 220,000 books. They have all gone. They had all perished before they were ten years old. It is only one book in a thousand that can outlive the forty-two-year limit. Therefore why put a limit at all? You might as well limit the family to twenty-two children.

If you recall the Americans in the nineteenth century who wrote books that lived forty-two years you will have to begin with Cooper. You can follow with Washington Irving, Harriet Beecher Stowe, Edgar Allan Poe. And there you have to wait a long time. You come to Emerson and you have to stand still and look further. You find Howells and T.B. Aldrich, and then your numbers begin to run pretty thin. And you question if you can name twenty persons in the United States who in a whole century have written books that would live forty-two years. Why, you could take them all and put them on one bench there. Add the wives and children and you could put the result on two or three more benches.

One hundred persons. That is the little, insignificant crowd whose bread and butter is to be taken away for what purpose, for what profit to anybody? You turn these few books into the hands of the pirate and of the legitimate publisher too, and they get the profit that should have gone to the wife and children.

When I appeared before that committee of the House of Lords the chairman asked me what limit I would propose.

I said, "Perpetuity."

I could see some resentment in his manner. And he said the idea was illogical, for the reason that it has long ago been decided that there can be no such thing as property in ideas.

I said there was property in ideas before Queen Anne's time. They had perpetual copyright.

He said, "What is a book? A book is just built from base to roof on ideas, and there can be no property in it."

I said I wished he could mention any kind of property in this planet that had a pecuniary value which was not derived from an idea or ideas. He said real estate. I put a supposititious case, a dozen Englishmen who travel through South Africa and camp out. And eleven of them see nothing at all. They are mentally blind. But there is one in that party who knows what this harbor means and what the lay of the land means. To him it means that some day a railway will go through here, and there on that harbor a great city will spring up. That is his idea. And he has another idea, which is to go and trade his last bottle of Scotch whisky and his last horse blanket to the principal chief of that region and buy a piece of land the size of Pennsylvania. That was the value of an idea that the day would come when the Cape to Cairo Railway would be built.

Every improvement that is put upon the real estate is the result of an idea in somebody's head. The skyscraper is another idea. The railroad is another. The telephone and all those things are merely symbols which represent ideas. An andiron, a washtub, is the result of an idea that did not exist before.

So if, as that gentleman said, a book does consist solely of ideas, that is the best argument in the world that it is property and should not be under any limitation at all. We don't ask for that. Fifty years from now we shall ask for it.

I hope the bill will pass without any deleterious amendments. I do seem to be extraordinarily interested in a whole lot of arts and things that I have got nothing to do with. It is a part of my generous, liberal nature. I can't help it.

I feel the same sort of charity to everybody that was manifested by a gentleman who arrived at home at two o'clock in the morning from the club and was feeling so perfectly satisfied with life, so happy and so comfortable. And there was his house weaving, weaving, weaving around. He watched his chance, and by and by when the steps got in his neighborhood he made a jump and climbed up and got on the portico. And the house went on weaving and weaving and weaving. But he watched the door, and when it came around his way he plunged through it. He got to the stairs, and when he went up on all fours the house was so unsteady that he could hardly make his way.

But at last he got to the top and raised his foot and put it on the top step. But only the toe hitched on the step, and he rolled down and fetched up on the bottom step, with his arm around the newel post.

And he said, "God pity the poor sailors out at sea on a night like this."

December 1906

∾ 71 ∾

In May of 1907, the *New York Times* reported on a talk Clemens gave at Government House in Annapolis, Maryland: "Mighty Mark Twain/Over-awes Marines/He Tells How the Minions of/Government Quail as They/Plan His Arrest/Potter A Great Man, Too/Philosopher Has Motorman's Au-thor-/ity—Good Grows Out of the 'With-/drawal' of a Watermelon."

Edwin Warfield was governor of Maryland.

THE WATERMELON

Yes, I have been arrested. I was arrested twice, so that there could be no doubt about it. I have lived many years in the sight of my country an apparently uncaught and blameless life, a model for the young, an inspiring example for the hoary-headed. But at last the law has laid its hand upon me.

Mine was no ordinary offense. When I affront the law I choose to do so in no obscure, insignificant, trivial manner. Mine was a crime against nothing less than the federal government. The officers who arrested me were no common, or garden, policemen. They were clothed with the authority of the federal Constitution.

I was charged with smoking a cigar within a government reservation. In fact, I was caught red-handed. I came near setting a stone pile on fire.

It is true that the arrest was not made effective. One of the party whispered to the marines what Governor Warfield was going to say, and did say, in introducing me to the audience at my lecture—that I was one of the greatest men in the world. I don't know who proposed to tell that to the marines but it worked like a charm. The minions of the law faltered, hesitated, quailed, and today I am a free man. Twice they laid hands upon me, twice were overcome by my deserved reputation.

Perhaps I ought not to say myself that it is deserved. But who am I to contradict the governor of Maryland? Worm that I am, by what right should I reverse the declared opinion of that man of wisdom and judgment whom I have learned to admire and trust?

I never admired him more than I did when he told my audience that they had with them the greatest man in the world. I believe that was his expression. I don't wish to undertake his sentiments but I will go no further than that—at present. Why, it fairly warmed my heart. It almost made me glad to be there myself. I like good company.

Speaking of greatness, it is curious how many grounds there are for great reputations—how many different phases, that is to say, greatness may take on. There was Bishop Potter. He was arrested a few months ago for a crime similar to mine though he lacked the imagination to select United States government property as the scene of his guilty deed. Now, Bishop Potter is a great man. I am sure he is, because a streetcar motorman told me so. A motorman is not a governor of Maryland, but then Bishop Potter is not a humorist. He could hardly expect a certificate like mine.

I rode with the motorman one day on the front seat of his car. There was a blockade before we got very far, and the motorman, having nothing to do, became talkative.

"Oh, yes," he said, "I have a good many distinguished men on this trip. Bishop Potter often rides with me. He likes the front seat. Now there's a great man for you—Bishop Potter."

"It is true," I responded. "Dr. Potter is indeed a mighty man of God, an erudite theologian, a wise administrator of his diocese, an exegete of—"

"Yes," broke in the motorman, his face beaming with pleasure as he recognized the justice of my tribute and hastened to add one of his own. "Yes, and he's the only man who rides with me who can spit in the slot every time."

That's a good story, isn't it? I like a good story well told. That is the reason I am sometimes forced to tell them myself. Here is one, of which I was reminded yesterday as I was investigating the Naval Academy. I was much impressed with the Naval Academy. I was all over it. And now it is all over me. I am full of the navy. I wanted to march with them on parole. But they didn't think to ask me. Curious inattention on their part. And I just ashore after a celebrated cruise.

While I was observing the navy on land I thought of the navy at sea and of this story, so pathetic, so sweet, so really touching. This is one of my pet stories. Something in its delicacy, refinement and the elusiveness of its humor fits my own quiet tastes.

The time is two A.M. after a lively night at the club. The scene is in front of his house. The house is swaying and lurching to and fro. He has succeeded in navigating from the club. But how is he going to get aboard this rolling, tossing thing? He watches the steps go back and forth, up and down.

Then he makes a desperate resolve, braces himself, and as the steps come around he jumps, clutches the handrail, gets aboard, and pulls himself safely up on the piazza. With a like maneuver he gets through the door. Watching his chance, he gains the lowest step of the inside staircase and painfully makes his way up the swaying and uncertain structure. He has almost reached the top when in a sudden lurch he catches his toe and falls back, rolling to the bottom.

At this moment his wife, rushing out into the upper hall, hears coming up from the darkness below, from the discomfited figure sprawled on the floor with his arms around the newel post, this fervent, appropriate and pious ejaculation, "God help the poor sailors out at sea."

I trust this matter of my arrest will not cause my friends to turn from me. It is true that no matter what may be said of American public morals, the private morals of Americans as a whole are exceptionally good. I do not mean to say that in their private lives all Americans are faultless. I hardly like to go that far, being a man of carefully weighed words and under a peculiarly vivid sense of the necessity of moderation in statement. I should like to say that we are a faultless people but I am restrained by recollection. I know several persons who have erred and transgressed—to put it plainly, they have done wrong. I have heard of still others—of a number of persons, in fact—who are not perfect.

I am not perfect myself. I confess it. I would have confessed it before the lamentable event of yesterday. For that was not the first time I ever did wrong. No. I have done several things which fill my soul now with regret and contrition.

I remember, I remember it so well. I remember it as if it were yesterday, the first time I ever stole a watermelon. Yes, the first time. At least I think it was the first time, or along about there. It was, it was, must have been, about 1848, when I was thirteen or fourteen years old. I remember that watermelon well. I can almost taste it now.

Yes, I stole it. Yet why use so harsh a word? It was the biggest of the load on a farmer's wagon standing in the gutter in the old town of Hannibal, Missouri. While the farmer was busy with another—another—customer, I withdrew this melon. Yes, "I stole" is too strong. I extracted it. I retired it from circulation. And I myself retired with it.

The place to which the watermelon and I retired was a lumberyard. I knew a nice, quiet alley between the sweet-smelling planks and to that sequestered spot I carried the melon. Indulging a few moments' contemplation of its freckled ring, I broke it open with a stone, a rock, a dornick, in boy's language.

It was green—impossibly, hopelessly green. I do not know why this circumstance should have affected me but it did. It affected me deeply. It altered for me the moral values of the universe. It wrought in me a moral revolution. I began to reflect. Now, reflection is the beginning of reform. There can be no reform without reflection.

I asked myself what course of conduct I should pursue. What would conscience dictate? What should a high-minded young man do after retiring a green watermelon? What would George Washington do? Now was the time for all the lessons inculcated at Sunday school to act.

And they did act. The word that came to me was "restitution." Obviously, there lay the path of duty. I reasoned with myself. I labored. At last I was fully resolved.

"I'll do it," said I. "I'll take him back his old melon."

Not many boys would have been heroic, would so clearly have seen the right and so sternly have resolved to do it. The moment I reached that resolution I felt a strange uplift. One always feels an uplift when he turns from wrong to righteousness. I arose, spiritually strengthened, renewed and refreshed, and in the strength of that refreshment carried back the watermelon—that is, I carried back what was left of it—and made him give me a ripe one.

But I had a duty toward that farmer as well as to myself. I was as severe on him as the circumstances deserved. I did not spare him. I told him he ought to be ashamed of himself giving his—his customers green melons. And he was ashamed. He said he was. He said he felt as badly about it as I did. In this he was mistaken. He hadn't eaten any of the melon. I told him that the one instance was bad enough, but asked him to consider what would become of him if this should become a habit with him. I pictured his future. And I saved him. He thanked me and promised to do better.

We should always labor thus with those who have taken the wrong road. Very likely this way the farmer's first false step. He had not gone far, but he had put his foot on the downward incline. Happily, at this moment a friend appeared, a friend who stretched out a helping hand and held him back. Others might have hesitated, have shrunk from speaking to him of his error. I did not hesitate nor shrink. And it is one of the gratifications of my life that I can look back on what I did for that man in his hour of need.

The blessing came. He went home with a bright face to his rejoicing wife and I—I got a ripe melon. I trust it was with him as it was with me. Reform with me was no transient emotion, no passing episode, no Philadelphia uprising. It was permanent. Since that day I have never stolen a water—never stolen a green watermelon.

May 1907

✎ 72 ✎

In the early summer of 1907 Clemens embarked on a triumphal tour of England, where he was entertained and lionized as though he was visiting royalty. In June he was given a luncheon by the Society of Pilgrims in London, which many distinguished people attended. Augustine Birrell, author, member of Parliament and chief secretary for Ireland, presided. In introducing Clemens, Birrell said:

"We all love Mark Twain, and we are here to tell him so. One more point—all the world knows it and that is why it is dangerous to omit it—our guest is a distinguished citizen of the great republic beyond the seas. In America his *Huckleberry Finn* and his *Tom Sawyer* are what *Robinson Crusoe* and *Tom Brown's School Days* have been to us. They are racy of the soil. They are books to which it is impossible to place any period of termination. I will not speak of the classics—reminiscences of much evil in our early lives. We do not meet here today as critics, with our appreciations and depreciations, our twopenny little prefaces or our forewords. I am not going to say what the world a thousand years hence will think of Mark Twain. Posterity will take care of itself, will read what it wants to read, will forget what it chooses to forget, and will pay no attention whatsoever to our critical mumblings and jumblings. Let us therefore be content to say to our friend and guest that we are here speaking for ourselves and for our children, to say what he has been to us.

"I remember in Liverpool, in 1867, first buying the copy, which I still preserve, of the celebrated *Jumping Frog*. It had a few words of preface which reminded me then that our guest in those days was called 'the wild humorist of the Pacific slope,' and a few lines later down, 'the moralist of the Main.' That was some forty years ago. Here he is, still the humorist, still the moralist. His humor enlivens and enlightens his morality, and his morality is all the better for his humor. That is one of the reasons why we love him. I am not here to mention any book of his—that is a subject of dispute in my family circle, which is the best and which is the next best—but I must put in a word, lest I should not be true to myself—a terrible thing—for his *Joan of Arc*, a book of chivalry, of nobility, and of manly sincerity for which I take this opportunity of thanking him.

"But you can all drink this toast, each one of you with his own intention.

You can get into it what meaning you like. Mark Twain is a man whom English and Americans do well to honor. He is the true consolidator of nations. His delightful humor is of the kind which dissipates and destroys national prejudices. His truth and his honor, his love of truth, and his love of honor, overflow all boundaries. He has made the world better by his presence. We rejoice to see him here. Long may he live to reap the plentiful harvest of hearty, honest human affection!"

Thomas Otway was an English dramatist; Thomas Chatterton an English poet; Charles Eliot Norton was an American author, editor and professor of art history; and Joseph Dalton Hooker was an English naturalist, botanist and surgeon.

AFFECTION

Pilgrims, I desire first to thank those undergraduates of Oxford. When a man has grown so old as I am, when he has reached the verge of seventy-two years, there is nothing that carries him back to the dreamland of his life, to his boyhood, like recognition of those young hearts up yonder. And so I thank them out of my heart. I desire to thank the Pilgrims of New York also for their kind notice and message which they have cabled over here.

Mr. Birrell says he does not know how he got here. But he will be able to get away all right, he has not drunk anything since he came here. I am glad to know about those friends of his, Otway and Chatterton—fresh, new names to me. I am glad of the disposition he has shown to rescue them from the evils of poverty, and if they are still in London I hope to have a talk with them. For a while I thought he was going to tell us the effect which my book had upon his growing manhood. I thought he was going to tell us how much that effect amounted to and whether it really made him what he now is. But with the discretion born of Parliamentary experience he dodged that, and we do not know now whether he read the book or not. He did that very neatly. I could not do it any better myself.

My books have had effects, and very good ones too, here and there, and some others not so good. There is no doubt about that. But I remember one monumental instance of it years and years ago. Professor Norton of Harvard was over here, and when he came back to Boston I went out with Howells to call on him. Norton was allied in some way by marriage with Darwin.

Mr. Norton was very gentle in what he had to say, and almost delicate, and he said, "Mr. Clemens, I have been spending some time with Mr. Darwin in England, and I should like to tell you something connected with that visit. You were the object of it, and I myself would have been very proud of it, but you may not be proud of it. At any rate, I am going to tell you what it was and to leave to you to regard it as you please. Mr. Darwin took me up to his bedroom and pointed out certain things there—pitcher plants and so on—that he was measuring and watching from day to day. And he said, 'The chambermaid is permitted to do what she pleases in this room but she must never touch those plants and never touch those books on that table by that candle. With those books I read myself to sleep every night.' Those were your own books."

I said, "There is no question in my mind as to whether I should regard that as a compliment or not. I do regard it as a very great compliment and a very high honor that that great mind, laboring for the whole human race, should rest itself on my books. I am proud that he should read himself to sleep with them."

Now, I could not keep that to myself—I was so proud of it. As soon as I got home to Hartford I called up my oldest friend, and dearest enemy on occasion, the Rev. Joseph Twichell, my pastor, and I told him about that, and of course he was full of interest and venom. Those people who get no compliments like that feel like that.

He went off. He did not issue any applause of any kind and I did not hear of that subject for some time. But when Mr. Darwin passed away from this life, and some time after Darwin's *Life and Letters* came out, the Rev. Mr. Twichell procured an early copy of that work and found something in it which he considered applied to me.

He came over to my house—it was snowing, raining, sleeting, but that did not make any difference to Twichell. He produced the book, and turned the pages over and over until he came to a certain place, when he said, "Here, look at this letter from Mr. Darwin to Sir Joseph Hooker."

What Mr. Darwin said—I give you the idea and not the very words—was this: I do not know whether I ought to have devoted my whole life to these drudgeries in natural history and the other sciences or not, for while I may have gained in one way I have lost in another. Once I had a fine perception and appreciation of high literature, but in me that quality is atrophied.

"That was the reason," said Mr. Twichell, "he was reading your books."

Mr. Birrell has touched lightly—very lightly, but in not an uncomplimentary way—on my position in this world as a moralist. I am glad to have that recognition, too, because I have suffered since I have been in this town—in the first place, right away when I came here, from a newsman going around with a great, red, highly displayed placard in the place of an apron. He was selling newspapers, and there were two sentences on that placard which would have been all right if they had been punctuated, but they ran those two sentences together without a comma or anything, and that would naturally create a wrong impression, because it said, "Mark Twain arrives Ascot Cup stolen."

No doubt many a person was misled by those sentences joined together in that unkind way. I have no doubt my character has suffered from it. I suppose I ought to defend my character but how can I defend it? I can say here and now, and anybody can see by my face that I am sincere, that I speak the truth, that I have never seen that Cup. I have not got the Cup. I did not have a chance to get it.

I have always had a good character in that way. I have hardly ever stolen anything, and if I did steal anything I had discretion enough to know about the value of it first. I do not steal things that are likely to get myself into trouble. I do not think any of us do that. I know we all take things—that is to be expected—but really I have never taken anything, certainly in England, that amounts to any great thing. I do confess that when I was here seven years ago I stole a hat, but that did not amount to anything. It was not a good hat, and was only a clergyman's hat, anyway.

I was at a luncheon party, and Archdeacon Wilberforce was there also. I dare say he is Archdeacon now. He was a canon then. And he was serving in the Westminster battery, if that is the proper term. I do not know, as you mix military and ecclesiastical things together so much. He left the luncheon table before I did. He began this. I did steal his hat but he began by taking mine. I make that interjection because I would not accuse Archdeacon Wilberforce of stealing my hat, I should not think of it. I confine that phrase to myself. He merely took my hat. And with good judgment, too, it was a better hat than his. He came out before the luncheon was over and sorted the hats in the hall and selected one which suited. It happened to be mine. He went off with it.

When I came out by and by there was no hat there which would go on my head except his, which was left behind. My head was not the customary size just at that time. I had been receiving a good many very nice and complimentary attentions, and my head was a couple of sizes larger than usual, and his hat just suited me. The bumps and corners were all right intellectually. There were results pleasing to me—possibly so to him. He found out whose hat it was and wrote me saying it was pleasant that all the way home whenever he met anybody his gravities, his solemnities, his deep thoughts, his eloquent remarks were all snatched up by the people he met and mistaken for brilliant humorisms.

I had another experience. It was not unpleasing. I was received with a deference which was entirely foreign to my experience by everybody whom I met, so that before I got home I had a much higher opinion of myself than I have ever had before or since. And there is in that very connection an incident which I remember at that old date which is rather melancholy to me, because it shows how a person can deteriorate in a mere seven years. It is seven years ago. I have not that hat now.

I was going down Pall Mall or some other of your big streets and I recognized that that hat needed ironing. I went into a big shop and passed in my hat and asked that it might be ironed. They were courteous, very courteous, even courtly. They brought that hat back to me presently very sleek and nice, and I asked how much there was to pay. They replied that they did not charge the clergy anything. I have cherished the delight of that moment from that day to this. It was the first thing I did the other day to go and hunt up that shop and hand in my hat to have it ironed.

I said when it came back, "How much to pay?"

They said, "Ninepence."

In seven years I have acquired all that worldliness, and I am sorry to be back where I was seven years ago.

But now I am chaffing and chaffing and chaffing here, and I hope you will forgive me for that. But when a man stands on the verge of seventy-two you know perfectly well that he never reached that place without knowing what this life is—heartbreaking bereavement. And so our reverence is for our dead. We do not forget them, but our duty is toward the living, and if we can be cheerful, cheerful in spirit, cheerful in speech and in hope, that is a benefit to those who are around us.

My own history includes an incident which will always connect me with England in a pathetic way, for when I arrived here seven years ago with my wife and my daughter—we had gone around the globe lecturing to raise money to clear off a debt—my wife and one of my daughters started across the ocean to bring to England our eldest daughter. She was twenty-four years of age and in the bloom of young womanhood, and we were unsuspecting. When my wife and daughter—and my wife has passed from this life since—when they had reached mid-Atlantic, a cablegram—one of those heartbreaking cablegrams which we all in our days have to experience— was put into my hand. It stated that that daughter of ours had gone to her long sleep.

And so, as I say, I cannot always be cheerful, and I cannot always be chaffing. I must sometimes lay the cap and bells aside and recognize that I am of the human race like the rest and must have my cares and griefs. And therefore I noticed what Mr. Birrell said—I was so glad to hear him say it—something that was in the nature of these verses here at the top of this:

> *He lit our life with shafts of sun*
> *And vanquished pain.*
> *Thus two great nations stand as one*
> *In honoring Twain.*

I am very glad to have those verses. I am very glad and very grateful for what Mr. Birrell said in that connection. I have received since I have been here, in this one week, hundreds of letters from all conditions of people in England—men, women and children— and there is in them compliment, praise and, above all and better than all, there is in them a note of affection. Praise is well, compliment is well, but affection—that is the last and final and most precious reward that any man can win, whether by character or achievement, and I am very grateful to have that reward.

All these letters make me feel that here in England, as in America, when I stand under the English flag I am not a stranger. I am not an alien, but at home.

June 1907

❧ *73* ❧

On July 4, 1907, Clemens spoke at a banquet of the American Society, London. About five hundred people attended. Mortimer Durand was an English writer, statesman and ambassador to the United States.

FOURTH OF JULY

Once more it happens, as it has happened so often since I arrived in England a week or two ago, that instead of celebrating the Fourth of July properly as has been indicated, I have to first take care of my personal character.

Sir Mortimer Durand still remains unconvinced. Well, I tried to convince these people from the beginning that I did not take the Ascot Cup. And as I have failed to convince anybody that I did not take the cup, I might as well confess I did take it and be done with it. I don't see why this uncharitable feeling should follow me everywhere and why I should have that crime thrown up to me on all occasions. The tears that I have wept over it ought to have created a different feeling than this. And besides, I don't think it is very right or fair that, considering England has been trying to take a cup of ours for forty years—I don't see why they should take so much trouble when I tried to go into the business myself.

Sir Mortimer Durand, too, has had trouble from going to a dinner here, and he has told you what he suffered in consequence. But what did he suffer? He only missed his train and one night of discomfort, and he remembers it to this day.

Oh, if you could only think what I have suffered from a similar circumstance. Two or three years ago in New York with that Society there which is made up of people from all British Colonies and from Great Britain generally, who were educated in British colleges and

British schools, I was there to respond to a toast of some kind or other. And I did then what I have been in the habit of doing from a selfish motive for a long time, and that is, I got myself placed No. 3 in the list of speakers—then you get home early.

I had to go five miles up river and had to catch a particular train or not get there. But see the magnanimity which is born in me, which I have cultivated all my life.

A very famous and very great British clergyman came to me presently, and he said, "I am away down in the list. I have got to catch a certain train this Saturday night. If I don't catch that train I shall be carried beyond midnight and break the Sabbath. Won't you change places with me?"

I said, "Certainly I will."

I did it at once. Now see what happened. Talk about Sir Mortimer Durand's sufferings for a single night! I have suffered ever since because I saved that gentleman from breaking the Sabbath—yes, saved him. I took his place, but I lost my train, and it was I who broke the Sabbath. Up to that time I never had broken the Sabbath in my life, and from that day to this I never have kept it.

Oh, I am learning much here tonight. I find I didn't know anything about the American Society. That is, I didn't know its chief virtue. I didn't know its chief virtue until his Excellency our Ambassador revealed it—I may say exposed it. I was intending to go home on the thirteenth of this month but I look upon that in a different light now. I am going to stay here until the American Society pays my passage.

Our Ambassador has spoken of our Fourth of July and the noise it makes. We have got a double Fourth of July, a daylight Fourth and a midnight Fourth. During the day in America, as our Ambassador has indicated, we keep the Fourth of July properly in a reverent spirit. We devote it to teaching our children patriotic things—reverence for the Declaration of Independence. We honor the day all through the daylight hours, and when night comes we dishonor it.

Presently, before long—they are getting nearly ready to begin now—on the Atlantic coast, when night shuts down, that pandemonium will begin, and there will be noise and noise and noise all night long, and there will be more than noise, there will be people crippled, there will be people killed, there will be people who will lose their eyes, and all through that permission which we give to irresponsible boys to play with firearms and firecrackers and all sorts of dangerous things. We turn that Fourth of July, alas, over to rowdies to drink and get drunk and make the night hideous, and we cripple and kill more people than you would imagine.

We probably began to celebrate our Fourth of July night in that way one hundred and twenty-five years ago. And on every Fourth of July night since, these horrors have grown and grown, until now, in our five thousand towns of America, somebody gets killed or crippled on every Fourth of July night, besides those cases of sick persons whom we never hear of, who die as the result of the noise or the shock. They cripple and kill more people on the Fourth of July in America than they kill and cripple in our wars nowadays. And there are no pensions for these folk.

And, too, we burn houses. Really we destroy more property on every Fourth of July night than the whole of the United States was worth one hundred and twenty-five years ago. Really our Fourth of July is our day of mourning, our day of sorrow. Fifty thousand people who have lost friends or who have had friends crippled receive that Fourth of July, when it comes, as a day of mourning for the losses they have sustained in their families.

I have suffered in that way myself. I have had relatives killed in that way. One was in Chicago years ago, an uncle of mine, just as good an uncle as I have ever had, and I had lots of them, yes, uncles to burn, uncles to spare. This poor uncle, full of patriotism, opened his mouth to hurrah, and a rocket went down his throat. Before that man could ask for a drink of water to quench that thing, it blew up and scattered him all over the forty-five States. And really now, this is true, I know about it myself. Twenty-four hours after that it was raining buttons, recognizable as his, on the Atlantic seaboard. A person cannot have a disaster like that and be entirely cheerful the rest of his life.

I had another uncle, on an entirely different Fourth of July, who was blown up that way, and really it trimmed him as it would a tree. He had hardly a limb left on him anywhere. All we have left now is an expurgated edition of that uncle. But never mind about these things. They are merely passing matters. Don't let me make you sad.

Sir Mortimer Durand said that you, the English people, gave up your colonies over there, got tired of them, and did it with reluctance. Now I wish you just to consider that he was right about that and that he had his reasons for saying that England did not look upon our Revolution as a foreign war, but as a civil war fought by Englishmen.

Our Fourth of July, which we honor so much and which we love so much and which we take so much pride in, is an English institution, not an American one, and it comes of a great ancestry. The first Fourth of July in that noble genealogy dates back seven centuries lacking eight years. That is the day of the Great Charter, the Magna Carta, which was born at Runnymede in the next to the last year of King John, and portions of the liberties secured thus by those hardy Barons from that reluctant King John are a part of our Declaration of Independence, of our Fourth of July, of our American liberties.

And the second of those Fourths of July was not born until four centuries later, in Charles the First's time, in the Bill of Rights. And that is ours, that is part of our liberties. The next one was still English, in New England, where they established that principle which remains with us to this day, and will continue to remain with us—no taxation without representation. That is always going to stand, and that the English Colonies in New England gave us.

The Fourth of July, and the one which you are celebrating now, born in Philadelphia on the 4th of July, 1776—that is English too. It is not American. Those were English colonists, subjects of King George III, Englishmen at heart, who protested against the oppressions of the Home Government. Though they proposed to cure those oppressions and remove them, still remaining under the Crown, they were not intending a revolution. The revolution was brought about by circumstances which they could not control.

The Declaration of Independence was written by a British subject, every name signed to it was the name of a British subject. There was not the name of a single American attached to the Declaration of Independence. In fact there was not an American in the country in that day except the Indians out on the plains. They were Englishmen, all Englishmen. Americans did not begin until seven years later, when that Fourth of July had become seven years old, and then the American Republic was established. Since then there have been Americans. So you see what we owe to England in the matter of liberties.

We have, however, one Fourth of July which is absolutely our own, and that is that great proclamation issued forty years ago by that great American to whom Sir Mortimer Durand paid that just and beautiful tribute—Abraham Lincoln. Lincoln's proclamation, which not only set the black slaves free, but set the white man free also. The owner was set free from the burden and offense, that sad condition of things where he was in so many instances a master and owner of slaves when he did not want to be. That proclamation set them all free. But even in this matter England suggested it, for England had set her slaves free thirty years before, and we followed her example. We always followed her example, whether it was good or bad.

And it was an English judge that issued that other great proclamation and established that great principle that when a slave, let him belong to whom he may, and let him come whence he may, sets his foot upon English soil, his fetters by that act fall away and he is a free man before the world. We followed the example of 1833 and we freed our slaves, as I have said.

It is true, then, that all our Fourths of July, and we have five of them, England gave to us. Except that one that I have mentioned, the Emancipation Proclamation. And, lest we forget, let us all remember that we owe these things to England.

Let us be able to say to Old England, this great-hearted, venerable old mother of the race, you gave us our Fourths of July that we love and that we honor and revere. You gave us the Declaration of Independence, which is the Charter of our rights. You, the venerable Mother of Liberties, the Protector of Anglo-Saxon Freedom, you gave us these things. And we do most honestly thank you for them.

July 1907

ᘿ 74 ᘾ

The Savage Club, London, gave a dinner for Clemens that same month, July 1907, at which he was presented with a portrait of himself signed by all the club members attending the dinner. Harold Frederic was an American writer and London correspondent of the *New York Times*. The chairman, in introducing Clemens, said he had read parts of Clemens's works to Frederic during the latter's last illness.

WEARING WHITE CLOTHES

M r. chairman and fellow savages, I am very glad indeed to have that portrait. I think it is the best one that I have ever had, and there have been opportunities before to get a good photograph. I have sat to photographers twenty-two times today. Those sittings added to those that have preceded them since I have been in Europe (if we average at that rate) must have numbered one hundred to two hundred sittings. Out of all those there ought to be some good photographs. This is the best I have had, and I am glad to have your honored names on it.

I did not know Harold Frederic personally but I have heard a great deal about him, and nothing that was not pleasant and nothing except such things as lead a man to honor another man and to love him. I consider that it is a misfortune of mine that I have never had the luck to meet him. And if any book of mine read to him in his last hours made those hours easier for him and more comfortable, I am very glad and proud of that.

I call to mind such a case many years ago of an English authoress, well known in her day, who wrote such beautiful child tales, touching and lovely in every possible way. In a little biographical sketch of her I found that her last hours were spent partly in reading a book of mine, until she was no longer able to read. That has always remained in my mind, and I have always cherished it as one of the good things of my life. I had read what she had written, and had loved her for what she had done.

Stanley apparently carried a book of mine feloniously away to Africa, and I have not a doubt that it had a noble and uplifting influence there in the wilds of Africa, because on his previous journeys he never carried anything to read except Shakespeare and the Bible. I did not know of that circumstance. I did not know that he had carried a book of mine. I only noticed that when he came back he was a reformed man.

I knew Stanley very well in those old days. Stanley was the first man who ever reported a lecture of mine, and that was in St. Louis. When I was down there the next time to give the same lecture I was told to give them something fresh, as they had read that in the papers.

I met Stanley here when he came back from that first expedition of his which closed with the finding of Livingstone. You remember how he would break out at the meetings of the British Association and find fault with what people said, because Stanley had notions of his own and could not contain them. They had to come out or break him up, and so he would go round and address geographical societies. He was always on the warpath in those days, and people always had to have Stanley contradicting their geography for them and improving it. But he always came back and sat drinking beer with me in the hotel up to two in the morning. And he was then one of the most civilized human beings that ever was.

I saw in a newspaper this evening a reference to an interview which appeared in one of the papers the other day, in which the interviewer said that I characterized Mr. Birrell's speech the other day at the Pilgrims' Club as "bully." Now, if you will excuse me, I never use slang to an interviewer or anybody else. That distresses me. Whatever I said about Mr. Birrell's speech was said in English, as good English as anybody uses. If I could not describe Mr. Birrell's delightful speech without using slang I would not describe it at all. I would close my mouth and keep it closed, much as it would discomfort me.

Now that comes of interviewing a man in the first person, which is an altogether wrong way to interview him. It is entirely wrong because none of you, I, or anybody else, could interview a man, could listen to a man talking any length of time and then go off and reproduce that talk in the first person. It can't be done. What results is merely that the interviewer gives the substance of what is said and puts it in his own language and puts it in your mouth. It will always be either better language than you use or worse, and in my case it is always worse. I have a great respect for the English language. I am one of its supporters, its promoters, its elevators. I don't degrade it. A slip of the tongue would be the most that you would get from me. I have always tried hard and faithfully to improve my English and never to degrade it. I always try to use the best English to describe what I think and what I feel, or what I don't feel and what I don't think.

I am not one of those who in expressing opinions confine themselves to facts. I don't know anything that mars good literature so completely as too much truth. Facts contain a deal of poetry. But you can't use too many of them without damaging your literature. I love all literature. And as long as I am a doctor of literature—I have suggested to you for twenty years I have been diligently trying to improve my own literature. And now, by virtue of the University of Oxford, I mean to doctor everybody else's.

Now I think I ought to apologize for my clothes. At home I venture things that I am not permitted by my family to venture in foreign parts. I was instructed before I left home and ordered to refrain from white clothes in England. I meant to keep that command fair and clean, and I would have done it if I had been in the habit of obeying instructions. But I can't invent a new process in life right away. I have not had white clothes on since I crossed the ocean until now.

In these three or four weeks I have grown so tired of gray and black that you have earned my gratitude in permitting me to come as I have. I wear white clothes in the depth of winter in my home but I don't go out in the streets in them. I don't go out to attract too much attention. I like to attract some, and always I would like to be dressed so that I may be more conspicuous than anybody else.

If I had been an ancient Briton I would not have contented myself with blue paint, but I would have bankrupted the rainbow. I so enjoy gay clothes in which women clothe themselves that it always grieves me when I go to the opera to see that, while women look like a flower bed, the men are a few gray stumps among them in their black evening dress. These are two or three reasons why I wish to wear white clothes. When I find myself in assemblies like this, with everybody in black clothes, I know I possess something that is superior to everybody else's. Clothes are never clean. You don't know whether they are clean or not, because you can't see.

Here or anywhere you must scour your head every two or three days or it is full of grit. Your clothes must collect just as much dirt as your hair. If you wear white clothes you are clean, and your cleaning bill gets so heavy that you have to take care. I am proud to say that I can wear a white suit of clothes without a blemish for three days. If you need any further instruction in the matter of clothes I shall be glad to give it to you. I hope I have convinced some of you that it is just as well to wear white clothes as any other kind. I do not want to boast. I only want to make you understand that you are not clean.

As to age, the fact that I am nearly seventy-two years old does not clearly indicate how old I am, because part of every day—it is with me as with you—you try to describe your age, and you cannot do it. Sometimes you are only fifteen. Sometimes you are twenty-five. It is very seldom in a day that I am seventy-two years old. I am older now sometimes than I was when I used to rob orchards, a thing which I would not do today—if the orchards were watched.

I am so glad to be here tonight. I am so glad to renew with the Savages that now ancient time when I first sat with a company of this club in London in 1872. That is a long time ago. But I did stay with the Savages a night in London long ago, and as I had come into a very strange land and was with friends, as I could see, that has always remained in my mind as a peculiarly blessed evening, since it brought me into contact with men of my own kind and my own feelings.

I am glad to be here and to see you all again, because it is very likely that I shall not see you again. It is easier than I thought to come across the Atlantic. I have been received, as you know, in the most delightfully generous way in England ever since I came here. It keeps me choked up all the time. Everybody is so generous, and they do seem to give you such a hearty welcome.

Nobody in the world can appreciate it higher than I do. It did not wait till I got to London, but when I came ashore at Tilbury the stevedores on the dock raised the first welcome—a good and hearty welcome from the men who do the heavy labor in the world and save you and me having to do it. They are the men who with their hands build empires and make them prosper. It is because of them that the others are wealthy and can live in luxury. They received me with a "Hurrah!" that went to my heart. They are the men that build civilization, and without them no civilization can be built.

So I came first to the authors and creators of civilization, and I blessedly end this happy meeting with the Savages who destroy it.

July 1907

✏ 75 ✏

After declining a dinner offered by the lord mayor of Liverpool because he was being so heavily feted in London, Clemens was persuaded to change his mind. He went to Liverpool on July 10, 1907, together with Thomas Power O'Connor (Tay Pay). That evening the lord mayor tendered him a lavish banquet in the town hall. Clemens did not partake of the twelve-course dinner and assorted wines and brandies. The *Liverpool Daily Post* of the next day explained why, but first it honored Clemens with headlines: "Mark Twain in Liverpool/Dines with the Lord Mayor/Distinguished Company at the Town Hall/Characteristic Speech by the Humorist."

After listing some of the prominent people who attended, the article noted, "When the guests reached the cloakroom they were informed by prominent printed notices that Dr. Clemens would arrive at the dinner between eight and half-past. It appears that Mark, having had a sleepless night, and feeling fatigued as the result of his journey down from London, had retired to bed for a brief rest at the London and North-Western Hotel before attending the dinner. At twenty-five minutes past eight o'clock, when the menu had been all but gone through, the Lord Mayor left the hall, and a few minutes later escorted Mark into the presence of the company, who received him very warmly. Mark was smoking the inevitable cigar."

The speech he gave that evening was one of the most felicitous and moving that Clemens ever made. About a fortnight later O'Connor, the Irish politician, journalist and founder of *T.P.'s Weekly*, described its effect on the large audience.

"It may seem impossible to write anything new about Mark Twain; and yet I believe I have something to say about him that has never been said before. He is known as the great humorist; as the great master of tears as well as laughter; as the great reasoner—as shown in his dissection of the Christian Science myth; as a great controversialist—witness his scathing exposure of the atrocities of King Leopold in the Congo; but I have never yet seen any mention of the fact that he is one of the great orators of his time.

"This fact first dawned upon me when I heard him speak at the lunch over which Mr. Birrell presided. He had made a speech [titled "Affection" in the present volume] for half an hour or so which consisted entirely of rollicking jokes which sent the whole company into fits of laughter; and everybody might have expected that he was going to end on this note—that, in fact, he had no other note on which he could play but this. And then all of a sudden, with a transition so easy and so natural that you scarcely perceived it at first, he dropped the cap and bells, and one saw into the depths of the man.

"Like so many great humorists, Mark Twain is often sad; like all men of strong and deep emotion, he is incapable of recovering from some of fortune's wounds. And there are two wounds from which he has not recovered—from which he never will recover—the death of his wife and the death of his daughter, Susan. It was to these great sorrows that suddenly he referred, and at once there came over the gathering, which had been shouting its tumultuous laughter a moment before, that great, deadly stillness which is always the truest sign of an audience being stirred to its uttermost depths. And it was not merely the beautiful language in which this reference to his great trouble was clothed that thrilled the audience, it was the perfect delivery and management of his voice which has a great gamut of melodies—a voice the most perfect singer or actor might envy. And then it was that I realised how tremendous was Mark Twain's power over an audience; and how richly he was endowed with that divine afflatus which makes one man able to play on every chord of the hearts of hundreds or thousands of other men who listen to him. It was to me almost a revelation.

"But it was at the banquet given by Lord Mayor Japp in Liverpool last week that I saw the final proof that Mark Twain ought to have been an orator by occupation as well as a writer."

O'Connor then quoted from his introduction of Mark Twain, in which he stressed Clemens's determined and successful efforts to pay all his debts to the penny.

"I omit the brilliant witticisms with which the greater part of Mark Twain's reply was occupied; everybody is now accustomed to the fact that there is no living man can approach him in a humorous after-dinner speech; what I want to insist on is the other side—the purely oratorical side of the man.

"Therefore do I come at once to the serious passages in which the great speech finally ended. I had—as has been seen—alluded to the historic lecturing tour he had taken to pay the debt which another man had accumulated for him in the business of publisher, and this is how he alluded to the fact; it will be seen how recurrent is the memory of that beautiful character who was the lodestar of his life."

Here O'Connor quoted the part of Clemens's speech in which the latter credited his wife for insisting that he pay one hundred cents on the dollar.

"You can realise how suddenly all the temper of that audience was transformed, and how this beautiful and touching allusion to that wondrous type of all the stern sense of right, combined with all a woman's tenderness and devotion, moved the great audience which Mark Twain was addressing.

"From that moment forward, the speech was not mere speech; it was a rich symphony. He approached at last a peroration, the like of which I have rarely heard. Here it is."

And then O'Connor gave the last part of the speech, beginning with "Home is dear to us all."

"A wonderful bit of literature, you will see at once; but that is not the reason I transfer it to these columns; it is because of the extraordinary way in which it was delivered, and its marvelous effect.

"The audience sat suddenly in spellbound and almost painful silence, and the voice rang out on the stillness—very quiet, very self-controlled, but clear as the bells whose chimes reach you on a far-off hill from the belfry in the chapel of your native town. And at last the audience could restrain itself no longer; and when in rich, resonant, uplifted voice Mark Twain sang out the words: 'I am the Begum of Bengal a hundred and twenty-three days out from Canton,' there burst forth a great cheer from one end of the room to the other. It seemed an inopportune cheer, and for a moment it upset Mark Twain, and yet it was felicitous in opportuneness. Slowly, after a long pause, came the last two words—like that curious, detached and high note in which a great piece of music sometimes suddenly and abruptly ends—'Homeward bound.' Again there was a cheer; but this time it was lower; it was subdued; it was the fitting echo to the beautiful words—with its double significance—the parting from a hospitable land, the return to the native land—wail and paean, paean and wail. It is only a great littérateur that could conceive such a passage; it is only a great orator that could so deliver it."

Rubert William Boyce was a professor of pathology at the University of Liverpool. The Waterbury was a cheap American watch popular at the time. John Henniker Heaton was a member of Parliament and a leading promoter of penny postage.

THE *BEGUM OF BENGAL*

M y Lord Mayor, my Lord Bishop. And gentlemen. I want to thank you, my Lord Mayor, for the welcome which you have given me tonight. And I thank these gentlemen for their hearty response in which they have received the toast. And I will thank—any other name? I only know him by "Tay Pay." I have another name, Langhorne, but it really doesn't belong to me. Then you have a telegram from Professor Boyce, who says he still has a watch. That comes of having a fleeting reputation. I came to this country distinguished for honesty. And then somebody took that Ascot Cup just as I arrived, which has thrown a gloom over my whole stay here and will provide sorrow and lamentations for my friends on the other side. And now I am held responsible for the regalia which has been stolen from Dublin Castle. What will become of my reputation if I do not get out of the country very soon? I do not know. People say it is a curious coincidence that the Ascot Cup and the regalia from Dublin Castle should have been stolen during my stay. And so it is. I was going to Dublin. Fortunately for the rags of my reputation, I could not get there.

And you say, what is this? It is rumor. Nobody comes out and charges me with carrying out that robbery. It is mere human testimony, and it does not amount to testimony, it is merely rumor, circumstantial evidence, mere human speech, assertion, rumor and suspicion. But circumstantial evidence is the best evidence in the world.

Once a month for five hundred years certain officers whose function it is go down the cellars in Dublin Castle and there they find the safe in which the precious jewels are kept, and take them out one by one daily just to see that they are all right, and put them back in the safe. They have been doing this for five hundred years and they have got so used to it that they did not shut up the safe. I should like to know whether that is a good safe and a valuable safe. That is an important feature for me, because with the reputation I have got now, all the circumstantial evidence would point to the fact that if I took anything at all I would not merely have carried off the regalia but the safe along with it.

All this is testimony in my favor, and yet Professor Boyce is afraid to bring along his watch, which is probably only a Waterbury, and an old one at that.

Mr. O'Connor has furnished you information that enabled you to understand that I have been a jack-of-all-trades. That is quite true. He said a word about my father. He was a lawyer, but my father was entitled to more words than that. He was another of my kind. He was not just merely a lawyer, but in that little village on the banks of the Mississippi, when I was a boy, he was mayor of the town, the chief of police, the postmaster, the one policeman, and the sheriff

who had to hang all the malefactors. In fact, he was the entire government—concentrated. Now, you can't pass by a man like that
with just a word.

Mr. O'Connor spoke of my brother too. Well, my brother and I
were twins. He was born ten years before I was, a little discrepancy
that never could be accounted for. It was the intention that that
brother of mine should be a lazy person. I know that perfectly well.
But somehow or other it missed fire and I was born that way instead. I have been lazy ever since and indolent, while that brother,
the twin, he was full of energy and the spirit of labor. Whatever he
put his hand to he worked at it hard and faithfully, and the result
was—the result was he could never make a living anyhow.

I can't help being frivolous tonight, because I have followed out
my instructive and natural custom this afternoon by having a sleep
and resting myself. Whenever I am rested and feeling good I can't
help being frivolous. It is only when I am weary and worn out and
discouraged that the time comes for me to take a hold on great national questions and handle them. I wanted to talk real instructive
wisdom tonight. But this rest has intervened and put it all out of my
mind.

I have been two or three weeks discussing cheap penny international postage with Mr. Henniker Heaton and I have told him all I
know about it. And now he knows nothing about it himself. I said I
was born lazy, but I was born wise also, and the only time I ever lost
a situation, the only time I was ever discharged from a post, was in
San Francisco more than forty years ago when I was a reporter on
the *Morning Call*. I was discharged just that once in my life, and the
only thing they could bring against me was that I was incompetent
and incandescent and inharmonious and everything they could think
of in three syllables. But mainly I was lazy and inefficient.

That was the only time anybody ever found fault with me for a
thing like that. It was occurring all the time. In fact it was monoto-
nous, and it was no use picking out a thing like that.

According to Tay Pay, I have been a little of everything. This time
I am an ambassador. I like that position very well. I don't mind it as
it has not a salary attached to it, because a salary limits your energy.
It does mine always. I would rather be free to do my ambassadorial
work after my own fashion, and I intend to keep up this ambas-

sadorial business right along. Whenever I find a chance of encouraging the good feeling between this old mother country and her eldest child over there, I intend to put in my word and keep up the ambassadorial work.

The University of Oxford in making me a doctor has added one more function to my numerous functions. And somebody asked me a rather pointed question. "Was it not rather a delicate thing to make you a Doctor of Literature? Are you competent to doctor literature? Had you not better doctor your own a little?"

That is all wrong. I have been doctoring my own literature. It is only now by the authority of Oxford that I propose to doctor other people's, and I hope you will see results.

Why, I have always had an interest in literature outside my own concern. I have always been ready to give a helping hand to a rising young author. I saved one poet in San Francisco forty years ago and I don't forget it. I did a good turn to that poet. I was ready to doctor him or anybody else. Well, he wasn't much of a poet—a kind of a poet good enough for the early days on the Pacific. He was not prosperous, and he was named Eddystone. We called him Eddystone Lighthouse. That was sarcasm. He was not a lighthouse. He was in trouble and I came to the young man's help. I was a reporter but I was likely to lose the employment at any time, and I knew it would be such a good thing for me if I could do something rather extraordinary to keep ahead of the other papers.

Well, the young poet got discouraged. His poetry began to be a drug. He could not sell it. And by and by when he could not give it away his circumstances were desperate, and he came to me as a friend and wise adviser, and he proposed to commit suicide.

I told him it was a good idea. It was a good idea in various ways. It would relieve him from writing poetry and it would relieve the community from reading it and it would give me a chance with my newspaper, I being the only other person present at the suicide—I would take care of that.

He was a little sorry to see me so enthusiastic. I could not help that. My heart was in it. We discussed methods, and I told him the most picturesque was the revolver to blow his brains out with. He did not like that idea very much but I reconciled him to it.

But we did not have any money to buy a revolver, and we went round to the place with the three balls. There was a revolver there, just the right thing, but we could not borrow that revolver without furnishing some money. I told the gentleman that this was the only chance the young man had. But he was that kind of man that you could not persuade at all—a man who has no human sympathy although it does not cost anything.

Then I suggested drowning to my friend. That would be a neat thing. It could not be as fine for me as the other, but drowning was good enough when you could not get anything better. So we went out to the seashore, and he did not like the looks of the water, and wanted me to try how it would go. But no, I was not in that line at all.

Then a most curious thing—one of the strangest things, a thing you would never imagine at all—happened. From some ship that had foundered perhaps a thousand miles away there came an object of some interest at that moment. There were, in fact, two events gradually coming together. While this young man was brooding and contemplating suicide there was a life preserver floating in from that ship. A life preserver for a man who was about to commit suicide!

It looked ridiculous at first but we took the life preserver to the pawnbroker and traded with him for the revolver. And then we made all the arrangements. But he didn't like to put the firearm to his forehead.

I said, "It will be over in a minute" and this seemed to reassure him, for he bucked up and blew his brains out.

People said it wasn't brains. But it was. There was not much of it. But it was real gray matter, which is supposed to constitute intelligence so far as it can.

Well, that was the making of that boy. Why, when he got well all obstructions were gone! And I have thought many times since that if poets when they get discouraged would blow their brains out they could write very much better when they get well.

I landed in this town of Liverpool thirty years ago, the first time I ever put my foot on English soil, and I had an adventure. As a matter of fact, Liverpool is connected with one or two adventures of a very pleasant sort. I went to the outside edge of the town and I saw the scenery, the blocked-up windows to escape the window tax, and various other exciting things, and finally I took a cab and drove around.

The man was a very good-natured, pleasant, middle-aged Scotchman, and he asked where he should drive me to. I said anywhere, just around for an hour or two hours. He drove me a little way and then stopped and asked me again.

Well, I wanted to think—I was full of some great project. And finally when this had occurred several more times, in desperation I said, "Oh, take me to Balmoral."

I did not say a word, and I did not pay any attention to where he was going. I wanted to think. I did not know where I was. I was away somewhere in the country, and I hailed him and asked him where he was going. And he said, "On the way to Balmoral." So he was.

I got him to turn round and get back to Liverpool if he could, to catch a train for London if possible. When we got back I asked him what I had to pay, and he said—well, it was equivalent to four hundred dollars. I asked him if he was in earnest and he said he was, as outside the city he could charge any reasonable price. He said that Balmoral was four hundred miles away, and it would be four hundred dollars.

It seemed a sorry and embarrassing situation. I proposed to go before the rulers of the city or his Majesty or something of that sort to lay the case and he did. I said he had made a mistake, and the authorities said he had a right to charge anything reasonable. It seemed a large sum he had charged, and they said it was not the cabman's fault—it was four hundred miles to Balmoral and four shillings a mile was not unreasonable, especially as he would have to come back at his own expense.

Well, the man acted very handsomely. He compromised for twelve dollars. Though stupid tradition says that Scotchmen did not profess a sense of humor, I say that that man has a sense of humor.

What was Tay Pay's early statement that requires refutation? [O'Connor, "I said that you had been a financier."]

I was, but I am not now. I didn't succeed in it. He also mentioned another matter, and he paid me the compliment to mention that at the time when I was bankrupt, heavily in debt, I paid every dollar.

This is often mentioned, very pleasing to me to hear, and I feel that I ought to get on my feet and tell you all about it, how my business man, my longheaded commercial friend said, "In this bankruptcy business you pay thirty cents to the dollar and you go free."

Now, a man can easily be persuaded to go outside the strict moral line but it is not so with a woman and a wife.

My wife said, "No, you shall pay a hundred cents to the dollar and I will go with you all the way."

And she kept her word. Let us give credit where credit is due, and it is more due to her than to me.

I don't think I will say anything about the relations of amity existing between our two countries. It is not necessary, it seems to me. The ties between the two nations are so strong that I do not think we need trouble ourselves about them being broken. Anyhow, I am quite sure that in my time and in yours, my Lord Mayor, those ties will hold good, and please God, they always will. English blood is in our veins, we have a common language, a common religion, a common system of morals, and great commercial interest to hold us together.

Home is dear to us all, and now I am departing to my own home beyond the ocean. Oxford has conferred upon me the loftiest honor that has ever fallen to my share of this world's good things. It is the very one I would have chosen as outranking any and all others, the one more precious to me of any and all others within the gift of man or State. During my four weeks' sojourn here I have had another lofty honor, a continuous honor, an honor which has flowed serenely along without obstruction through all these twenty-six days, a most moving and pulse-stirring honor—the heartfelt grip of the hand, and the welcome that does not descend from the pale, gray matter of the brain but rushes up with the red blood of the heart. It makes me proud and it makes me humble too.

Many and many a year ago I read an anecdote in Dana's *Two Years Before the Mast*. It was like this. There was a presumptuous little self-important man in a coasting sloop engaged in the dried apple and kitchen furniture trade, and he was always hailing every ship that came in sight. He did it just to hear himself talk and to air his small grandeur.

One day a majestic Indiaman came plowing by with course on

course of canvas towering into the sky, her decks and yards swarming with sailors, bearing a rich freight of precious spices, lading the breezes with gracious and mysterious odors of the Orient. it was a noble spectacle. And of course the little skipper popped into the shroud and squeaked out a hail.

"Ship ahoy! What ship is that? And whence and whither?"

In a deep and thunderous voice the answer came through the speaking trumpet.

"The *Begum of Bengal,* a hundred and twenty-three days out from Canton. What ship is that?"

Well, it just crushed that poor little creature's vanity, and he squeaked back most humbly.

"Only the *Mary Ann,* fourteen days out from Boston, with nothing to speak of."

Oh, what an eloquent word, that "only," to express the depths of his humbleness. That is just my case. Just one hour, perhaps, in the twenty-four—not more—I pause and reflect, and then I am humble. Then I am properly meek, and for a little while I am only the *Mary Ann,* fourteen days out, charged with vegetables and tinware.

But during all the other twenty-three hours my vain self-complacency rides high, and then I am a stately Indiaman, plowing the great seas under a cloud of canvas, and laden with the finest words that have ever been spoken to any wandering alien in this world, and then my twenty-six happy days seem to be multiplied by five, and I am the *Begum of Bengal,* a hundred and twenty-three days out. And homeward bound.

July 1907

76

Clemens was invited to attend the Jamestown Exposition in Jamestown, Virginia, on Fulton Day, September 23, 1907. In introducing Clemens, Lieutenant Governor Ellyson of Virginia said, "The people have come here to bring a tribute of affectionate recollection for the man who has contributed so much to the progress of the world and the happiness of mankind." As Clemens walked down to the platform the applause grew louder and louder. He raised his hand for silence but was so moved he was unable to speak for a while. He tried to speak once. The audience, noticing how moved he was, cheered once more.

Admiral Purnell Frederick Harrington was an American naval officer.

ADMIRAL HARRINGTON

I am but human, and when you give me a reception like that I am obliged to wait a little while I get my voice. When you appeal to my head I don't feel it, but when you appeal to my heart I do feel it.

We are here to celebrate one of the greatest events of American history, and not only in American history but in the world's history. Indeed it was—the application of steam by Robert Fulton. It was a world event. There are not many of them. It is peculiarly an American event, that is true, but the influence was very broad in effect. We should regard this day as a very great American holiday.

We have not many that are exclusively American holidays. We have the Fourth of July, which we regard as an American holiday, but it is nothing of the kind. I am waiting for a dissenting voice. All great efforts that led up to the Fourth of July were made not by Americans but by English residents of America, subjects of the King of England.

They fought all the fighting that was done, they shed and spilt all the blood that was spilt, in securing to us the invaluable liberties which are incorporated in the Declaration of Independence. But they were not Americans. They signed the Declaration of Independence. No American's name is signed to that document at all. There never was an American such as you and I are until after the Revolution, when it had all been fought out and liberty secured, after the adoption of the Constitution, and the recognition of the independence of America by all powers. While we revere the Fourth of July (and let us always revere it and the liberties it conferred upon us), yet it was not an American event, a great American day.

It was an American who applied that steam successfully. There are not a great many world events, and we have our full share. The telegraph, telephone and the application of steam to navigation—these are great American events.

Today I have been requested, or I have requested myself, not to confine myself to furnishing you with information, but to remind you of things, and to introduce one of the nation's celebrants. Admiral Harrington here is going to tell you all that I have left untold. I am going to tell you all that I know, and then he will follow up with such rags and remnants as he can find, and tell you what he knows.

No doubt you have heard a great deal about Robert Fulton and the influences that have grown from his invention. But the little steamboat is suffering neglect. You probably do not know a great deal about that boat. It was the most important steamboat in the world. I was there and saw it. Admiral Harrington was there at the time. It need not surprise you, for he is not as old as he looks. That little boat was interesting in every way.

The size of it. The boat was one [consults Admiral] . . . he said ten feet long. The breadth of that boat [consults Admiral] . . . two hundred feet. You see, the first and most important detail is the length, then the breadth and then the depth. The depth of that boat was [consults again]. The Admiral says it was a flat boat. Then her tonnage—you know nothing about a boat until you know two more things: her speed and her tonnage. We know the speed she made. She made four miles—and sometimes five miles. It was on her initial trip—on August 11, 1807, that she made her initial trip, when she went from [consults Admiral] Jersey City to Chicago. That's right. She went by way of Albany. Now comes the tonnage of that boat. Tonnage of a boat means the amount of displacement. Displacement means the amount of water a vessel can shove in a day. The tonnage of man is estimated by the amount of whisky he can displace in a day.

Robert Fulton named the *Clermont* in honor of his bride. That is, Clermont was the name of the county seat.

I feel that it surprises you that I know so much. In my remarks of welcome of Admiral Harrington I am not going to give him compliments. Compliments always embarrass a man. You do not know anything to say. It does not inspire you with words. There is nothing you can say in answer to a compliment. I have been complimented myself a great many times, and they always embarrass me. I always feel that they have not said enough.

The Admiral and myself have held public office, and were associated together a great deal in a friendly way in the time of Pocahontas. That incident where Pocahontas saves the life of Smith from her father, Powhatan's, club, was gotten up by the Admiral and myself to advertise Jamestown. At that time the Admiral and myself did not have the facilities of advertising that you have.

I have known Admiral Harrington in all kinds of situations—in public service, on the platform, and in the chain gang now and then. But it was a mistake. A case of mistaken identity. I do not think it is at all a necessity to tell you Admiral Harrington's public history. You know that it is in the histories. I am not here to tell you anything about his public life, but to expose his private life.

I am something of a poet. When the great poet laureate Tennyson died and I found that the place was open I tried to get it. But I did not get it. Anybody can write the first line of a poem but it is a very difficult task to make the second line rhyme with the first. When I was down in Australia there were two towns named Johnswood and Par-am. I made this rhyme.

> *The people of Johnswood are pious and good;*
> *The people of Par-am they don't care a* ———.

I do not want to compliment Admiral Harrington, but as long as such men as he devote their lives to the public service the credit of the country will never cease. I will say that the same high qualities, the same moral and intellectual attainments, the same graciousness of manner, of conduct, of observation and expression have caused Admiral Harrington to be mistaken for me. And I have been mistaken for him.

A mutual compliment can go no further, and I now have the honor and privilege of introducing to you Admiral Harrington.

September 1907

77

In December of 1907 the Pleiades Club of New York gave a dinner in honor of Clemens. General Nelson Appleton Miles was an American soldier for more than forty years.

GENERAL MILES AND THE DOG

It is hard work to make a speech when you have listened to compliments from the powers in authority. A compliment is a hard text to preach to. When the chairman introduces me as a person of merit, and when he says pleasant things about me, I always feel like answering simply that what he says is true. That it is all right. That, as far as I am concerned, the things he said can stand as they are. But you always have to say something, and that is what frightens me.

I remember out in Sydney once having to respond to some complimentary toast, and my one desire was to turn in my tracks like any other worm and run for it. I was remembering that occasion at a later date when I had to introduce a speaker. Hoping then to spur his speech by putting him, in joke, on the defensive, I accused him in my introduction of everything I thought it impossible for him to have committed. When I finished there was an awful calm. I had been telling his life history by mistake.

One must keep up one's character. Earn a character first if you can. And if you can't, then assume one. From the code of morals I have been following and revising and revising for seventy-two years I remember one detail. All my life I have been honest—comparatively honest. I could never use money I had not made honestly. I could only lend it.

Last spring I met General Miles again and he commented on the fact that we had known each other thirty years. He said it was strange that we had not met years before when we had both been in Washington. At that point I changed the subject, and I changed it with art. But the facts are these.

I was then under contract for my *Innocents Abroad* but did not have a cent to live on while I wrote it. So I went to Washington to do a little journalism. There I met an equally poor friend, William Davidson, who had not a single vice, unless you call it a vice in a Scot to love Scotch. Together we devised the first and original newspaper syndicate, selling two letters a week to twelve newspapers and getting $1 a letter. That $24 a week would have been enough for us if we had not had to support the jug.

But there was a day when we felt that we must have $3 right away, $3 at once. That was how I met the General.

It doesn't matter now what we wanted so much money at one time for. But that Scot and I did occasionally want it. The Scot sent me out one day to get it. He had a great belief in Providence, that Scottish friend of mine.

He said, "The Lord will provide."

I had given up trying to find the money lying about, and was in a hotel lobby in despair when I saw a beautiful unfriended dog. The dog saw me too and at once we became acquainted. Then General Miles came in, admired the dog and asked me to price it. I priced it at $3. He offered me an opportunity to reconsider the value of the beautiful animal but I refused to take more than Providence knew I needed. The General carried the dog to his room.

Then came in a sweet little middle-aged man, who at once began looking around the lobby.

"Did you lose a dog?" I asked.

He said he had.

"I think I could find it," I volunteered, "for a small sum."

"How much?" he asked.

And I told him $3.

He urged me to accept more but I did not wish to outdo Providence.

Then I went to the General's room and asked for the dog back. He was very angry, and wanted to know why I had sold him a dog that did not belong to me.

"That's a singular question to ask me, sir," I replied. "Didn't you ask me to sell him? You started it."

And he let me have him. I gave him back his $3 and returned the dog, collect, to its owner. That second $3 I carried home to the Scot and we enjoyed it. But the first $3, the money I got from the General, I would have had to lend.

The General seemed not to remember my part in that adventure, and I never had the heart to tell him about it.

December 1907

ॐ *78* ॐ

In January of 1908 the Lotos Club gave a dinner for Clemens in New York, Frank R. Lawrence, club president, presiding. It would be the last Lotos Club dinner in his honor. The coyly produced menu included Innocent Oysters Abroad, Roughing It Soup, Fish Huckleberry Finn, Joan of Arc Filet of Beef, Hadleyburg Salad and Pudd'nhead Cheese. Robert Percival Porter was an American journalist. Hamilton Mabie was an American author and editor.

I WAS BORN FOR A SAVAGE

I wish to begin this time at the beginning lest I forget it altogether. That is to say I wish to thank you for this welcome that you are giving and the welcome which you gave me seven years ago and which I forgot to thank you for at that time. I also wish to thank you for the welcome you gave me fourteen years ago, which I also forgot to thank you for at the time. I hope you will continue this custom to give me a dinner every seven years before I join the hosts in the other world. I do not know which world.

Mr. Lawrence and Mr. Porter have paid me many compliments. It is very difficult to take compliments. I do not care whether you deserve the compliments or not, it is just as difficult to take them. The other night I was at the Engineers' Club and enjoyed the sufferings of Mr. Carnegie. They were complimenting him there. There it was all compliments. And none of them deserved. They say that you cannot live by bread alone. But I can live on compliments.

I do not make any pretense that I dislike compliments. The stronger the better. And I can manage to digest them. I think I have lost so much by not making a collection of compliments to put them away and take them out again once in a while. When in England I said that I would start to collect compliments. And I began there and I have brought some of them along.

The first one of these lies—I wrote them down and preserved them. I think they are mighty good and extremely just. It is one of Hamilton Mabie's compliments.

He said that La Salle was the first one to make a voyage of the Mississippi. But Mark Twain was the first to chart, light and navigate it for the whole world. If that had been published at the time that I issued that book [*Life on the Mississippi*], it would have been money in my pocket. I tell you it is a talent by itself to pay compliments gracefully and have them ring true. It's an art by itself.

Here is another compliment—by Albert Bigelow Paine, my biographer. He is writing four octavo volumes about me and he has been at my elbow two and one-half years. I just suppose that he does not know me, but says he knows me.

He says, "Mark Twain is not merely a great writer, a great philosopher, a great man. He is the supreme expression of the human being, with every human strength—and weakness."

What a talent for compression. It takes a genius in compression to compact as many facts as that.

W.D. Howells spoke of me as first of Hartford, and ultimately of the solar system, not to say of the universe.

You know how modest Howells is. If it can be proved that my fame reaches to Neptune and Saturn that will satisfy even me. You know how modest and retiring Howells seems to be. But deep down he is as vain as I am.

Mr. Howells had been granted a degree at Oxford, whose gown was red. He had been invited to an exercise at Columbia, and upon inquiry had been told that it was usual to wear the black gown. Later he had found that three other men wore bright gowns. And he had lamented that he had been one of the black mass, and not a red torch.

Edison wrote, "The average American loves his family. If he has any love left over for some other person he generally selects Mark Twain."

Now here's the compliment of a little Montana girl which came to me indirectly. She was in a room in which there was a large photograph of me. After gazing at it steadily for a time, she said, "We've got a John the Baptist like that."

She also said, "Only ours has more trimmings."

I suppose she meant the halo.

Now here is a gold miner's compliment. It is forty-two years old. It was my introduction to an audience to which I lectured in a log schoolhouse. There were no ladies there. I wasn't famous then. They didn't know me. Only the miners were there, with their breeches tucked into their boot tops, and with clay all over them. They wanted someone to introduce me, and they selected a miner, who protested, saying,

"I don't know anything about this man. Anyhow, I only know two things about him. One is, he has never been in jail. And the other is, I don't know why."

There's one thing I want to say about that English trip. I knew his Majesty the King of England long years ago, and I didn't meet him for the first time then. One thing that I regret was that some newspapers said I talked with the Queen of England with my hat on. I don't do that with any woman. I did not put it on until she asked me to. Then she *told* me to put it on, and it's a command there. I thought I had carried my American democracy far enough. So I put it on. I have no use for a hat, and never did have.

Who was it who said that the police of London knew me? Why, the police know me everywhere. There never was a day over there when a policeman did not salute me and then put up his hand and stop the traffic of the world. They treated me as though I were a duchess.

The happiest experience I had in England was at a dinner given in the building of the *Punch* publication, a humorous paper which is appreciated by all Englishmen. It was the greatest privilege ever allowed a foreigner. I entered the dining room of the building, where those men get together who have been running the paper for over fifty years.

We were about to begin dinner when the toastmaster said, "Just a minute. There ought to be a little ceremony."

Then there was that meditating silence for a while, and out of a closet there came a beautiful little girl dressed in pink, holding in her hand the original of a cartoon of me, published in the previous week's paper: Mr. Punch offering me welcome to England.

It broke me all up. I could not even say "Thank you." That was the prettiest incident of the dinner, the delight of all that wonderful table.

When she was about to go I said, "My child, you are not going to leave me. I have hardly got acquainted with you."

She replied, "You know I've got to go. They never let me come in here before. And they never will again."

That is one of the beautiful incidents that I cherish.

January 1908

When Clemens had ended the speech, and while he was still being cheered by the audience, Colonel Porter brought out the red-and-gray gown of Clemens's Oxford honorary doctorate and made him put it on. The audience rose. Looking down admiringly at himself, Clemens said,

"I like that gown. I always did like red. The redder it is the better I like it. I was born for a savage. Now, whoever saw any red like this? There is no red outside the arteries of an archangel that could compare with this. I know you all envy me. I am going to have luncheon shortly with ladies, just ladies. I will be the only lady of my sex present. And I shall put on this gown and make those ladies look dim."

❧ *79* ❧

To my knowledge, this is the first time the following speech is being reprinted. It was given on Thursday evening, April 9, 1908, in Hamilton, Bermuda, and was published in the Hamilton *Royal Gazette* two days later with headlines that read "Lecture at the Colonial/Opera House/Mark Twain on 'Caprices of/Memory'/Large Audience." It was made at a fundraising benefit for the Bermuda Biological Station and Aquarium to an audience that included the Governor of Bermuda, the Governor General of Canada, and the Chief Justice of Bermuda (H. C. Gollan).

Clemens, who was familiar with the islands, had been in Bermuda some six weeks for a rest. Goodwin Gosling was the secretary of the Bermuda Biological Society.

CAPRICES OF MEMORY

I gather from what the Chief Justice has said that Bermuda is about the right place to establish a Biological Station. Not only are the waters rich in fish, but I understand that the fishes themselves take an interest in the Aquarium and are ready to help. I saw in a fish pond, yesterday, thirteen very choice fish of superb colors, that were all caught in a rat trap in one night. The rat trap had been baited for rats. It was stood on the edge of the fish pond, and a dog got to playing with it, and tumbled it into the pond, and in the morning thirteen valuable fish were found in the trap. I think Mr. Goodwin Gosling told me that all the fishes in the Aquarium were caught in a rat trap.

I intend to talk to you this evening about the caprices of memory. Each of our senses has a memory of its own. It seems to me that the memory has a way of treasuring things which are apparently of no value at all, and discarding many things which are valuable. I know it is so in my case. I remember things that happened in my childhood which are of no apparent value. They stayed with me faithfully until I was seventy-two years old. And yet I am not sure they were not of some value after all—in a moral sense and in the building up of my moral character and structure.

I remember now as if it were yesterday the first time I ever stole a watermelon. I think it was the first time. I stole that watermelon out of a farmer's wagon while he was waiting on another customer. I carried it out to the seclusion of the lumberyard and broke it open. It was green. The greenest watermelon that was ever raised in the Mississippi Valley. When I saw it was green I was sorry and I began to reflect. Seemed to me I had done wrong.

I thought, "Now, what ought a boy to do? What ought a right-thinking, clean-hearted, high-principled boy to do who has stolen a green watermelon? What would George Washington do?"

I said to myself, "There is only one thing for him to do. He must restore that stolen watermelon."

Not many boys would do that. I did. I rose up spiritually strengthened and refreshed and I carried it back and restored it to the farmer—what was left of it. And I made him give me a ripe one.

I was severe with him. I told him he ought to be ashamed of himself going around working off green watermelons on people who had confidence in him. I told him if he did not break himself of that habit he would not have any more of my custom.

He said it would not happen again, and I know it was a lesson to that man, and it was such a pleasure to me to reflect that perhaps I saved that man, set him on the right path with his face pointing toward ultimate righteousness.

Now, that was sufficient reward for me, and I got a watermelon besides. That is the way moral character is built up—by personal experience. When you commit a sin and you recognize it, it makes an impression and you will never commit just that sin again. I have never stolen a watermelon of that character since. All you have to do in order to become entirely pure is to commit all the sins there are. I have done that. Anybody can do it. Anybody can build up a perfect moral character. If I live a few more years I shall finish the list of crimes and I shall consider there is no one in the world like me.

I was kept at home one day. I was thirteen or fourteen years old. It was one Saturday afternoon and I was kept at home because of one of those experiments of mine in moral philosophy. I did have one little satisfaction. I had half a watermelon. I dug it out until only the shell remained and it formed a sort of canoe. It seemed a pity to waste that. I didn't know what to do with it.

I thought at last I would drop it on somebody's head. Three-story window. Every temptation. I watched people come along down below in order to pick out the right person. It is possible to drop a watermelon on the wrong man's head.

At last my younger brother came along. When I saw him I knew that he was delivered into my hands. I never took more interest in any work of art in the world than I did in measuring his distance from me, and his rate of progress. I held that canoe out of the window over his head. I could see him foreshorten until his nose and toes were on a line.

When I judged he was six feet from the point where the melon would land I released it. It was beautiful to see the operation of that exact calculation I made. It hit him right on top of the head. There was an explosion. The shell burst into a thousand pieces and chunks of it broke windows three miles around.

That taught me I was born for the military service. I joined the military forces at the beginning of the Civil War. I served a couple of weeks. I found there was going to be rain, and as they didn't like umbrellas I resigned.

My father—well, he was an austere man. A man of great importance, too. At this time he lived in a village on the banks of the Mississippi. He was a person of the biggest importance there. He was mayor, he was coroner and sheriff and chief of police, and he was the police himself. In fact he was everything. He was the concentrated government of that village.

I didn't think a great deal of his judgment. I didn't like to go to school. But he insisted on my going at most improper and inconvenient times. I preferred to go fishing, and whenever I went fishing without his permission it placed me in a delicate situation. I was likely to get belated and reach home late at night. Then there would be an account to settle, and I would be on the weak side of it.

One summer's day when it was a little too rainy to go to school, and not too rainy to go fishing, I thought I'd do that. I was gone all day, and at eleven o'clock at night I came back so tired and so worn out. Something had happened that afternoon I didn't know about. At that time—in 1849—there was an endless procession of wagons passing through our village day by day, bound for the California goldfields, and sometimes there would be trouble. There had been trouble this day. There had been a fight and one man had stabbed another to death by plunging a Bowie knife into his breast. My father was the coroner, among other things, and they took this dead man to my father's little office and stretched the corpse out in the middle of the floor—stripped to the waist.

Now, it was my custom when I arrived late to go and sleep in that little place. When I entered that little dark office at eleven o'clock and groped my way in and stretched myself out on the only settee there, I was so comfortable, so happy, so contented, so delighted. It was Paradise to me.

Before I dozed off my eyes began to get accustomed to the gloom of the place and I thought I could see the shape of somebody stretched out on the middle of the floor. My first impulse was to go there and touch it. I overcame that. It was a suspicious-looking shape. I tried to go to sleep but I couldn't. I became interested in the thing, and the longer I meditated over it and watched it the more uncomfortable I became. Then I thought I would try counting until the moonlight through the window arrived at that object, and I turned my face to the wall and counted. I counted ten, twenty, thirty. The moonshine was getting nearer and nearer, and as it got closer and closer my anxiety grew and grew.

I began to get alarmed. I was almost moved to get up and clear out of the place. But I was putting a test upon my personal courage. I was trying to gauge just how much personal courage I had and how much I lacked, so that I would know how to conduct myself in cases of emergency. So I said, "I will stay here until the moonlight reaches that thing."

I counted and counted and counted. I got so nervous at last. I thought I would count a thousand. I counted as long as I could. But when you are anxious you are apt to make a miscount and you have to commence all over again.

At last, when I could count no longer I turned over, and there in the moonlight lay the outspread marble hand of that murdered man. I never felt so embarrassed. I said, "I will wait." I wanted to see the rest. I turned over and counted and counted. I didn't know it was a murdered man. I knew it was a hand I didn't want there. I watched the moonlight creep up that white arm, further and further until it reached the shoulder, a tuft of hair, until there it was—a marble bust, with staring glassy eyes, with that great gash in the breast.

I went away from there. I don't mean to say I went in a hurry. I just went, that's all. I went out of the window. I took the sash along with me. It was more handy to take it than to leave it. In any emergency which has arisen from that day to this I have known the standard of my courage. I know when to drop out of the window.

By and by I went from that little village—that little sleepy village—to Nevada and eventually to California. I left behind me in that village one sort of life and went to another sort on the Pacific Coast. It was so quiet, so deadly quiet, in that village. Why, this town of Hamilton on Sunday is an insurrection compared to it. Half the people were alive and the other half were dead. A stranger could not tell them apart.

I went from that sort of society to Nevada and we stopped at Carson City. This new life I speak of was something I had not seen before at all—because a great movement like that gathers up the young spirited fellows of energy who go out into the world and make discoveries and make their fortunes in strange ways and in strange places. And the population of that town of Carson City in the sandy desert, under the shade of mountain peaks several thousand feet high, was a mixed one. It consisted of all sorts of people—clergymen and burglars, and highwaymen, lawyers and liars and everything which goes to make things lively and to make life a joy.

Among them were a great many of the predecessors of the cowboys who rode the Mexican saddle and swung the lariat. I saw these men come flying through the town every day, sitting their horses so easily, and as comfortable as in a rocking chair. The spectacle was picturesque and exhilarating to me who knew nothing about horses, and I wished I could be a horseman myself. I wished I could try that great art some day, to fly through the town with incredible swiftness and disappear next minute in a cloud of dust. I got possessed with the passion and desire to become a horseman.

One day there was a horse auction going on. A man rode up and down, up and down upon an old ruin of a horse which was full of admirable points—you could hang your hat on them anywhere.

"Going, going at twenty dollars, horse, saddle and bridle," exclaimed the auctioneer.

A man was standing by me, and I noticed he was looking me over with a great deal of interest. It flattered me, because I was not used to being looked over with interest.

Presently he said, "It's a pity to see such a noble steed like that going at such a low figure."

I said, "I thought so myself," and that I had a notion to bid.

He said, "You couldn't do a better thing. People might try to make you believe it's an American horse. It's nothing of the kind. That horse is a genuine Mexican blood."

I didn't know what a "Mexican blood" was but there was something about his way of saying it that made me want to possess a "Mexican blood."

I said, "Has that horse got any other advantages?"

"Advantages," he said. "I'll tell you in confidence that horse can out-buck any horse on this planet."

Well, I didn't know what bucking meant but I was eager to possess a bucking horse. I didn't wait any longer. I bid $36 and got him.

The auctioneer said, "Sold," and the other boys round about said, "Sold."

But still the horse was mine. It was the first time I ever owned a horse.

I said, "Take him to the livery stable. Tone him down. Harrow him. Do everything you can do to a horse. And give him everything in and out of season—oats or ice cream."

When he came out he interested himself in everything going on. He couldn't stand still. Wanted to be doing something right away. He just looked me over and appeared to be glad of my society. Some of the boys held him down by the head while the others held him to earth by the tail. I got on him. The minute I was in the saddle I was up in the air, and up and up and up. Came down and alighted in the saddle again. Up again and down again. He went through the maneuver until he was tired of it. I was ahead of him in that.

Finally he stood on his hind legs, just on his toe nails, looking at the scenery. I had hold of him around the neck. He had no ears. I thought I would slide down and get down the back way. I was too late. He resumed the original performance and shot me in the air. I would not like to say how high I did go. It would sound like exaggeration. But really, I came across birds up there.

When I came down he was gone. I have not practiced any horsemanship since. It was a valuable lesson I learned. It meant a great deal to me. I have been able to avoid horsemanship every since, and it has probably saved my life.

April 1908

~~ 80 ~~

In May of 1908 Clemens attended a banquet at the Waldorf-Astoria hotel in New York celebrating the opening of the new, uptown college buildings of the College of the City of New York. Bram Stoker was an English writer, and manager of Henry Irving, the English actor.

JUMPING TO CONCLUSIONS

I agreed when the mayor said that there was not a man within hearing who did not agree that citizenship should be placed above everything else, even learning.

Have you ever thought about this? Is there a college in the whole country where there is a chair of good citizenship? There is a kind of bad citizenship which is taught in the schools, but no real good citizenship taught. There are some which teach insane citizenship, bastard citizenship, but that is all. Patriotism! Yes, but patriotism is usually the refuge of the scoundrel. He is the man who talks the loudest.

You can begin that chair of citizenship in the College of the City of New York. You can place it above mathematics and literature, and that is where it belongs.

We used to trust in God. I think it was in 1863 that some genius suggested that it be put upon the gold and silver coins which circulated among the rich. They didn't put it on the nickels and coppers because they didn't think the poor folks had any trust in God.

Good citizenship would teach accuracy of thinking and accuracy of statement. Now, that motto on the coin is an overstatement. Those Congressmen had no right to commit this whole country to a theological doctrine. But since they did, Congress ought to state what our creed should be.

There was never a nation in the world that put its whole trust in God. It is a statement made on insufficient evidence. Leaving out the gamblers, the burglars and the plumbers, perhaps we do put our trust in God after a fashion. But, after all, it is an overstatement.

If the cholera or black plague should come to these shores, perhaps the bulk of the nation would pray to be delivered from it, but the rest would put their trust in the Health Board of the City of New York.

I read in the papers within the last day or two of a poor young girl who they said was a leper. Did the people in that populous section of the country where she was, did they put their trust in God? The girl was afflicted with the leprosy, a disease which cannot be communicated from one person to another. Yet instead of putting their trust in God they harried that poor creature, shelterless and friendless, from place to place exactly as they did in the Middle Ages, when they made lepers wear bells so that people could be warned of their approach and avoid them. Perhaps those people in the Middle Ages thought they were putting their trust in God.

The President ordered the removal of that motto from the coin, and I thought that it was well. I thought that overstatement should not stay there. But I think it would better read, "Within certain judicious limitations we trust in God," and if there isn't enough room on the coin for this, why, enlarge the coin.

Now I want to tell a story about jumping at conclusions. It was told to me by Bram Stoker and it concerns a christening. There was a little clergyman who was prone to jump at conclusions sometimes. One day he was invited to officiate at a christening. He went. There sat the relatives—intelligent-looking relatives they were. The little clergyman's instinct came to him to make a great speech. He was given to flights of oratory that way—a very dangerous thing, for often the wings which take one into clouds of oratorical enthusiasm are wax and melt up there, and down you come.

But the little clergyman couldn't resist. He took the child in his arms and, holding it, looked at it a moment. It wasn't much of a child. It was little, like a sweet potato. Then the little clergyman waited impressively, and then, "I see in your countenances," he said, "disappointment of him. I see you are disappointed with this baby. Why? Because he is so little. My friends, if you had but the power of looking into the future you might see that great things may come of little things. There is the great ocean, holding the navies of the world, which comes from little drops of water no larger than a woman's tears. There are the great constellations in the sky, made up of little bits of stars. Oh, if you could consider his future you might see that he might become the greatest poet of the universe, the greatest warrior the world has ever known, greater than Caesar, than Hannibal, than—er—er" (turning to the father)—"what's his name?"

The father hesitated, then whispered back, "His name? Well, his name is Mary Ann."

May 1908

81

In January of 1909 the New York Post-Graduate Medical School and Hospital invited Clemens to attend their annual dinner at Delmonico's in New York. George N. Miller, the president, in introducing Clemens referred to the latter's recent experience with burglars at his new home, Stormfield, in Redding, Connecticut.

DR. CLEMENS, FARMEOPATH

I am glad to be among my own kind tonight. I was once a sharp-shooter but now I practice a much higher and equally as deadly a profession. It wasn't so very long ago that I became a member of your cult, and for the time I've been in the business my record is one that can't be scoffed at.

As to the burglars, I am perfectly familiar with these people. I have always had a good deal to do with burglars—not officially, but through their attentions to me. I never suffered anything at the hands of a burglar. They have invaded my house time and time again. They never got anything. Then those people who burglarized our house in September. We got back the plated ware they took off, we jailed them, and I have been sorry ever since. They did us a great service. They scared off all the servants in the place.

I consider the Children's Theater, of which I am president, and the Post-Graduate Medical School as the two greatest institutions in the country. This school, in bringing its twenty thousand physicians from all parts of the country, bringing them up to date, and sending them back with renewed confidence, has surely saved hundreds of thousands of lives which otherwise would have been lost.

I have been practising now for seven months. When I settled on my farm in Connecticut in June I found the community very thinly .

settled. And since I have been engaged in practice it has become more thinly settled still. This gratifies me, as indicating that I am making an impression on my community. I suppose it is the same with all of you.

I have always felt that I ought to do something for you, and so I organized a Redding (Connecticut) branch of the Post-Graduate School. I am only a country farmer up there but I am doing the best I can. Of course, the practice of medicine and surgery in a remote country has its disadvantages but in my case I am happy in a division of responsibility. I practise in conjunction with a horse doctor, a sexton and an undertaker. The combination is airtight, and once a man is stricken in our district escape is impossible for him.

These four of us (three in the regular profession and the fourth an undertaker) are all good men. There is Bill Ferguson, the Redding undertaker. Bill is there in every respect. He is a little lukewarm on general practice and writes his name with a rubber stamp. Like my old Southern friend, he is one of the finest planters anywhere. Then there is Jim Ruggles, the horse doctor. Ruggles is one of the best men I have got. He also is not much on general medicine but he is a fine horse doctor. Ferguson doesn't make any money off him.

You see, the combination started this way. When I got up to Redding and had become a doctor I looked around to see what my chances were for aiding in the great work. The first thing I did was to determine what manner of doctor I was to be. Being a Connecticut farmer, I naturally consulted my farmacopia and at once decided to become a farmeopath. Then I got circulating about and got in touch with Ferguson and Ruggles. Ferguson joined readily in my ideas. But Ruggles kept saying that while it was all right for an undertaker to get aboard, he couldn't see where it helped horses.

Well, we started to find out what was the trouble with the community and it didn't take long to find out that there was just one disease and that was race suicide. And driving about the countryside I was told by my fellow farmers that it was the only rational human and valuable disease. But it is cutting into our profits, so that we'll either have to stop it or we'll have to move.

We've had some funny experiences up there in Redding. Not long ago a fellow came along with a rolling gait and a distressed face. We asked him what was the matter. We always hold consultations on every case, as there isn't business enough for four. He said he didn't know but that he was a sailor, and perhaps that might help us to give a diagnosis. We treated him for that, and I never saw a man die more peacefully.

That same afternoon my dog Tige treed an African gentleman. We chained up the dog, and then the gentleman came down and said he had appendicitis. We asked him if he wanted to be cut open, and he said yes, that he'd like to know if there was anything in it. So we cut him open and found nothing in him but darkness. So we diagnosed his case as infidelity, because he was dark inside. Tige is a very clever dog and aids us greatly.

As a practitioner I have given a great deal of my attention to Bright's disease. I have made some rules for treating it that may be valuable. Listen.

Rule 1. When approaching the bedside of one whom an all-wise President—I mean an all-wise Providence—well, anyway, it's the same thing—has seen fit to afflict with disease—well, the rule is simple even if it is old-fashioned.

Rule 2. I've forgotten just what it is but. . . .

Rule 3. This is always indispensable. Bleed your patient.

January 1909

ᘒ 82 ᘒ

In April of 1909 Henry H. Rogers, the financier and Clemens's friend, was honored at a businessmen's dinner for him in Norfolk, Virginia, the occasion being the completion of the Virginia Railway, which Rogers had financed. Clemens was introduced as "one who has made millions laugh— not the loud laughter that bespeaks the vacant mind, but the laugh of mirth, intelligent mirth, the mirth that helps the human heart and the human mind."

MR. ROGERS

I thank you, Mr. Toastmaster, for the compliment which you have paid me, and I am sure I would rather have made people laugh than cry, yet in my time I have made some of them cry. And before I stop entirely I hope to make some more of them cry.

I like compliments. I deal in them myself. I have listened with the greatest pleasure to the compliments which the chairman has paid to Mr. Rogers and that road of his tonight, and I hope some of them are deserved.

It is no small distinction to a man like that to sit here before an intelligent crowd like this and to be classed with Napoleon and Caesar. Why didn't he say that this was the proudest day of his life? Napoleon and Caesar are dead, and they can't be here to defend themselves. But I'm here.

The chairman said, and very truly, that the most lasting thing in the hands of man are the roads which Caesar built, and it is true that he built a lot of them, and they are there yet. Yes, Caesar built a lot of roads in England and you can find them. But Rogers has only built one road and he hasn't finished that yet. I like to hear my old friend complimented but I don't like to hear it overdone.

I didn't go around today with the others to see what he is doing. I will do that in a quiet time when there is not anything going on and when I shall not be called upon to deliver intemperate compliments on a railroad in which I own no stock.

They proposed that I go along with the committee and help inspect that dump down yonder. I didn't go. I saw that dump. I saw that thing when I was coming in on the steamer, and I didn't go because I was diffident, sentimentally diffident, about going and looking at that thing again—that great, long, bony thing. It looked just like Mr. Rogers's foot.

The chairman says Mr. Rogers is full of practical wisdom, and he is. It is intimated here that he is a very ingenious man, and he is a very competent financier. Maybe he is now, but it was not always so. I know lots of private things in his life which people don't know, and I know how he started. And it was not a very good start. I could have done better myself.

The first time he crossed the Atlantic he had just made the first little strike in oil, and he was so young he did not like to ask questions. He did not like to appear ignorant. To this day he don't like to appear ignorant, but he can look as ignorant as anybody. On board the ship they were betting on the run of the ship, betting a couple of shillings, or half a crown, and they proposed that this youth from the oil regions should bet on the run of the ship.

He did not like to ask what a half-crown was, and he didn't know, but rather than be ashamed of himself he did bet half a crown on the run of the ship, and in bed he could not sleep. He wondered if he could afford that outlay in case he lost. He kept wondering over it, and said to himself, "A king's crown must be worth $20,000, so half a crown would cost $10,000." He could not afford to bet away $10,000 on the run of the ship, so he went up to the stakeholder and gave him $150 to let him off.

I like to hear Mr. Rogers complimented. I am not stingy in compliments to him myself. Why, I did it today when I sent his wife a telegram to comfort her. That is the kind of person I am. I knew she would be uneasy about him. I knew she would be solicitous about what he might do down here, so I did it to quiet her and to comfort her. I said he was doing well for a person out of practice. There is nothing like it. He is like I used to be.

There were times when I was careless—careless in my dress when I got older. You know how uncomfortable your wife can get when you are going away without her superintendence. Once when my wife could not go with me (she always went with me when she could—I always did meet that kind of luck), I was going to Washington once, a long time ago, in Mr. Cleveland's first administration, and she could not go. But, in her anxiety that I should not desecrate the house, she made preparation. She knew that there was to be a reception of those authors at the White House at seven o'clock in the evening.

She said, "If I should tell you now what I want to ask of you, you would forget it before you get to Washington, and therefore I have written it on a card, and you will find it in your dress-vest pocket when you are dressing at the Arlington, when you are dressing to see the President."

I never thought of it again until I was dressing, and I felt in that pocket and took it out, and it said, in a kind of imploring way, "Don't wear your arctics in the White House."

You complimented Mr. Rogers on his energy, his foresightedness, complimented him in various ways, and he has deserved those compliments, although I say it myself, and I enjoy them all. There is one side of Mr. Rogers that has not been mentioned. If you will leave that to me I will touch upon that. There was a note in an editorial in one of the Norfolk papers this morning that touched upon that very thing, that hidden side of Mr. Rogers, where it spoke of Helen Keller and her affection for Mr. Rogers, to whom she dedicated her life book. And she has a right to feel that way, because, without the public knowing anything about it, he rescued, if I may use that term, that marvelous girl, that wonderful Southern girl, that girl who was stone deaf, blind and dumb from scarlet fever when she was a baby eighteen months old, and who now is as well and thoroughly educated as any woman on this planet at twenty-nine years of age. She is the most marvelous person of her sex that has existed on this earth since Joan of Arc.

That is not all Mr. Rogers has done. But you never see that side of his character, because it is never protruding. But he lends a helping hand daily out of that generous heart of his. You never hear of it. He is supposed to be a moon which has one dark side and the other bright. But the other side, though you don't see it, is not dark. It is bright, and its rays penetrate, and others do see it who are not God.

I would like to take this opportunity to tell something that I have never been allowed to tell by Mr. Rogers, either by my mouth or in print, and if I don't look at him I can tell it now.

In 1893, when the publishing company of Charles L. Webster, of which I was financial agent, failed, it left me heavily in debt. If you will remember what commerce was at that time you will recall that you could not sell anything and could not buy anything, and I was on my back. My books were not worth anything at all, and I could not give away my copyrights.

Mr. Rogers had long enough vision ahead to say, "Your books have supported you before, and after the panic is over they will support you again," and that was a correct proposition.

He saved my copyrights and saved me from financial ruin. He it was who arranged with my creditors to allow me to roam the face of the earth for four years and persecute the nations thereof with lectures, promising that at the end of four years I would pay dollar for dollar. That arrangement was made. Otherwise I would now be living out of doors under an umbrella, and a borrowed one at that.

You see his white mustache and his head trying to get white (he is always trying to look like me—I don't blame him for that). These are only emblematic of his character, and that is all. I say, without exception, hair and all, he is the whitest man I have ever known.

April 1909

A year later, on the afternoon of April 21, 1910, Clemens sank into a coma at Stormfield, his home at Redding, Connecticut. He had been suffering from heart trouble for some time. He was in his seventy-fifth year. According to Paine, he died "just at sunset" on that day. He was buried three days later in Elmira, New York.

Sources

Abbreviations
MTP—Mark Twain Papers, University of California (Berkeley)
MTS (10)—*Mark Twain's Speeches*, 1910
MTS (23)—*Mark Twain's Speeches*, 1923
NYT—*New York Times*

1. The Sandwich Islands. MTS (23).
2. Woman. MTS (10).
3. American Vandal Abroad. MTS (23).
4. Jim Wolfe. MTS (10).
5. Stanley and Livingstone. MTS (10).
6. London. MTS (10).
7. Sins of the Press. MTS (23).
8. There Is Hope for Us Yet. MTS (23).
9. Cigars. MTS (10).
10. Boggs. MTS (10).
11. New England Weather. MTS (10).
12. The Stirring Campaign. NYT, October 7, 1877.
13. Whittier's Birthday. MTS (23).
14. Nineteenth-Century Progress. *Dime Jolly Speaker*, #22, 1879, in Documents File 1879 in MTP.
15. The Corpse. NYT, April 11, 1879.
16. Science of Onanism. Privately printed edition of 100 copies, 1964, of which #28 is in MTP. Also *Fact* magazine, March–April 1964, as well as two different typescript copies in MTP.
17. General Grant and the Babies. MTS (23).
18. Innocent Plagiarism. MTS (23).
19. Republican Rally. NYT, October 27, 1880.
20. Speechless. MTS (10).
21. The Art of War. MTS (23).
22. Visit to Canada. NYT, December 10, 1881, reprinted from *Montreal Gazette*, no date.

23. Plymouth Rock and the Pilgrims. MTS (10).

24. A Ragged Ramshackle Vow. MTS (23).

25. Advice to Youth. MTS (23).

26. Woman, God Bless Her! *Modern Eloquence*, ed. by Thomas B. Reed, 1901, vol. 1.

27. Adam. MTS (23).

28. Turncoats. MTS (23).

29. The Dead Partisan. MTS (23).

30. Plethora of Speeches. MTS (23).

31. The Compositor. MTS (10).

32. Author and Publisher. San Francisco *Examiner*, May 12, 1887, re-printed from *New York World*, February 11, 1887. This was a clipping in Documents File 1887 in MTP.

33. An Author's Soldiering. *Masterpieces of American Eloquence*, 1900.

34. Bench Shows. MTS (10).

35. General Grant's English. MTS (23).

36. A Speech for All Occasions. *Boston Daily Globe*, December 21, 1887.

37. Reforming Yale. MTS (23).

38. Foolproof Scheme. Autobiographical Dictation, August 28, 1906, in MTP.

39. Foreign Critics. MTS (23).

40. The Druggist. San Francisco *Argonaut*, January 5, 1891.

41. Horrors of the German Language. MTS (10).

42. The Ausgleich. MTS (10).

43. Statistics. MTS (10).

44. Masters of Oratory. MTS (10).

45. On Being Morally Perfect. MTS (10).

46. Playing a Part. MTS (10).

47. Home Conditions. MTS (10).

48. My Real Self. MTS (10).

49. Disappearance of Literature. MTS (10).

50. Feeding a Dog on Its Own Tail. MTS (10).

51. New York. MTS (10).

52. The Anti-Doughnut Party. MTS (10).

53. Women's Rights. MTS (10).

54. Lincoln's Birthday. MTS (23).

55. Humor. NYT, December 1, 1901.

56. Progress in Medicine. NYT, March 9, 1902.

57. I Have Tried to Do Good. MTS (10).

58. How to Reach Seventy. MTS (10).

59. Lost Opportunity. MTS (10).

60. Jack Van Nostrand. MTS (10).

61. Private and Public Morals. MTS (10).

62. Lying. MTS (10).

63. The Gentleman. MTS (23).
64. Memories. MTS (10).
65. New York Morals. MTS (10).
66. The Sock. MTS (10).
67. A Wandering Address. MTS (10).
68. Simplified Spelling. MTS (10).
69. Stage Fright. MTS (10).
70. Copyright. MTS (23).
71. The Watermelon. NYT, May 12, 1907.
72. Affection. MTS (10).
73. Fourth of July. MTS (10).
74. Wearing White Clothes. MTS (10).
75. The *Begum of Bengal*. *Liverpool Daily Post*, July 11, 1907.
76. Admiral Harrington. MTS (10).
77. General Miles and the Dog. MTS (10).
78. I Was Born for a Savage. MTS (23).
79. Caprices of Memory. The Hamilton (Bermuda) *Royal Gazette*, April 11, 1908.
80. Jumping to Conclusions. MTS (10).
81. Dr. Clemens, Farmeopath. MTS (10).
82. Mr. Rogers. MTS (10).

Acknowledgments

It gives me pleasure to thank the following for suggestions and courtesies afforded me during the preparation of this volume: Murray Baumgarten, Frank J. Carroll, James Cohee, Catherine Doyle, Robert H. Hirst, David Kaun, Peter Kenez, John Lowrance, Joan M. Neider, Janet Pumphrey, Joseph Silverman, Paul Spriggs, Thomas Tenney, Joan Woodward (Christchurch, New Zealand), M. S. Wyeth, Jr.; and the Boston Public Library, the Canterbury Museum (of Christchurch), the Newspaper Section of the Library of Congress, the Liverpool City Libraries, the Firestone Library of Princeton University, the Mark Twain Papers and the Bancroft Library of the University of California at Berkeley, and the McHenry Library of the University of California at Santa Cruz. I am particularly indebted to Paul Fatout for his excellent book, *Mark Twain Speaking*, which he edited and which I have found most useful, and I am grateful to the faculty and staff of Stevenson College of the University of California at Santa Cruz for many kindnesses extended to me.

Index of Titles